An American Spirit

An American Epic

By Thomas Davis

An American Spirit
An epic poem by Thomas Davis

Copyright 2019 by Thomas Davis

Four Windows Press
231 N Hudson Ave.
Sturgeon Bay, WI 54235

davisetheltom@gmail.com
fourwindowspress.com

Dedication

For an American nation facing challenges that come out of the nation's history and the history of humankind

For Ethel, the love of my life

and Mildred Hart Shaw, my only mentor when I was young

Acknowledgement

Hepcat's Revenge, a small literary journal associated with the University of Wisconsin—Stevens Point, published two passages from *An American Spirit* on April 1995, Vol. 10, pp. 4-6. This was just after the Oklahoma City bombing of the federal building. At the time the Editor said that the poem was prophetic, since it was written before Timothy McVeigh's madness, anticipating an America that was coming into being. I cannot say that his insight has not proven its currency as time has passed. The central metaphor has been exaggerated rather than diminished. If anything violence and intolerance, as well as the reasons for those phenomena, have gotten worse.

Four Windows Press

Cover art by Ethel Mortenson Davis, "Anishinabe Warrior"

Printed in the United States using Garamond Type

Epigraph

The heavens themselves, the planets and this center,
Observe degree, priority, and place,
Insisture, course, proportion, season, form,
Office, and custom, in all line of order,
And therefore is the glorious planet Sol
In noble eminence enthroned and sphered
Amidst the other, whose medicinable eye
Corrects the ill aspects of planets evil,
And posts like the commandment of a king,
Sans check to good and bad. But when the planets
In evil mixture to disorder wander,
What plagues and what portents, what mutiny,
What raging of the sea, shaking of earth,
Commotion in the winds, frights, changes, horrors,
Divert and crack, rend and deracinate,
The unity and married calm of states
Quite from their fixture! Oh, when degree is shaked,
Which is the ladder to all high designs,
The enterprise is sick! How could communities,
Degrees in schools and brotherhood in cities,
Peaceful commerce from dividable shores,
The primogenitive and due of birth,
Preogative of age, crowns, scepters, laurels,
But by degree, stand in authentic place?
Take but degree away, untune that string,
and hark, what discord follows!. . .

from a speech by Ulysses in *Troilus and Cressida*
by William Shakespeare.
Act I, Scene III.

Table of Contents

—

Invocation
To the Epic Muse

The string's untuned! Degree, priority
And place, insisture, course, proportion, form,
Season, office, custom — all are made
Disordered, mutinous, as unified
As raging seas and shaking earth. Stability is shaked.
Commotion in the winds and changes, frights
Divert and crack, rend and deracinate.
The Clockwork Universe is dead![1] And God,
Our Father who art in heaven, does play dice[2].
Planck's constant[3] proves that Heisenberg's
Uncertainty[4] is fundamental in the universe.
We look at light as if it's made of waves,
Then see it's made of particles that smear.
Quarks[5] live! And yet, they're probability, a sea
That crests and falls, appears and disappears
Until, at last, crazily, uncertain, mad
With change that computations photograph,
Light is, we are, the universe exists.

I walk in Purgatory looking up
Toward the shining Earthly Paradise.
I long to see the Griffon bathed in light
Inside the Garden where the Tree of Good
And Evil grows. I long to feel the weights
Imposed upon me by the Angel Guardian
Before the Gate of Purgatory lifted off
My spirit as I rise toward a Purity of Heart. [6]

I long to be a Greek, like Kazantzakis[7], wild,
Sun on my head so that it's Song of Light
Can spray the earth, the global grape, with life.
I am Odysseus with my long, coarse hair
And body hardened by black brine, the great
Mind archer, the forty-footed dragon wreathed
With steaming blood, reflected light, and flame![8]

I follow Virgil as he presses on apace
With darkness-wrapped Aeneas and his friend
Achates through the rough-hewn citadel

Of Carthage being built by Dido, Queen.
The cloud that swirls before my eyes is magical.
I walk down city streets among a crowd
Unseen, amazed that none perceive me there.
Then, later on, I hear the voice
Of Mercury who bids me leave the joy
Of Carthage and my love for Dido's eyes
And go to found the Trojan city, Rome.[9]

But gravity bends space and time, and though
I am a poet, "redy to wenden on
My pilgrymage,"[10] and though I sit inside
This summer's heat and pray my muse: sing me . . .
"And through me tell the story of that man . . ."[11]
 and though I wish to find a hero large enough
To roam the wide world after he has sacked
The holy citadel of Troy, I am American,[12]
A polyglot whose being is becoming, he
Whose language was confused at Babel, he
Whose light was scattered on the face of earth,
Mankind whose particles act just like waves.
What mutiny runs through the song I sing!
Community and brotherhood contend
For order, shatters, builds, then bends to change.

As Sitting Crow kneels in his cold garage
He dreams that glory can be forged from pain.
He is the first American, black hair, black eyes.
Beside him, on the concrete floor, are stolen tires.
A part of living, reproducing, dying earth,
He sits inside the cold garage and dreams.
He laughs at death and wraps into its dark,
Holds fires of glory in his hands and throws
Out globes of flame into the darknesses
That plague his people's lives:

                              alcohol
And drug addiction, poverty, and squalidness
That wraps its cloak about the Reservation towns,
Each dawn so hopeless that it spreads a dull,
Blank dread inside the streaming morning light.
He dreams, and like a planet throned and sphered
By gravity, he bends time, government, and space

—

Into the universe that whorls out from his dream.
He strives to rent the fabric of America,
But makes, instead, a symbol of the way
That chaos builds complexity, which leads,
According to a probability distribution not
Yet computated, to a glory that might yet become.

O, listen to the winds inside my mind,
O muse, O Calliope, Moon Woman, water mixed
Into the Hippocrene's deep well where Pegasus
Once struck his hoof and made a drinking place
For poets mad enough to court their frenzied dreams.
Stir up my words inside the winds and make
A tempest strong enough to bear this tale.
I am a man and not a god. I wear the cloak
Humility has fashioned for my race
Of kindred hearts and spirits. Only you,
O muse, O Calliope, can let my song
Run wild among the stars and worlds found there.

I sing of war and of men at war . . .

An American Spirit, an American Epic, the poem:

"INDIANS HOLD ALEXIAN BROTHER'S[13] NOVITIATE"
  Headline from the *Shawano Evening Leader*,
  January 2, 1975

The Leader did not print on New Year's day.
On January second, nineteen seventy five,
"KESHENA, Wis. (UPI) —"
                    the story broke:

White Rabbit

He walked into the Gresham[14] bar. Talk stopped.
He was Menominee, and they were white.
White Rabbit shut the door, looked in their eyes.
Behind the bar, Pete, overweight, face pale,
Sent roots into the building's floors and froze,
His fear/White Rabbit's fear as palpable
And real as rope around a rabbit's neck.

Jim Speltz, the leader of the Gresham radicals,
His pistol on his hip, turned, shook his head.
He didn't look so mean. He looked as plain
As sparrows perched on fence posts in a field.
"No Indians come in here," he said. "This bar's
A white man's place."

        White Rabbit stared at him.
Speltz moved his hand toward his pistol's grip.
The men and Pete stared at the emptiness
That hovered in the air above the bar.

White Rabbit reached toward the prayer he'd said
Before he'd left the safety of his car,
But all his fierce intensity was gone.
Words struggled past the blood inside his throat
And strangled as the noose clenched deep in flesh.

THE ONLY GOOD INDIAN'S A DEAD INDIAN, the sign had said.

"I am an Indian," he said at last.

        Speltz stared,
Eyes brown like sparrow's eyes — a rabbit's eyes.

White Rabbit frowned his bitterness, his skin.
He turned and walked back out into the cold.
Speltz didn't move. White Rabbit didn't feel
The hotness of a bullet searing flesh.

He drew his pocketknife into the light,
Walked over to the rabbit, knocked the sign

Down on the ground, cut the hanging rope,
Looked at the birches, blackness of the pine,
Then got into his car and drove away.

The rabbit twitched, not quite alive, as cold
Seeped through its bloody fur into his heart.

God and Bill Winchell

He looked around the bar: beams hand-hewn, dark,
Brass beer taps, mugs and glasses clean
Beside the liquor bottles on the shelves.

He'd read, then listened to, the news last night.
Back east a woman, young, a mother, wrong
(She'd wanted cigarettes, she'd told the cops),
Had gone into a bar and met a woman-friend.
They'd had a drink, her friend had left, and then . . .
A man had grabbed her, stripped her naked, bra
And panties ripped from breasts and thighs,
Screams silence in the ears of fifteen men.

Four men had pinned her down atop the bar,
Forced flesh into her mouth and threatened her
To make her send them off to male ecstasy.
And then they raped her time and time again —
Men watching, silent as a prayer meant for God.
The woods about the bar, pine, maple, oak,
Rose up toward the morning fierce with cold.
He felt the force of life inside the woods.

He touched the bar. There was a truth, he thought.

In North Dakota Gordon Call, at dusk,
The darkness stained with lingering, soft light,
Had stood beside his pickup truck and son.
His blood was land and crops and growing fields:
The father and the son, their breath puffed out
Into the winter air. The wind was cold.

And then the headlights picking road ruts out,
The fumbling with the rifles, triggers cold
Enough to burn the fingers, shots as sharp
As needle points . . . and then the blood, the death
Of Gordon's son, two marshals sprawled on ground . . .
Then Gordon's fear, recrimination. He had killed,
And now, his son, the flesh of his flesh, spirit born
Inside the spirit that he was, was dead.
He'd searched for homemade justice with a gun.

16

Two marshals and his son, his boy, were dead.

But Gordon Call was still a fugitive,
A voice of justice crying out against
The darkness buried in the nation's heart.
He'd had the guts to stand beside a road
One winter day and make a righteous stand.

Bill wondered how the men who'd watched the rape
Felt now. They'd feel unclean, he thought. They'd feel
Ashamed, perhaps, and wrong.

                          There was a God.
At least a few would feel their shame and wrong.

White Rabbit's Vision

White Rabbit sat upon Hard Maple Hill
Amidst the sugar maple trees that stood
In snow as straight and wonderful as women's grace.
He looked into the sky and saw his world:

Outside the tribe the white man's world was full
Of people, cars, confusion, running here and there,
Towns jammed with buildings clanging with the sounds
Of money changing hands.

                    Inside the tribe
The world was bright, the Reservation's trees,
Soils, streams all blending to a unity
Of universe: the deer, the butterflies,
Mice, plants, earth, Indian essence, growth.

But deep inside the brightness, hidden deep
Inside the unity, an angry, writhing snake
As black as night without a moon or stars
Kept striking at the brightness, swallowing
Light, letting Indian/white-man poisons ooze.

His hair was long and black; his eyes were black.
His face was longer than it should have been.
He wasn't oval like the moon or bright like stars.

Hill cold was deep inside his sitting flesh.

He felt the snake inside him, felt the dark
That writhed and twisted at the jumbled world
Beyond the snake and brightness.

                    In the trees
The sugar sap was sleeping. In the snake

The darkness slept, as cold and waiting as the hill.

Wraiths

1

John Israel sat behind his Army surplus desk.
He felt his age. He'd slogged through farmer's fields
For twenty years collecting votes, and now
He wished the goddamned world would go away.

2

His coffee sat inside its cup and stared at him.

3

His thoughts skipped restlessly. He'd left for home,
But every time he'd climbed into the squad,
Grim wraiths, wings black and hollow like bat's wings,
Had haunted him the minute that he'd crawled inside.

At first he'd felt excited, wrapped into events.
The late night call from young Joe Stims, his family;
Jane as she struggled out of sleep to stare at him;
The drive through empty streets past antiseptic lights,
And then the frantic calls until Judge Gordon Myse,
Phone cradled in his hand, eyes lost, tried frantically
To end the standoff during morning light.

But then the wings inhabited the squad.
They didn't even whisper as they moved.
A tinge of darkness edged into the day.

In Tigerton Bill Winchell's boys bought guns
To help bring God into the government.

4

A faceless deputy sprawled dead beside
A country road, his face a mask of bone,
No nose or mouth or eyes, just blood and bone.

5

Eight miles away the Indians at the Novitiate
Held fast against the men the Governor had sent.
At first he'd thought that Sitting Crow would face
Reality and end his foolishness,
But then the media had found an untapped line
Into the monastery and spent the day
Bestowing hours of television time
On men and women who had never dreamed
They'd have the chance to make the evening news.
The Governor had called and forced John's hand.
The Sheriff had to take control or else . . .

Last night they'd shot a mule. A needed meal
Had grazed into the sights of Indian guns.

6

The mule guts spilled out from their cavity,
Snow splotched with steaming beads of blood.
The mulish spirit rose mist-white into the air.

7

At night a calculating Sitting Crow
Slipped people through the swamps, the net of cops,
To safety past the reservation's line.

8

And then there was the Rajah, preaching peace
While taking wealth from converts to his cause.
His neighbors claimed he worked his followers
Half dead and then forced fasts that lasted weeks.

9

A child's bones stared at John, its eyes too large.
The child held out its arms. It smelled so strong
Of sickness that it made John's stomach churn,
A urine smell, a smell of coming death.

10

He didn't know. He would have known once, walked
Into the jail on winter mornings, talked with those
Behind iron bars, and then drove out to Birnamwood
And Gresham, Cecil, Tigerton, and Bonduel
To feel the temperatures inside his world.

11

The phone rang, hollow in the courthouse emptiness.
John, startled, forced his hand toward the phone.

"You'd better get out here," Thorn said. He paused.
The silence strained at John. "I called your house.
Your wife's half nuts. You've got to get some sleep."

John sighed. "I'm on my way," he said. "Hold on.
I'll get the story in the squad."

                         He ran.
Streets looked unreal as red lights stroked walls, curbs.
He crossed the river bridge past fields of snow.

A truck sped down an empty country road.
A man had talked his way through roadblocks, smashed
Through bales of hay placed on the empty road.
The radio whined, crackled at John's nerves.
The wraith wings didn't whisper, whispered in the squad.
The truck stopped. Five kids jumped from the truck.

12

John's men brought guns into the air
And shot into the backs of Indian kids.
A sea of blood surged out into the night.

13

"Don't shoot!" John croaked into the mike. "Don't shoot!"

He wheeled the squad into the Novitiate yard.
The Novitiate loomed limestone white in front of him.

14

His overheated truck steamed, whistled at the night.
He slumped into the car seat, his head
Too large and heavy for his neck to hold.

The Indian kids were screeching crazily.
They'd run the gauntlet of the white man's guns!

15

The big, dark man was talking quietly to Thorn,
His back to John, wrists cuffed behind his back.
Thorn seemed distracted, filled with rage and dread,
An Indian cop imprisoned by a white man's badge.

John grabbed the man and spun him round and glared.
The Indian's black, calm eyes stared back at him.

He'd been a friend of Ivanhoe's for thirty years.
Once Ivanhoe had worked for John, a deputy
As tough and loyal as Burt Samuelson or Thorn.
John felt the wraith wings flutter dark and wild
"You God damned fool," John said. "You God damned fool!"

Not moving, Ivanhoe smiled, pride in his eyes.

The Potentials of Violence

Jim left the bar, guts churning, rage abuzz.

The Indian buck had walked into the bar,
His straggly, iron gray hair in braids, eyes bold.

Two hundred years ago the government
Had paid a bounty when you'd killed an Indian buck,
But now ancestors of the braves who'd felt
White steel as flesh sliced bloody scalp from hair
Walked through the doors of bars where signs proclaimed
The white man's dominance, his sanctuary.

The old man was a fool, his dignity,
Humiliation funny in the face of rage.
But Jim and every white man in the bar
Had felt their impotence, their inability
To chase the Indian from the bar afraid.

They'd stood, hands on their guns, and felt like fools.
They'd thought about reporters and the flood
Of cameras, words, and questions that would plague
Them if they kicked the old fool in his groin.

And now Jim's gut ached: the old man's eyes.
Jim's hands ungripped and gripped the steering wheel.

He wasn't superman. He couldn't let
Himself unravel from a single incident.
He knew himself for what he was: a small
Man caught inside a world too big for him:
the stones upon a Great Lakes beach, the rich
Deciduous forests shaved from dairy farms,
The land a continent linked to a continent,
The oceans of the world and other continents,
Each land-place filled with restless, saddened men.

He railed against injustices, pain,
And plotted out his small revenges on the world.
His tongue lashed out at television cameras, rage
The language that he spewed into his life.

Someday, perhaps, he'd get the chance to pay
Back insult with a bullet lodged into a heart.

He felt his daughter's breasts against his chest,
Her frantic struggling an irritant,
The fabric of her blouse and bra so thin
He knew he'd rip them, finding nakedness.
He felt the power of his manhood hard as iron.
Her eyes were overlarge, more white than brown.
The brandy pounded in his swimming head.
She twisted, tearing off her blouse, her bra
A fiery red against her smooth, white skin.

He felt half faint. His need, her fear, the booze . . .

She hadn't screamed. She hadn't say a word.
She'd looked into his eyes, down at his jeans.
She'd caught her breath, then turned and ran outside.
His rage-desire churned. He loathed himself.

He turned the Buick off the pavement down
The gravel road that ended at the farm.
The darkness ebbed and flowed about the car.

He had to make life right. The Indian didn't count.
He had to flee the newsmen's search for facts.
He had to be alone. He had to be
If wrongs he'd done could ever be erased.

Lena

Before dawn Lena left the cold Novitiate
And slipped down to the river's banks to wash her hair.
The final stars of night were glory in the skies,
And though the cold crunched sharp beneath her feet,
She still felt warm. Her worries of the day before
Had melted in the silence of the night.

She knew men watched her from the night-black woods.
Across white river ice one stamped at cold.
Their guns were much too cold to touch with flesh.

She knelt beside the hot spring's steaming mist
And felt the earth's cold/heat upon her face.
She wondered, if she really washed her hair,
Would ice bead white as frost into its raven-blue?

The day before sporadic shooting, meaningless
Inside a world immense with snow and cold,
Had made anxiety an ache inside her gut.
Last night she'd sought out Sitting Crow,
Unzipped his sleeping bag before eyes blinked from sleep,
And let him rise inside her ice-cold hands.

He'd touched her breasts and made her nipples hard,
Reached deep inside her ache, touch kneading down
Despair black in the cold Novitiate walls.
Warmth spread inside her folds, and then his weight
Was thrusting down inside her tightened flesh
His swelling hard, insistent, rhythmical.
Release, hot wetness, gentle moaning, soft . . .

She knelt down in the snow and threw her hair.
She shivered as spring's heat shocked cold through arms.
She'd never felt such cold-fire-fear before.
She threw her head back, splashing water, ice
Into the cold, her face a mask of cold.

She felt exultant. She was Indian, free!
The whites had seized her lands. They'd trampled feet
On ashes of her dead. Now Sitting Crow

25

Was sitting in the dark Novitiate.
Men watched her, holding guns too cold to touch.

All history trailed blood behind its march.

She turned and ran toward the fireplace fires
That burned all day and night against the cold.
Mixed with the raven of her hair, ice gleamed
As dawn broke gray and cold above the earth.

Banshee

Kim laughed, a banshee loose upon the earth.
He danced into the oak Novitiate doors
And whooped and yelled to feel his victory.
The Sheriff's guns had melted in the hands
That pointed them at him. The Sheriff's men
Were cowards, chicken livered yellow, dumb
As turkeys just before their heads came off.

"O macho man!" he called himself. "A fox
Whose wiles are greater than the Sheriff's guns.
Whoo Hooo!" he shouted out. "Ay yie! Ay yie!"

And then he saw Aunt Lena's angry face.
A crazy-looking Superstar and Horse,
Their eyes alight with his, Bob Buck's, Todd Dunn's,
Sam Wellington's, and Marsha Sam's exploit,
Were laughing at him as he capered like
The Trickster celebrating feats of trickery.
But then he had to face his Aunt's black eyes.
She moved. He moved. She blocked the hallway door.

She didn't speak at first. She tried to summon words.
"What do you think you're doing here?" she raged.
"You could have died out there. Those men have guns!"

She looked at Superstar and Horse. They frowned
As if they disapproved of kids who'd hide
Beneath a tarp, then brave a hundred guns,
But both of them had shining, praising eyes.

As Lena tried to think about Kim's being there,
Sam slipped behind her, goosed her, yelled, and danced
Into the doorway. Kim and Marsha grinned
And dashed past Lena yodeling their joy.

The five of them danced frantic past dim rooms.
Cheers echoed down the empty marble halls.
Kim found the stairs and climbed the steps by twos
Until he stood beside a window on the second floor.
He pried the window open, looked toward

Where Ivanhoe had parked the truck they'd rode
To victory and screeched at white men out of sight.

"I'm just fourteen!" he yelled. "A man of fourteen made
You look like stupid fools!"

          The others stood beside
Him throwing taunts at men they couldn't see.

"Menominee were warriors once again," Kim thought.
He looked at Marsha, put his arm around
Her shoulders, smiled with joy, and thought, "By God.
I am a warrior from a warrior tribe."

By God, she had a slender bod, he thought.

He screeched so loud his voice grew hoarse. He turned
As Lena caught him by his braids and pulled.
He tried to get away, then cursed his Aunt.
Bob, Todd, and Sam had taken off like deer,
But Marsha held her ground beside her man.
As Lena looked at them she shook her head.

"We've got to talk to Sitting Crow," she said.
She made Kim look at her. "I'll have your hides
If Sitting Crow decides to make me baby-sit you guys!"

Kim smiled. No woman's hand could hold him down.
He was the fox who'd made the Sheriff look a fool.
"We're meeting Sitting Crow?" he asked. He felt
His heart take off as if it were a goose.
"I get to meet with Sitting Crow?" he asked again.

He stood up straight and looked at Marsha's eyes.
What would kids locked in school think if they knew
That he was near to meeting Sitting Crow?
"Lead on, Aunt, lead," he said as Marsha choked
A giggle in her throat.

          His Aunt looked down at him.
The men outside had made it plain they'd use
Their guns if Warriors didn't leave the building soon.

—
28

She yanked her nephew's braids and smiled inside
To hear him yelp his protest to the world.

Portrait of a Demagogue
At Work

Before he went downstairs, Bill Winchell looked
Into the late night sky. He didn't see the moon,
Though silver light was mingled with the cold.
Instead, he gathered in himself, each thought,
Each breath a wandering fire he willed into his cause.
At last he turned and strode downstairs, his boots
A sharp retort against the red linoleum.

The thirty men who'd brought their beers downstairs
Stopped talking when they saw his burning eyes.
An hour before they'd joked and laughed, souls glad
To have day done. As Thelma moved about,
Vivacity sparked laughter, elbows into ribs,
And thoughts they'd never dare to think at home.
But now their faces, white and ethnic, felt his truth.

He felt his fire, felt revelations building deep.
He pushed the doubts he felt about himself,
Just after waking, up the stairs into the bar.

Behind the folding table at the back,
Three-dozen M-1s lined the off-white plaster wall.
Beside the table army-issue hand grenades
Protruded, large, green metal eggs, into the light.

Bill bowed his head in prayer, tried to cleanse
Himself of pride while gathering the fires
He'd stored inside himself into a storm of words.
He looked into men's eyes and sadly shook his head.

"The words of wisdom are as nails," he said. "They're nails
That those who know the Truth have got to drive
Into the hearts of those who cannot see."

He paused, his voice intense, yet soft. He sent
His spirit gently out into the room,
Surrounding, probing, reaching for a dominance.

"Back East a woman walked into a bar.

Four men, their filth abomination, raped
A woman for an hour," he said. He paused.
"And in that bar the four men weren't alone.
Some fifteen other men drank beer and cheered
As men drove rods into the woman's womb."

He paused. He'd said his troubled thoughts,
And now the men were troubled, foreheads creased.

"This is the land our fathers risked their lives
To settle, reaching for a dignity
Denied them elsewhere in the world," he said.
"They brought their wives and daughters to this land
Fired up by hopes for decency, God's grace.

"This is what we Americans have wrought:
A bar where fifteen men can stand and cheer
Four animals as they debase and rape
A mother, wound her, take away her dignity!"

The tension in the room was building. Strong
With rage he felt their rage reverberating back,
His will, their will enough to shake the universe.

"There's evil strong enough to take our farms," he said.
"And give them to the corporations and the banks,
An evil strong enough to rape the lives
Our fathers and our mothers built for us.

"That woman in that bar back east, so far away,
Is not so different from the men inside this room.
We've each been raped. We've stood and let the government
Tell us the hours we work each day are not our own.
They bleed us with their taxes, then force loans
By making sure the hours we work won't pay enough
To feed our families. Then they come with documents
That say that we're not anything, that we're
No better than the dirt beneath their heels
When they're out drinking in a bar back east.

"And in their big political conventions words
Of hope are roared in mockery of us,
The ones that grow their bread and build their homes."

31

Bill paused, light headed from his voice's rage.
The men were nodding, caught inside his argument.
He smiled as silence settled down into the room.
He felt triumphant, justified. He'd caught the fire.
It held the possibility of birth,
Of rousing up the nation with its old ideals.

"We've got our guns and hand grenades," he said.
"We've had enough of helplessness. We've known our land,
And now the bankers, government, and Jews . . ."

He paused, his thought unfinished, forcing thought.

"These words are rods I want to pound like nails
Into your flesh: Our enemy is here.
But we have guns and won't be raped again.
We're like the country's early patriots.
We'll make our stand for right on Bunker Hill[15].
The government's apologists can cheer
And put away the shame they feel, but we are men,
And like the Indians, we will fight to keep our land.
We aren't a helpless woman in a bar
Back east who can't fight four large, bestial men."

His voice hushed down into a whisper, peace.
Nobody clapped. He never let them clap.
Their eyes were shining, though. They shook his hand.
He felt the Truth he'd said inside of them.
Someday the fire he'd sparked would be unleashed.
They'd stand before a bonfire with their eyes on God.

At last they drifted from the room toward their farms.
He turned the downstairs lights off, climbed the stairs,
And sat behind the bar he'd owned for thirteen years.

The time was coming soon, he told himself.
The dark was pregnant with the time to come.

Rajah

Nine children, faces bright, sat at the Rajah's feet.
He'd worn his robe this morning, and the folds
That pooled out from his sitting stool pleased him.

"No life is different from its nature," Rajah said.
"This paradox is deep and wonderful.
Like ice burned tongues or filling hunger's emptiness.
For though each nature will be what it is,
Creation still must shape and alter us
Until we're part of God's great harmony."

He smiled, the act of teaching pleasing him.
This cold land's people were prepared for truth.
A warmer land would make his flesh feel good,
But cold drove people inward, forcing thoughts
Beyond their flesh toward a core sublimity.

He turned as Dawn, his newest follower,
Slipped quietly into the room, flesh full.
In days to come she'd shrink into her womanhood,
Becoming spare as thought was disciplined.
The Rajah smiled at her. Her breath was hard and short.
She couldn't seem to keep arms at her sides.

"What is it child?" He asked.

                              Her chest heaved, gasping air.
"They've got Celest," she said. "They took Celest.
I saw them grab her. Two of them. She screamed.
They threw her in their car. Then drove away. I screamed . . ."

He felt her panic welling up inside his peace.
The image of Celest, her screams, was in the room.
He felt fear flow into the children at his feet.
"You've got to stop," he told Dawn. "Calm yourself."

Her blue eyes blinked. She shut her mouth, then gasped.
The children looked at him. Confusion, fear,
Dawn's panic made them seem emaciated, small.

"Go to your rooms," he said. "I am the Rajah. Peace."
"In shaping, each must face disrupted lives."

Obedient, they left. He looked at Dawn.
She'd started quivering, arms clutched against her breasts.

"Come child," he said.

        She walked across the room.
He put his hand out, let his warmth move into her.
Her tenseness fought against his spirit's calm.

Then, unexpectedly, a black, despairing rage
Made legs feel weak and boiled into his chest.
He'd left behind in India the petty government
Determined to define what made a holy man.

"The evil, vicious fools!" He raged. "They're after me!
The Rajah! Shaper! Alterer! The evil fools!"

Beneath his hand Dawn tensed, then left the room,
The universe,

        as catatonic shock
Stunned through her legs and heart into her brain.

The Rajah, frightened, looked into her empty eyes.

The Darkness Emanating From A Fire

Kim walked into the marble dining-hall.
Before him Lena paced as if she were
A cougar proud of how her body moved.
Beside him Marsha held Kim's hand, her eyes
Much larger than they'd been before they'd tossed
The tarp aside and ran past men with guns.

Impassive, Sitting Crow stared stonily at Kim.
He looked like fire, thin, swift, and pliable.
Eyes smoldered darkness, starlight lost to dark.
The darkness emanated from the fire
And wrapped the spirits standing near with flames.

Kim stood before his hero as his Aunt
Went up and linked her arm into his arm.
Kim wasn't quite afraid, but still, his heart
Was hammering so loud he wasn't sure
That he would hear what Sitting Crow would say.

Defiant, angry, Sitting Crow looked down at Kim
And felt the wrong: two youngsters in a hall
Surrounded by whites armed with loaded guns.
He felt the crumbling of his plans: kids locked
Into a deathtrap when they should have been at school.

The silence stretched. "What are you doing here?" he asked.

Kim smiled. His spirits rose, a falcon hovering
In air above the river's granite cliffs.
He was the macho man! The man who'd run
Like wind before the barrels of the white man's guns!
"We're joining you," he said. "We know you're right,
And so we've come to join the warriors strong
Enough to face the white man's cops and guns."

He looked at Marsha, pleased at what he'd said.
She smiled at him, the perfect woman joined
To him because she liked the man he was.

His anger burning, Sitting Crow leaned close.

"We've vowed to die," he said. "Whites won't believe
We're mad enough to let you die with us.
They know the Indian heart, how Indians feel
About their children, how we'll give our lives,
Or dreams or freedom or our souls for them.
We've got to slip you past the cops into the woods.
We understand your courage and resolve,
But I . . . the warriors, cannot let you stay with us."

Beside Kim, Marsha pressed against his side.
Kim felt the wildness whirling in his brain
And felt the way the world felt upside down.
They'd gotten through two roadblocks, braved aimed guns,
And now were told they were a bunch of kids.
He shuffled on the marble floor in tune
With all his free abandon brimmed with light.

"We've got a right, like you, to die," he said.
His knees were jittery and faltering.
He didn't have the right to lecture Sitting Crow.
The man was like a God, a fearless heart.
"We're not a bunch of little bratty kids.
I'm not about to hang my ass in front
Of white men's guns again until they blaze
Like John Wayne's pistols through the doors downstairs.
You can't make me or Marsha or my Aunt
Betray what we've decided in our hearts."

His will contending with his anger, Sitting Crow
Looked stonily into the young man's eyes.
"You're young," he said. "Filled up with who you are.
The truth is, all the evil in the whites
Can't be erased by killing all the whites.
We need a conversation where our race
Impresses natural rights too long denied."
He looked at Lena. "If you try to stay
I'll have to ask your Aunt to take you home."

Kim didn't look toward his Aunt. Eyes flashed.
As Lena looked at Kim she felt undone.
She felt the currents wild in Sitting Crow.
She wouldn't let him face his trials alone.
Kim stared at Sitting Crow and tried to make

Him blink, but deep inside, the warrior fires
Leaped back and forth between the spirit-world,
The real-world, the drum of war a symphony
That drew its music from tree roots and rock.

Kim felt himself drawn down to a wilderness:
Chaotic songs of spirit, life, and death.
He saw the fibrillation of the crow's black heart,
Felt quill-roots sprouted on the crow's hunched back.

He ripped his eyes away from Sitting Crow's.
"I am the crazy fool who'll snatch, from air,
A bullet, spit it back into the shooter's eye,"
He sang. "I'll find a stone and shatter it
Into a million bits by laughing like
The crazy man, the macho man I am!"

He grabbed ahold of Marsha's hand and ran
Into the halls that ran in mazes north and south.
He didn't want to face the madness black
Inside the shaman's power-singing eyes.
He felt toward a darkness where there was
No Sitting Crow, no rage, no shining eyes.

Negotiation

The phone: Once. Twice. Then Lena answered angrily.
She couldn't find her nephew anywhere.
The ringing, as she tried to think about
A place where kids could hide, was startling.

"John Israel here," John said. "I'd like to talk
To Sitting Crow."

          At daybreak he and Thorn had strung
A phone line from a pole into the barn.
Upon a bale of hay the phone looked alien
Inside the world of barn beam gray, dust motes,
Straw, darting swallows, dairy cows, manure.
John searched for absolution from the dust.
His stomach knotted tight into his nerves.

Her eyes cold, Lena looked at Sitting Crow
And let the Sheriff feel her silence through the line.
The porcelain-black telephone was old.
Yet, she and Sitting Crow, Horse, Superstar,
Had talked to newsmen from around the world.

Beside her Sitting Crow was looking out
Toward the barn to where the Sheriff sat.
He didn't look at Lena. Finally she smiled.
She thought about her moment of defiant joy
Beside the spring the day before. Her voice grew shrill.
"We're cold in here," she said. "We're out of food.
You let those kids get past you. You're responsible.
He'll talk to you when we've got food and heat."

"I can't do that," John said. "Unless you'll throw
Your guns away and come out peacefully.
I don't want anyone to die. Tell Sitting Crow."

She looked at Sitting Crow. His spirit shone
With fierce, bright light. He took the offered phone.
"Our treaty rights say Catholic orders owning land
Contiguous to Indian lands must use their land
Or give it to the Tribe," he said. "This land's unused,

38

So what we've taken's ours by treaty rights."

John sighed and shook his head. He felt the wraiths
Inside the barn, their fluttering a whispered song.
"I told you truth," he said. "I got the priests
To meet the Tribal Chair, and she reviewed
The costs of keeping up the Novitiate
And told the priests the Tribe could not accept the cost."

"The Chair is not the Tribe." He spit his words.
"We want the land signed over to the Tribe.
You white men never understand our ways.
An Indian takes a gift of beads and signs
A paper that he doesn't understand
And signs away his people's natural rights,
And by your law whites own what can't be owned."

John sighed into the line. "I'm not a judge,"
He said. "Those arguments belong in court.
Right now we need to find a compromise.
You want to live. Nobody has to die."

"We've taken vows of death," said Sitting Crow.
"We've pledged our flesh to Mother Earth."

John's stomach churned. Sour acid burned his chest.
"But Sitting Crow. . ." he said.

                              As Sitting Crow
Glared from the force of what he'd said, he turned
To Lena, handed her the phone and smiled.
He grasped his rifle's barrel, stared toward the barn.

"Our deaths be on your head, white man," she said.
"The children here need food. They need to feel
Their parent's love again before they die."
She hung the phone up, looked at Sitting Crow,
And smiled. He smiled, determination in his eyes.

Soon Israel would face the truth. He'd send
His men back home or make a killing-ground.
In Sitting Crow the Indians had a warrior chief.
He loved, but knew his heritage was death.

———

She touched his shoulder. "Now we'll know the white man's heart."
Inside her words she hid the question: Will
You make me babysit the kids back home?
She wouldn't let him die away from her.

He turned back to his window, gun in hand.

Inside the barn's gray dusk John held the phone.
He'd slept an hour at dawn. He fought against
The blood that welled before his eyes from earth.

Out in the light the blood would go away.
Out in the light the earth could heal itself.

The Judas Kiss

1

The mist hung brown and heavy near the stream.
Six moved through brush so tangled that it seemed
As if they'd never find the rendezvous.
They held their Uzies[16] close, their senses strained
To catch a sound of movement in the brush.

Perched in a maple on the river's banks,
Bill Winchell smiled to see them in the brush.
The biting cold invigorated him.
The six were West Virginians that had flown
In yesterday and Donn Truesdale, a local boy.
One moved as if he'd been in Viet Nam.
He looked as feral as a mountain cat —
Bill held the net-rope in his hand, breath held.
The six men crept toward his maple perch.
The tree trunk sang a song of bark and leaves.

He jerked the rope. The net fell from its perch
And trapped the man who'd been in 'Nam. The others turned.
He fired four shots. A splotch of orange appeared
On everyone but Truesdale, the net-caught man.
The combat madness made Bill feel invincible.
He climbed, half dropped out of the tree and rolled.
An Uzi chattered, bullets painting ground.

He came up firing, shooting paint into the net
The young Virginian had almost escaped.
Donn Truesdale squeezed another round, but missed.
Bill jumped, got Truesdale in his sights, and fired.
With agony, splotched orange, the farmer died.
Bill sang his victory beneath his breath.

2

Bill sat inside the bar, beside the stove,
And radiated satisfaction, moved
By words that rose and fell in tides of thought.
He felt into the nation's depths of soul.

41

He watched as Thelma moved about the bar.
She stirred men like he stirred them. As she moved
Half looked at her, her breasts; the others turned
Away from her to obviate desire.
The room was overflowing with his followers.
Their energy was restless, moving, filled
 With manly fire that made them good Americans.

He sat alone amidst the crowd of men.
He felt the pistol jumping in his hand and saw
Donn Truesdale's face as paint struck home its death.
Donn's eyes rolled, frightened, wild, inside his head.
Bill loved the young man, loved how passionate
His agony had been. The man had thought he'd won,
And then he'd lost and felt the pain of loss.
He was a true American, a man
Who knew how easily the moneymen
And Jews corrupted all the country's good.

Sam Ludwig got up from a group of men
From Baraboo and brought his German beer to Bill.
More right-hand man than follower, he was
A German, born into the land he farmed.

"You got away again today," he said.

Bill looked in Sam's eyes; then Sam looked away.
"I won't be beat, you know," he said, his voice intense.

"I know. Donn Truesdale thinks you've got a spell."

The thought pleased Bill. He felt invincible.
"God's word's invincible," he said. "I'm not.
Donn had a shot, but missed. I marked him like
The Lord marked Cain."

                    Sam looked at Bill again.
His eyes were dark from years of worrying.
"The bank's said that they're going to foreclose,"
He said. "They won't give me a loan to plant this spring."

The clean, fierce fire of hate stirred Bill's insides.
"We've got to move while Gordon Call's still free,"

He said. "We've got to show the infidels
Who run this rotten governmental mess
That men still walk the earth!"

                      The helplessness
Sam felt fell from him. With a smile he touched Bill's hand.
"You lead; I'll follow you to hell and back," he said.

Bill's fire leaped like the pistol marking men
With death by make-believe. His soul sang silently.

He clasped Sam's hand and watched as Thelma moved.
She made teeth ache with fire. She felt his eyes.

3

Donn Truesdale came into the bar at twelve.
Bill's mark of Cain had been washed off. He looked
Half fey, blue eyes booze-bright. He saw Bill by the stove.
His face lit up. Beneath his skin a candle had been lit.

"My man!" he hollered. Like a ship in heavy seas
He plowed through men toward Bill's eyes and Sam.
As Thelma bumped against his weave, Donn stepped
Aside, then slid behind her wake to get to Bill.
"You got me good today," he said. He grinned.
"I had you dead to rights, but I'm the one that died."

Bill smiled, eyes closed. "I like to win," he said.

The young man's smile dissolved into a frown.
Bill felt the tension rising, felt the mania
That swept across Donn Truesdale's flushed, hot face.
His fingers tightened on the net-rope, nerves
As taut and tuned as lion muscles primed
To spring toward an unsuspecting prey.

Donn put his hands down on the tabletop.
"I am in love with you," he said to Bill, voice slurred
And sweet as honey stolen from a hive.

Sam scraped his chair's legs back. Bill, riveted,
Stared at Donn's shining eyes. His heart was wild.

Donn's lips came close to his across the tabletop.
Bill felt transfixed. He felt as if he were the Christ
Before Gethsemane[17]. Donn's lips touched his.
The kiss's passion stirred Bill's soul and made
It twist and turn inside a brutal winter wind.
The bar was silent. Prophecies were loose.
The pioneers wrenched from their roots and marched
Into the wilderness, the promised land.
The farmers left the land and threw their lives
Into the concrete towered city citadels,
Their spirits shriveled by the masses they became.

Bill's cheeks flamed red. He felt the shame
The Truesdale boy had brought into the bar.
"You've got a lust no man should have," he said.

Donn looked as if he'd taken lead, not paint,
Into his heart. His blue eyes filled with tears.
He shook his head. "I'm not a queer," he said.
He looked confused confronting Bill's harsh eyes.

Sam looked from Bill to Donn to Bill again.
Bill got up, walked toward the basement stairs.

He was enraged, eternally defiled
By someone he had treated like a son.

White Rabbit's Fields

1

At home White Rabbit sat inside his chair.
Through kitchen windowpanes the world seemed warm,
The winter's snow, ice, cold outside, away.
In dimming evening light the pines, dark, green,
Had living presences, their mystery
Enfolded in the beauty of the world.

The way the night was creeping from the sky,
Black shadows spilled from trees, unsettled him.
He'd watched night spread a thousand, thousand times,
An interacting dance invoking strong, dark moods,
But he had never felt such strong disquiet — all
His earth-soul tense from feelings darker than the night.

The incident at Pete's Bar haunted him.
The rabbit, eyes glazed dull with death, hung by its neck,
His vision of the snake dreamed while he sat
Inside the winter cold atop Hard Maple Hill . . .
The world was skewered, bent away from where
It should have been, his earthen self a leaf
Torn from its branch by winds so strong they ripped
Tree roots and toppled pines to forest floors.

The radicals who'd seized the Novitiate
Had stirred the white man's passions to a boil.
The winds were stronger than they'd been for years.
The tribe would feel the white man's furious wrath.

And why? He knew the radicals. His memories:

White Rabbit pulled the ginseng root from sand
And handed it to Superman, a medicine
Of power, quickening a woman's womb,
Or stirring men to life when they had shrunk
Into an instrument for getting rid of piss.

As Superman looked at the root, his blue eyes shrunk.
"We've spent three days out in the woods," he snarled.

"So far we've got a quarter bag of roots."

"I told you at the house," White Rabbit said.
"You picked a bad year. Ginseng needs good rains.
This year's too dry. The wild root makes whites pay.
The farmers plant the roots and grow it as a crop.
I am a gatherer, traditional Menominee."

"I'll murder you like you're a dumb-assed goose,"
The young man said.

            White Rabbit shrugged.
"I can't create what isn't there," he said.
"I'm not a shaman."

            Superstar pulled out
His pistol, snub-nosed, ugly, black, and waved.
"You are the champion ginseng gatherer,
The last great shaman living with the tribe."
He leered. "Let's see how well you gather death."

White Rabbit stared impassively, his heart
Alive with fear. He didn't flinch as Superstar
Brought down the pistol barrel to his head.
He said an ancient Indian chant, "Go walk
In beauty that the beauty may be you."

The pistol's ugly barrel stared at him.
It seemed to be as massive as the rock
On Highway 47 that the old chiefs said
Contained the soul of all Menominee.
The pistol didn't waver. Superstar's
Hand gripped the gun-butt; finger touched
The trigger. Time grew outward from the space
White Rabbit occupied to stop the sun.
At last the barrel wavered, pointed down.
White Rabbit looked at Superstar. His eyes were dull.
"You're Indian; I'm an Indian. I can't kill you."

White Rabbit didn't move. He waited. Superstar
Threw down the garbage bag of ginseng roots
And walked away.

But what was life? His hands
Alive with digging up the ginseng roots
That Superstar had thought were worth his death?

2

Tu Fu stood motionless above him, watching hands
Enriched by Mother Earth dig up the ginseng root
He'd left for this, their thirty-year old ceremony
Of digging up the season's last forked root.

"You look so peaceful in your garden place,"
Tu Fu said softly.

As White Rabbit pulled
The root out from the ground he thought of Superstar.
Sky scattered through the canopy of pine.

"Last month a young man nearly murdered me,"
He said. "He stuck his gun into my face.
In thoughts my spirit seems alive to death.
I want to sleep at night, but can't. I don't feel joy
In digging through the richness of the earth."

Tu Fu's eyes narrowed, then his shoulders slumped.
"I didn't look," he said. "I've known you thirty years,
And still, I didn't look."

"He was Menominee.
"He said he'd sell the roots to you."

"To me?"
Tu Fu asked sharply. "I buy the root from you.
You made this garden. I have always thought
The root should come from hands that feel the earth."

"That doesn't trouble me," White Rabbit said.
"He'd heard of you, that's all. The tribal young
Are always chasing spirit-wisps and ghosts.
What troubles me is that he let me live
Because, he said, we're brothers of the skin."

"You have a race," Tu Fu said. "Sometimes blood

Burns brightly, like a fiery sunset sky."

"But he could think of killing me," White Rabbit said.
"There's blood in that, but no true sense of tribe.
He would have taken everything I am
To make his life a little easier."

Tu Fu looked at the root White Rabbit held.
"The poet says," he said. "Why fuss about your age;
The young are still too young to know the dead.
They see they are forever. Chill winds blow.
They feel the wind and bare their chests and laugh.
You see that death is death. To them it's mist and fog."

"But we should still support their mindlessness?"

Tu Fu smiled quietly. "The young man failed
To dig the ginseng roots," he said. "You've put
The plants into this soil behind your house
For forty years. He didn't find your garden place."

The dark had gathered up the forest pines
And made them shadows black against the sky.
The snow was touched by starlight, dark, yet white.
A year ago the radicals had been a bunch of kids.
But now they were proclaiming war against
The whites and glory to Menominee.

White Rabbit felt a need to feel the hearts
Inside the radicals. He was an ancient man.
In youth he'd lived at schools the white man ran.
They'd cut his hair and took his language, banned
It from his tongue, and tried to make him less
Than what he knew he was, an Indian boy.

He'd loved his tribe: the Pow Wows with their men
Bird-feathered, rolling laughter, language used
Before the white man found this wilderness.
He'd married young and wept when Wanda died.
He'd loved his life as strongly as a man can love.

But what now? What was life? His destiny?
Inside his canopy of pines his garden grew.

He harvested the power of his ginseng roots.
He walked into the white man's world and drove
A white man's car and heard the Indians' rage.
He knew that Superstar was radical,
A leader with a liquid, dancing tongue.

White Rabbit was an elder, old enough to know
That wars were for the young. But still, he yearned
To wipe away the eyes Jim Speltz had spit at him.
He yearned to heal the hurt that Superstar
Had metamorphosed into rage. He yearned.
He was too old to dream a warrior's death.

The darkness wrapped itself inside his heart.
He sat inside his kitchen on his chair
And stared into the endless fields of dark.

The Altar

1

John parked outside the Methodist's brick church
And blankly stared at dark oak, double doors.
At last, still empty, cold, he left the squad
And climbed the church's steps and went inside.

He'd never been a man with burning faith.
He'd tried to live his life by Christian principles,
But in his heart of hearts he couldn't see
Jehovah's power hidden in the nuclear
Exchange that made a million, million suns
Across a universe too huge to comprehend.

But still, his troubles mounting, here he was
Inside God's holy temple, waiting for God's voice
To shake the doors and smoke to fill the air
And seraphim[18] to fly to him with fire.
He slipped into a pew and looked at altar wood.
He strained to see Manoah's altar cut from rock
And shaped, truncated, like a pyramid.[19]
He longed to see, in flames, an angel rising up
Toward the light of heaven, in his heart
A flame of faith that scorched his doubts.

But in the chapel's peace no fire was lit.
His long dead mother looked at him and said
That if the Lord had wanted man to fly,
He would have grafted, on our shoulders, wings.
The altar, carved from wood, impermanent,
Substantial only if faith's eyes were clear,
Was not enough. He'd heard what Sitting Crow had said:

"We've taken vows of death," he'd said to John.
"We've pledged our flesh and life to Mother Earth."

A child's skull-sockets staring at his eyes,
Its eyes so large they sunk into skull emptiness . . .

The men the Governor had sent held guns

A sound behind him made him jump. He turned
And smiled to see Skye Frays. The minister
Was dressed as always: Brown coat, string tie, brown slacks.
He looked at John, a question in his eyes.
"John Israel?" he asked. "In church?" He smiled.
"I never thought I'd see the holy day."

John bit his lip and frowned. "I'm here," he said.
He opened up his arms and grinned expansively.
"Manoah's altar shimmers in my mind,
And seraphim meld with the altar flame."

Skye frowned, sat down, and looked into John's eyes.
"Sounds like you've loads of trouble on your mind,"
He said. "You need a sympathetic ear?"

What did he want? John asked himself. He looked
Up at the altar, felt the purity.
He conjured up black wings inside the barn's soft light.
"I'm troubled, Skye," he said. "Menominee's gone mad.
The Governor's as nervous as a mother hen.
The whites who think that being white is being right
Are rattling sabers like a tribe of fools,
And I can't sleep at night." He looked at Skye.
"I've got these demons in my brain, and when I run . . ."

Skye searched John's face. He didn't try to speak.
Possession by a demon wasn't possible.
"I've ministered Menominee for fifteen years,"
He said at last.

                    John nodded, waiting. Skye looked up
Toward the stained glass windows pouring light
Into the chapel. Christ was looking down
Upon the two of them, his hands outstretched.
"I'm glad you're Sheriff, John," he said. "You've got
A conscience I can trust. The radicals
On either side won't make you spill their blood.
There's death in Sitting Crow, and everything
I've spent a lifetime working at will fail
If that young man achieves his martyrdom."

"The demons aren't a dream," John said. "They're real."

The mule's guts spilled into the snow still splotched
With beads of blood. Its life-hot organs steamed.

Skye touched John's hand, looked at his haunted eyes.
He shook his head and tried to find the Psalm:
>"They even sacrificed their sons
>And their daughters to demons,
>And shed innocent blood,
>Even the blood of their sons and daughters,"[20]

He said. John shivered uncontrollably.

A sea of blood surged out into the night.

"God's real?" he asked.

      Skye looked at Christ. Light stained
through robe and eyes and fell on them. "He's real," he said.

What could he do? He was a minister,
And John had come to see him in his church.
He couldn't doubt his faith. He wouldn't doubt his faith.

John looked at Skye and tried to find Skye's faith.
He looked toward the altar, tried to see
A seraph standing on the altar's wood.
But even if he saw, what then? Could he believe?
Or would they haunt him like the demons haunted him?
Flames danced upon the altar's wood. A pile of ash.

2

The Rajah climbed the church's steps aflame
With holiness. He burned with rage and hate
To think about the evil that had made
His following a target of his enemies.
He passed through doors into the spirit-heart
Of Christianity and felt his calm
Inside the storm that made him tremble rage.
He felt the Christian holiness confront his holiness.

He stood inside the chapel's foyer, face
Implacable, will burned into the flame he was.
He'd not accept the violation of his universe
Caused by the cowards who had snatched Celest.
He'd face the Sheriff, make him face the crime
Committed, then mold justice to his will.

The minister beside the Sheriff turned and watched
The Rajah move into the chapel with the force
Of wind and river water striking cliffs of stone.
The minister put out his hands, dismayed
To see the flame around the Rajah's head.
How could he see what was impossible?
The Rajah sang with power, inner peace.
He wouldn't fail. As God was great and good
Inside His universe, he wouldn't fail.

3

John turned and looked toward the church's doors.
An angry Rajah stormed into the chapel, face
Contorted from his rage.

                            What now? John asked.
He tried to conjure angels up to dance
Upon the altar, but the world churned in a dance
That had no end. The order he had always sought
Had died with Sitting Crow at Joe Stim's house,
And now he couldn't even find his peace
Inside the sanctuary of a church.

        "May the day perish on which I was born,
He quoted softly, gently to himself
        May that day be darkness; may God above not seek it,
        nor the light shine upon it.
        May darkness and the shadow of death claim it . . ."[21]

4

Skye stood as if he'd seen the Devil come.
His jaw was open. Stunned, his eyes were round,
And in his rage at violation, pain,
He balled his fist into the pew's hard wood.

The Rajah's eyes were black as anthracite.
Skye put his hands out, shook his head to stop
The desecration of the chapel's peace.
He saw the flame about the Rajah's head.
"No, no," he said. "Not now. Not now." This was
God's creature too, not evil flesh, but still . . .

He tried to drive the Rajah's force away.
The Sheriff needed God, and Skye was charged
With shepherding men to a state of grace.

The Rajah stopped and shook his fist at John.
Small beads of sweat were shining in his beard.

Skye rose and placed himself, his ministry,
Between the Rajah and the Sheriff, but then he froze.
His neck hair bristled like a wind-blown prairie's grass.
He felt the light behind him, felt the fire
Of miracles about to come into his life.
He turned:

            The altar was aflame with light,
On fire, but still, it didn't burn. Skye sat back down.
Time disappeared into the dancing flame.
The Rajah, Sheriff, and his church were lost
Inside the radiance of miracle.

5

The Rajah's tried to sear the Sheriff with his eyes.
"Inside this Christian church!" he spat. "While thieves
Have snatched a soul away from home. My home!
What are you doing here? I never thought
That you were drunk on Christianity!"

John didn't move, but stared into the Rajah's eyes.
He felt the wrongness in the way the Rajah spoke.
The Rajah glared at John. A bird of prey,
He made John's fears well up inside his head.

"What's wrong?" John asked.

            The Rajah felt the universe

About him in the chapel, tried to concentrate
The currents flowing through the universe
Into his burning fire. The minister was lost in dreams.
He'd sat down in a pew. The Rajah wouldn't let
The church's evil touch his holy fire.

"What's wrong?" he mocked. "A woman disappears.
You're Sheriff; still, you ask, "What's wrong?" He jabbed
His hand at empty air and snarled his rage.
"An enemy has struck a wooden stake
Into my heart! I've got to strike back quick!"

John didn't take his eyes from Rajah's eyes.
Celest Speltz had been kidnapped from a parking lot,
But something else was wrong. He felt the wrong.
"I still don't understand," he said. "You've got
To calm down, make more sense. Unless you tell
Me what you're getting at, I'll sit right here
Until I'm not confused. You understand?"

The Rajah felt the flame he was flare up
Into a ball of lightning wild with sizzling light.
He felt the earth's crust shift, volcanic fires
And sulfur spewing death into the air.
"Celest is gone!" he shrieked. "She's gone! She's gone!
Two men have taken her against her will!"

John stared into the Rajah's furious eyes.
John's Indian problems were enough. Now this.
He didn't need to face the Rajah while
He tried to end the Warrior problem peacefully.
"Did someone see the kidnappers?" he asked.
"What if Celest decided that you're not
God's fountainhead? What if she's left your house?"

The Rajah's flame subsided, dying down
Into a blackness blacker than a moonless night.
Beneath his hand Dawn tensed, then left the room,
The universe. His face contorted as he strained
To discipline his rage. What right had Dawn
To leave like that? So suddenly he felt bereaved?
"Dawn Friends was with Celest at noon," he said.
"Celest was kidnapped on a grocery shopping trip.

We have to find Celest. I ask you, please."

John glanced at Skye. The minister was lost.
Light shined upon the minister's rapt face.
He looked enraptured, more than just a man.
John tried to turn toward the altar, but the Rajah's hand
Tugged at his sleeve. John looked back at the eyes
That glared at him and tried to see beyond
The Rajah's rage into the man's uncertainty.
"Where's Dawn?" John asked. He got up from the pew.

The Rajah frowned. He looked insane.
"The evil fools," he raged. "The evil's after me!
The Rajah! Shaper! Alterer! The evil fools!
You can't see her. She's sick." He tapped his skull.
"The violent men who took Celest have sickened her."

John didn't move. He didn't think he'd feel
Alive again. He felt the power of the faith in Skye,
But still, he'd never seen a single sign from God,
Not once in all the years he'd spent on earth.
"Dawn saw Celest's abductors capture her,"
He said. "You told me that. What's going on?"

The Rajah stood inside the stained glass window's light
With Christ above him shining like a sun.
"I am a holy man!" he screamed.

      "God comes forth in the sign of Arousing!
      The Arousing's image is thunder!
      It rises out of depths
      And soars into the stormy sky —

      "White hind legs gleam from afar as horses run!"

                                 "Your church
      Is water, ditches, ambush, penetrating moon,
      Blood sign, abysmal melancholy, sick,
      Hearts, earache, bending, thief of hearts and souls!

I am a holy man!" he screamed. "A holy man!"

Skye's face had paled. He gripped the pew wood's rail.

John felt the spirits loosed into the world and heard
Their wailing in the silent air. He grabbed
The Rajah's arm and marched him from the church.
"I am a holy man," the Rajah said. "You understand?"

6

John pushed the Rajah through the door away from Skye.
He had to get the two of them apart.
His need was powerful enough to make
Him feel as if he couldn't take another breath.
He looked back at the chapel. Fire danced bright
Upon the altar. In the flames two angels danced!
He wasn't mad. He wouldn't let the song
Of madness make his life spin off its course.

7

The fire around the altar died. It whooshed
Toward the heavens, brightening so strong
And fast that Skye was blinded by its glare —
Awash in miracle, Skye felt as if his life
Had culminated in a moment too intense
For human understanding. With a carefulness
Inborn from years of service to the poor,
He walked up to the altar, touched its wood
And wondered why the flames had blessed a man
Who'd never preached to worshipper-filled pews —

And then he turned.

        Where was John Israel?
The Rajah? Panic struck him, made his heartbeat wild.
They'd surely seen. They had to testify
Or else the miracle would not be manifest.
He'd lost all sense of time. The miracle
Had overwhelmed his fear at seeing how
The Rajah threatened John's pursuit of faith.

Skye was a shepherd. Yet, a miracle
Had turned his eyes into himself, the altar's flame.
What kind of miracle was that? They'd surely seen,
But they were gone. What had he done? What fire

——
57

Had made him blind to confrontation in his church?

He touched the altar's wood again and felt
Its purity beneath the roughness of his hands.
He'd seen a miracle, he told himself. A miracle.

The Death of Gordon Call

Alone inside the dark apartment, Bill
Stared absently at fields of moonlit snow.
He didn't want to see the beauty burned
Into the brightness of the winter night.
Below him, in the bar, the late night sounds
Of Thelma closing drifted up the stairs.

He felt like Job[22], tormented by the words
Of Bildad[23]:

> "A noose is hidden for him on the ground,
> and a trap for him in the road.
> Terrors frighten him on every side,
> and drive him to his feet.
> His strength is starved,
> and destruction is at his side.
> It devours patches of his skin;
> the firstborn of death devours his limbs."[24]

He felt Donn Truesdale's kiss upon his lips.
He felt revolted by a man he'd once
Have trusted with his life. What meanings made his fire?

His voice rolled. Then Donn Truesdale, others, heard,
But, in the end, his power had its boundaries.
A drunken man, like Truesdale, came into the bar,
Declared unmanly love out loud, then kissed . . .
He touched his shame-burned face and cringed.
No matter how omnipotent his words . . .

He listened, hoping Thelma would come up the stairs.
Donn Truesdale was his enemy. He longed to press
To woman-warmth. He checked the calendar
And set the clock to ring before dawn's light.

When Thelma stepped onto the stairs, he smiled.
He was a man. Tomorrow morning words
He breathed would agitate the nation's soul.
He was the prophet of America.
He saw the bones Ezekiel[25] saw dry on the earth,

59

And he would preach on bones. They'd take on flesh.
Black evil wouldn't rot the nation's heart.
He'd call his followers, They'd not defile themselves.

He waited in the bed for Thelma wrapped
Into the passion of his fiery prophecies.

2

He watched the sun rise from the bar. He felt
Unsettled even though the sun rose glorious.
He thought of Thelma in the bed upstairs,
But even thoughts of Thelma left him tense.

He left the window, turned the radio
To WTCH[26] to hear the news.
He'd listened every morning since Menominee
Had seized the desolate Novitiate.
The Indian seizure of religious property
Was proof of how the country brinked on ruin.

But then his blood ran cold.

                    "Today, down South
In Arkansas, Gordon Call, accused
Of killing federal marshals on his North Dakota farm,
Has died in yet another bloody battlefield.
No details are available, but Arkansas
Officials have confirmed that Call is dead.
Two local men that had harbored Call
Since he fled from North Dakota have also died.
According to these first reports . . ."

                            Bill sat
Down on a barstool. Clouds. Dark sky. Dark earth.
He sat in blackness, struggling to understand.
The radio droned soundlessly, the smooth
Announcer's voice a sound that was no sound.
He was a prophet. In his words truth raged
And worked to set men free. But Gordon Call

Was dead.

        The man who'd given up his son
Was dead — Bill Winchell sat in Tigerton . . .

He stared at hands. He'd farmed until he'd found
His gift for prophecy and sermon-fire.
He'd tilled the earth and been a part of earth.
And now the martyr Gordon Call, who'd worked
To found a movement big enough to shake
The bureaucrats and Jews, was dead, was dead.

He was a man. He wasn't queer. He wouldn't weep.
He'd sing like Daniel[27] had of ending times.
He'd see God's retribution visited upon the bankers, Jews,
And Truesdale. He would find a river water bright
With sun and purify the nation, clothing life
With linen white enough to dazzle human eyes.

He sobbed. He saw the mark of Cain[28] he'd splashed
On Truesdale's head. He'd been defiled. Defiled.

Bill wailed his rage into the quietness.
He heard the fear in Thelma as she called to him.

He shouted, "Gordon Call's been killed!" He faced
The dark; the glory of an angel's light grew bright.
Inside his darkness Thelma's arms embraced his pain.
He hadn't heard her come downstairs to him.

His words would shake Americans. He was a man.
He wouldn't fail like Gordon Call had failed.
He'd sing destruction. Words would change the world.

His hand touched Thelma's head. Her hair was glorious.
She held him as he rocked upon his stool.

Sam Ludwig

Sam Ludwig squeezed between the Holstein's sides.
Patched black on white, the Holstein's bristly hair
Was stiff against chest, belly as he slid
Back from his stretch to clunk the stanchion shut.
Cow heat made skin feel grafted to manure,
Dusked morning light, hay-oat smells, ice-caked cracks
Between the barn door's weathered boards, stone walls.
Above the fifty milkers, bags veined, full of milk,
A pale, soft mist rose spirit-like in morning dark.

He felt alive inside the barn. Two hundred years ago
His father's father had begun to clear the fields.
The barn was history, continuance,
A place of life where rock foundations sealed
The Ludwig generations' lives into the farm.
No doubts lived in the barn. The Holsteins stalled,
He closed their stanchions, touched heat, shoveled oats.
The Holsteins ate; he milked; he sold their milk,
And seasons came and went as surely as the sun.

The long continuance of Ludwigs on the land
Was ending. Fifteen years ago he'd caught
The fever spread by farm economists: efficiency
Is profit. Larger acreage makes efficiency.
Caught in the magic logic of the times,
He'd visited the red brick Tigerton's First Bank
To mortgage out his family's history.
When interest rates had soared to twenty-plus percent,
He'd visited the bank again, his profits spent
To pay the interest. In the shining lobby of the bank
He'd seen his future: Auctioneer spieled words,
Their gavels slammed onto the auction block
As he was sold in pieces to his neighbors, friends.
The banker, Chad LeConne, face wreathed in smiles,
Behind the auctioneer, the red brick bank
Saved from the threat of assets lost by men
Who'd lost ability to pay their loans.

He'd found Bill Winchell then, the preacher singed
With visions of the farmer's apocalypse.

He'd sat in Bill's dark bar and listened hard.
Bill raged against the bankers, Jews, and government.
While listening, rage seized him, made him more
Than what he really was. It justified
His place inside his family's history
And gave him reasons for his failure with the farm.
It let him sleep as money worries piled
On top of money worries, price of milk
Descending as recession gripped the farms.

He knew that Bill was crazy in his rage.
He knew that he had been a fool to let
Greed charm with thoughts from men who'd never farmed.
But craziness was easy. You had a drink,
Then went downstairs, and let yourself believe.

Hate was an easy thing to hold inside your hands.
It put the blame on heads unseen, on enemies.

Two hundred years of Ludwigs on the land.

Sam reached into the oat bin, let the oats
Run through his fingers back into the bin.
What could he do? Confront that he was less
Than all the Ludwig men who'd worked the farm?

The Germans claimed you had to have a gift
To work the land, to harvest crops in fall.
They claimed that countries lived and died by sons
Of farmers choosing land or city life.
The bankers and the government were warped
Into their wondrous economic arguments.
They understood how money ebbs and flows.
They didn't understand how ebbs and flows
Broke lives, destroying family histories,
Unleashing storms of hate into the world.

Sam picked a shovel from the barn's north wall
And started shoveling the piles of dark manure
Into the automatic cleaner built with loans.
The barn was like a giant womb, its life
Protected from the storms loose in the world.
A Holstein tail, encrusted with manure,

Slapped at his face. He stepped back, saw the cow
Had turned her head to look at him. He laughed.

Falcon

Kim flew upstairs, a falcon loosed, wild winged,
His spirit fierce with eyes that searched for prey.
Behind him Sam, Bob, Todd, and Marsha tried
To keep up with the beating of his wings.
He reached the tower, opened up the window, stood
Inside the window's open space, arms raised.
"I am the man!" he shouted. "I'm an eagle, feathers tipped
With spirit-power! Everything I am you're not.
So shoot me if you're not a sniveler!"

Horse stood back from the window half amused,
Half irritated by Kim's teenage rage.
He should have been surprised to see the kids,
But somehow wildness seemed inevitable.
Kim shook his head and shrieked so long and wild
An echo bounced back from the riverbank.

Horse waited for Kim's voice to die, then pulled
The window shut. "You through?" he asked.

                                        Kim glared.
Horse flinched to feel the young man's pain. He squatted down.
"You gonna say what's wrong with you?" he asked.

Grim, Wanda didn't take her eyes off Kim.
"Your Sitting Crow's decided we're just kids,"
She spat. "He told us that we had to go back home."

Horse looked at her. Black hair fell down her back,
And if she wasn't yet a woman, time
Would let her grow into the promise that she had.
He'd always felt the need to ease pain others felt.

"You don't like Sitting Crow's decision then?"
He asked.

        "You're right," Kim snarled. "We don't!
We made this work in spite of guns we faced,
And now the man I've thought was God looks down
And tells us that our guts are meaningless.

—
65

The white man won't believe you'll all choose death
If we're not safe, like little kids, at home."

Horse turned and looked at Todd, his neighbor's son.
"That true?" he asked.

Todd smiled. "Damned right," he said.

Horse tried to gauge the tension shimmering.
He looked toward the woods where frozen men
Stood tired because, determined, Sitting Crow
Had set to change the course of history.
He wondered how they felt so cold their feet were numb
And wondered what they thought about the fact
They'd let the kids slip through security.

"It's difficult," he said at last. "You're here;
You've got the courage of a Sitting Bull . . .
You've heard Tecumseh's name?" he asked.

Kim kept on glaring with his jumpy nerves.
"We're not a bunch of idiots," he said.
"All five of us are on the honor role."

Horse looked up sharply, then, chagrined, smiled ruefully.
He'd failed, then dropped out in the seventh grade.
"You know the Prophet[29] too?" he said.

Bob shrugged.

Horse said, eyes glazed with dream-weight of his thoughts:
"The way the Warriors feel is Sitting Crow
Is like Tecumseh[30] and the Prophet fused.
He's not too comfortable to be around,
But he can see things normal men can't see.
You watch him like I've watched him, filled with doubt
That he can manage what he says he can,
And then you see how truths come from the web
Of future history that only he can see."

"What are you saying?" Marsha asked. "What does
It have to do with us?"

Horse looked at her.
He thought of kids sprawled dead on marble floors.
Kim looked as if he'd detonate again.

"The strategy that Sitting Crow's defined,"
He said, a prayer chanting underneath his breath.
"Is that, before we trapped ourselves in here,
We'd dedicate our spirits, clothed in hope,
To speaking truth about our people's poverty.
We swore an oath to ring ourselves with cops
And court and honor death inside our hearts.
You didn't know about our vows before
You forced your way in here and can't be held
To what you didn't know. We all believe
That as the world finds strength in our resolve
Its winds will shift until we're caught in storms
Of death, or life, depending on man's will.
If Sitting Crow's the man I say he is,
You need to ask a question of yourselves,
How can you serve the best the cause he serves?"

Kim's rage had dissipated as Horse spoke,
And now his eyes were shining with a feral light.
"We'll take the oath," he said. "We're not afraid.
What makes you think that just because we're young
We have no right to fight for what we want?"

Horse shook his head. He hadn't won. His voice
A wind's breath rustling over dying leaves.

"I'm not a Sitting Crow," Horse said. "I can't
See all the streams that flow through earth and sky."

Kim stared at Horse. Bob, Marsha, Sam, and Todd:
They stared at Horse. He'd been afraid to speak.
He felt their anger building up again.

"I am the macho man!" Kim said, his rage
Unbound, and wild, again. "A crazy man!
I'll whip a tail around your tail and make
It eat you like a serpent with its fangs
And mouth attached behind its rattling end!"

What could Kim do? He was a kid. A kid!
He looked at Marsha, saw the fear she felt.
"At fourteen Juliet[31] was dead," he said.

He turned, a falcon, wheeling, hating bonds.
He screeched his war cry, ran toward the stairs
And started spiraling toward the basement, down.

The Sense of Angels

1

Inside the squad the Rajah folded, deep
Into the vortex swirling in his head.
His rage was gone. The world was bitter. Life was pain.
His self became a mote, two double helix strands.
He turned into an emptiness — no thirst,
Desire, dreams, pleasure, sorrow, hate, or love.
He sat beside John Israel and lost
The living threading him to white-man's-justice ways.
He sat as motionless as stone until blood slowed.
Stone-silence cloaked the universe of suns, dark peace.
He felt the Sheriff move inside the car.
The Sheriff was a mote inside the mote
That flowed inside two double helix strands.

2

John drove into the Red Owl[32] parking lot.
He couldn't see. Two fiery angels danced,
Their faces bright as morning stars in skies
Whose darkness trembles with the coming dawn.
He turned and looked into the Rajah's eyes.
Strange dreams were swimming large. Dilated eyes.

"What now?" John asked.

              The Rajah didn't move.
He looked like stone. John tried to see the man
Who'd come into the chapel like a storm.
The Rajah looked emaciated, old.
John shrugged his shoulders, turned the engine off.
He tried to leave the angels in the car.
He'd longed to see them. Still, they troubled him.
Their wings beat silently against the winter air;
Their eyes were bright with fire from holy fires.
He felt like singing joyful winter hymns.
His walking seemed a dance of body parts.

Why was he at a common grocery store

Instead of in the chapel struck by miracles?
The Rajah was a fraud, a leech that stripped
His followers of everything they owned
And then wrapped sermons deep into their bones.

The store was shining with the angel's light.
John felt as if he walked in light, man blessed by God.
He tried to focus on the job at hand,
But nothing in the store seemed real. Breath thinned.
He felt as if he'd lost his humanness.

And then, the light was gone. He was a man.

The miracle had lived, then died, and now?
The absence of the angels made him feel
Bereft, a nothingness, a man so dark
With flame his life was etherized, a stone.

Glen Morgan's son stood like a penitent
"You got those Indians from the old Novitiate?"

Bewildered by his loss of angel light,
John stared into the boy's brown, common eyes.
"What makes you ask me that?" he asked. "So what?"

"Those Indians got no right to church's property.
The church has given schools and welfare checks.
The Indians ought to stay at home and keep away
From property owned by the church and whites.
They need to go to jail for what they've done."

John shook his head. He tried to understand
The hate he saw curled up inside the boy —
A snake as shining white as cobra fangs.
"So many live in poverty," he said.

The ring of shopping carts slammed carelessly.
The checkers at the checkout stands were swamped.
Sales rang as ceaselessly as ocean's waves.
He longed to feel the sense of miracle.
How had he lost the angels' grace? His grace?

The boy still looked at him.

"You work here every day?"

The boy said yes.

                "You ever see Celest Speltz here?"
John looked into the boy's brown eyes again.
"You see somebody make her get into a car?"
He asked, then held his breath. He didn't want
To hear the words the Morgan boy would say.

"This afternoon," the boy said. "Like a damned.
This Lincoln opened up and swallowed her
Before she even had the time to scream.
The lady with her made an awful fuss.
I thought she'd die right in the parking lot."

John put his hand out on the dog food bags.
He shook his head, turned from the boy, and walked.
The Warriors. Now the Rajah. Eyes emaciated, black.
The murdered mule began to caper like
A colt above its carcass in the winter air.

3

The Rajah, deep inside a river's heart,
The double helix winding through its stones,
His yearnings, sufferings, desirings lost,
Stirred from his trance and felt the winter cold.
He saw the Sheriff in the Red Owl store.
He'd found Celest had been abducted, bound.
The Rajah tried to feel the outrage felt
While climbing up the church's evil steps,
But all the storms he'd built into himself
Were drowned by river waters from his trance.
He felt unsteady, weakened first by fire,
Then by immersion in the waters of his peace.
He touched the car's white metal hood, then walked
Toward the place where Dawn slept quietly.

He knew who'd seized Celest. His trance had tapped
Into the universe's harmony.
He saw the man dressed in the clothes that farmers wore,

71

His face as plain as fence-post sparrows perched
Above a field that stretched toward a woods.

He made his promise, forged in trance, his force.

4

John left the store with acid in his mouth.
The Rajah represented complications bruised
Into a weave of complications, spider webs.
A woman, shorn of sense, wrapped in the Rajah's web,
Had been abducted, whisked away by men
Who drove a big, black car with windows tinted black.
The whole thing made no sense. Celest Speltz, born
And raised in Shawano, had no money, friends . . .
John shook his head. For all the years he'd served
As Sheriff, no one time had made so little sense.
He'd even had to find a small girl's body drowned,
But always there were reasons: carelessness
Or greed or hate. He'd always understood.

John didn't like the feelings loose in him.
He felt like turning from the squad and walking off
Into the sunset, never turning back.
He longed to find the miracles he'd lost.

He walked across the parking lot, then stopped.

The Rajah wasn't in the squad. He'd left.
John cussed beneath his breath, then got
Into the car and radioed for Thorn.
The whirlwind funneling about John made
His head spin with its unpredictability.

Why had he seen the angels as his world
Ran like a herd of lemmings to its doom?
He didn't really like himself, he thought.
He felt as hollow as the hollow men:

> "Shape without form, shade without color,
> Paralyzed force, gesture without motion."[33]

"Thorn there?" he asked. Thorn was, at least, his friend.

Deprogramming

1

Jim stood outside the quiet living room
And wondered what he'd have to face inside.
His confrontation with the Indian in the bar
Had ceased to knot his gut, and now he thought
He'd have the guts to face the storm to come.

Trent Warren was a thought he'd carefully thought out.
Whites had their rights. His daughter had a right
For freedom from her father's sorry reins.
Perhaps he should have waited for this reckoning.
The Indian troubles marked him as a man to watch.
He'd meant to keep his silence when he'd heard
That Indian radicals had seized the old Novitiate,
But lifetime habits seldom died that easily.
The newsmen from Green Bay had egged him on
Until he'd splashed his views across the media.

And Trent had told him all their plans were delicate.
He'd warned him of this evening, too. But still,
He'd gone ahead. They'd go through hell to find
His daughter's soul, he'd been informed, and then
They'd go through hell again to give her back
The mind and soul that she had once controlled.

He could remember her before his wife had died,
So lovely that she was a melody.

Religious perverts didn't reason out their truths.
They had their visions and their dreams;
They drilled themselves into themselves
And then began to drill themselves into their followers.

Jim Speltz was ignorant. He didn't understand
What Trent had spent so many evenings telling him.
He wasn't clean. He'd tried to rape her once,
One year from when his lovely wife had died.
She'd run away before he'd pinned her down.
She'd left him wallowing inside his shame.

73

His only pride was in his white man's skin.

He loved Celest, felt shame at all his weaknesses,
And was determined, just this once, to give
The white man's right: a free, sound, thinking mind.

2

Inside the living room Celest glared hate.
She looked bedraggled, hair once shiny, dull.
Jim saw the change. She'd always been so strong!
She used to strip the cow's pink tits as fast
As he could strip once suction pumps were gone.

"You. You!" she hissed, spit dribbling on her lips.
"I'm twenty-one. You can't do this! I'll call the cops!
I'll see you dead before you ruin my life again!"

She fought against the ropes they'd tied her with.
She seemed as if she'd break before his eyes.

Trent, sitting in a corner on a wooden chair,
Moved Jim into a chair that faced Celest.
Jim's hands were shaking. Trent had told the truth.
For years he'd scourged the cults of followers
Whenever parents had the guts to back him up.
But now Jim's daughter's violence seemed too absolute.

"This is your father, isn't he?" Trent asked.

"He raped me once!" she screamed. "He tell you that!?
He's not my father. Rajah's everything!
You're raping me right now! You've kidnapped me.
My God, you're raping me! You're raping me!"

She screamed and rocked her body back and forth.
Jim sat inside the noise and felt his sweat.
He felt sick. Trent had told him, but the screaming made
Him want to get up from the chair and run away.
He hadn't known a woman could feel such pain.

Trent sat, impassive, waiting for the screams to stop.

Jim didn't move. The screams subsided into sobs.
Time shrunk into a noise too small to hear.

"This is your father, isn't he?" Trent said again.

Celest stopped whimpering. She stared at Trent.
"I say he is," she asked. "You'll let me go?"

Trent shook his head. "He tried, while drunk,
To rape you once. He has to live with that.
He's glad you ran away from him that time.
He is your father, though. You've got to tell me that.
Then, for a while, we'll let you sleep. You're tired."

Celest looked up at Jim, her hate fierce flames.
He hadn't been so bad a father? Just one awful slip?
They'd be inside the living room for days.
Jim looked at how they'd boarded up the window frames.

Celest spit on the carpet. "He's my Dad,
All right," she said. "Not spirit. Just the flesh."

She looked back at the floor, her spit slime green.

Relieved, Jim's tension shattered with her words.
Trent didn't move. They'd fight a war, he'd said.
They'd win, then lose, then win again until
Celest had found herself. And then they'd know
They'd done the thing they should have done.

He hoped the cops were so ensnared by drums
They'd not have time to search and find Celest.

Jim slumped back in his chair. My God, he thought.
I need a drink. Celest glared hate at him.

The Tree's Laughter

1

Bill strode into the basement, eyes afire.
He saw Donn Truesdale in a back row seat.
Sam Ludwig, looking ill, sat, like a rock,
In front of Truesdale, vengeance in his eyes.

Bill glared at Truesdale, set his Bible down,
And launched into his sermon's righteousness.
"We are American," he said. "That means we're kings.
We have our virtues, dominance, powers not
Just titular. We are American!"

He slammed his fist onto the tabletop.
He'd captured them! Their eyes had gathered fire.
He hadn't lost his hold with Truesdale's kiss.

"But by decrees that none of us have heard,
Another has in-gathered to himself
All-power even though we've never had a vote.
This man is not a man. You know his works.
He lends you money with a smile, then comes
To claim knee-tribute, land, your future, homes,
The life that make us what we are, true men.
I've looked him in the eye; you've looked at him,
And we have heard his words ring in our ears.
But what if I should tell you, cast his yoke away?"

He felt them stir, felt how they felt about his words.
He celebrated where they couldn't see his joy.
"Will you submit your necks and choose to bow?"
He roared. He let the silence stretch out thought.
"You won't if I know hearts and minds," he said.
"You won't if you but know the men you are.
You're Sons of Heaven, owned by no group-man,
Americans who only follow orders when they're just.
The law is not our Lord, does not enslave
The men inside this room ordained to rule!"

He paused again and looked at them, their faces rapt.

"We must prepare ourselves," he said. "The hour
Will come when we must stand as men against
The government, the bankers' Jew conspiracy.
They're not our Father who's on heaven's throne.
And in that hour when we must stand as men,
I'll call you home, and we will stand, Americans
Upon a field where battle rages with a rage
Unseen since Hitler[34] died inside his bunker's walls!"

He looked at them. He did not doubt himself.
He was a prophet, born to greatness, fire.
His force would change the course of history.
He could restore the Constitution's truth.
Sam Ludwig looked as fierce as warriors bound
To serve with Saul[35] before the start of David's[36] reign.
Turk Thomas looked as if he'd disappeared
Into the glory Bill was promising.
Bill looked at them, and then turned silently
And walked upstairs. Where Gordon Call had failed,
Bill Winchell would succeed. He had a prophet's fire.

2

Outside, Bill left the road and walked into the woods.
He felt the glory of a winter evening's cold.
His spoken words still clung to him, a light
As strong as glory granted by the Lord.

Two miles or so into the woods he stopped
And found an elm untouched by elm rot, stood
Beneath its branches, felt the holy fire
Reverberating from his spirit to the tree.

>"Vindicate me, O God,
>And plead my cause against an ungodly nation;
>Oh, deliver me from the deceitful and unjust man!
>For you are God of my strength;
>Why do you cast me off?
>Why do I go mourning because of the oppression of my enemy?"[37]

The trees about him stirred. He felt their fire,
And then he felt . . . their enmity. Their enmity?
The trees were from the hand and breath of God.

He touched the elm, felt power cached in wood.
A pine tree moved across the land in mist,
Its needles knives designed to slice men's flesh.
He thought of Gordon Call and how he'd died
Inside a storm of bullets shot by frightened men.
He felt his manhood stir to life, breath torn.
He thrust himself at Thelma's womanhood
Inside a mind unhinged by weirding stress.

The trees were older than the Psalm he sang.
They sang of love and death and moved in mist.
He twisted in the grip of madness, endless rage.
Trees sent their ancient thoughts to touch his soul.
More ancient trees, the blackthorn, whitethorn, stood
Beside him, plotting ploys against their enemies.

God frowned. The trees were like the golden calf.
Bill felt the sting of God's displeasure, felt
The song of victory the trees boomed, words
Drawn from their roots, the living soils of earth.

His followers were men of soil, of trees.
He prayed for God's deliverance and peace.
He was a man of God, American.
Americans were bound by no earth covenant.
Donn Truesdale's kiss had threatened him, his soul.
The trees were seeking allies for a war.
He was a man of God, a true American.
He wasn't mad. He wasn't mad. He wasn't mad!

His fire flared out toward the oak and pine.
The maples, poplars, beech trees stirred to life.
He felt their holiness. He turned away.
The trees were merely trees. They couldn't tear
From frozen soil and march against his enemies.
He'd never found the purity of God he craved.
He wasn't mad. He was a prophet righting wrongs.

3

The Indians were to blame, he thought. They'd roused
A spirit from their past, and now earth walked.
The snow crunched softly as he walked through trees.

What did it mean, his vision in the woods?
The world was changing. He could feel the change.

His heart was pounding as he left the woods.
Donn Truesdale was suddenly in front of him,
The man possessed by loneliness and fear.
His eyes were large and white; his skin was pale.

"Donn," Bill said harshly. Truesdale stood his ground.
"I didn't mean to anger you," he said.
"I'd had too much to drink, that's all it was.
I didn't like the fact I always die . . ."

                              Bill glared angrily.
"Men don't kiss men," Bill said. "You felt desire.
Abominations walk the earth these days."

Donn's face screwed up. He fought back brimming tears,
I won't cry here. I won't. I won't. I won't.
Bill sneered to see the weakness in the man.
Donn looked into the winter sky's harsh dusk.
"What if I'm queer?" Donn choked the mangled words.
"I love the fact you've got the guts to raise your voice
Against the fools who've turned this country wrong.
I don't desire your body. I'm in love.
Those two emotions aren't the same at all."

His voice trailed off into the dying light.
"You felt like Thelma kissing me," Bill said.

Donn shoved his hands into his pockets, shrugged.
"You're crazy, man," he said. He kicked at snow.

Bill's eyes grew hard with rage. Behind him trees
Were singing songs so powerful they deafened him.
He'd hurt Donn Truesdale, bad. He shook his head.
"You're nothing but a queer," he said. "I'll not
Submit myself to your unnatural desires.
You're part of all the rot that's swallowing
This country piece by piece. You'll never get
Another chance to make me look a laughingstock."

The trees were laughing, jubilant, alive.

He tried to shake their voices from his head.

"I am a son of God," he told them.

                           Donn's eyes flashed.
"You're just an old man demon-occupied," he said.
"So what if I am gay? That doesn't mean
That I'm not human, don't deserve respect."

Bill felt his fire build up a lovely rage.
"I'll get you for your impudence!" he screamed.
"You'll know the shame you've visited upon yourself!"

Donn looked into the eyes he once had loved.
They broiled complexities that weren't controlled.
Donn walked toward the bar and left Bill where he stood.

The elm tree shook its bare, dark branches in the wind
And laughed and laughed and laughed and laughed and laughed.

Bill felt the mocking in the laughter, felt the hate.
Abomination, demons were unbound.

Sitting Crow and Love

He crawled out of his sleeping bag. Cold air
Against his naked body; life confirmed through pain.
He shivered uncontrollably, eyes closed.

He pulled his shorts on, stepping over men
And women snuggled dark into their warmth,
Went to a window rimmed with frost, looked out
To where the barn's dark hulk hid deputies.

A shining worm of death streaked through the sky.
It burrowed down into sky's coal-dark soil.
As Sitting Crow's heart hammered from the cold,
He saw his death, the raven circling above
Flesh tissue sealed to earth's stone heaviness.

He saw the way the Indian kids looked dead.
They sprawled beside the Warriors, crusted frost
A peppering of white in raven Indian hair.

The night was dark and huge, a universe
That breathed in rhythms larger than the mind.
He'd told the newsmen on the telephone
That, for the Indian, death was destiny.
He'd told them blood contained a hallowing
Of spirit consecrated to an hour of death.
He'd told them that the state would stain its hands
With blood or hand a victory to their revolt.

An owl swooped from its perch upon an oak,
Wings ghostly as its talons reached the ground.
The moment of the mouse's death was still.
No noise. No movement. Universe asleep.
He felt the owl's small heart inside his heart,
The quick exhilaration of its flight, the prize,
The sustenance that made another day of life.

In air beside him Lena, naked, eyes so bright
They seemed to burn away the dark, materialized.
He looked at her and wept to know that soon
The white man would become a raving beast.

Kim looked at him with sightless eyes in death.
There were a thousand precedents: The deaths
Of Iroquois, Cheyenne, Blackfeet, Sioux, Navajo,
Apache, Passamaquoddy, Choctaw, Cherokee,
Pueblo, Chippewa, Oneida, Eskimo, Menominee,
Societies the white man didn't want to understand.

The modern Indian needed martyrs strong
Enough to make the white man face his wrongs.
He didn't want to die. In Lena's life was life,
A sweetness pure as frost encircled moon.

But still: his people and their history,
The pain they knew while living in the slums
Of Neopit, Milwaukee, Minneapolis,
Chicago, New York City, Los Angeles,
The times of blood when Indians died while struggling
Against the white man's march across the continent.

The darkness held the rhythms of his life.
It bound men, Lena, women, Indian kids.
Long worms of light went burrowing night soils.

He frowned to think of worms and death; he yearned
To leave the window and the barn that hulked
With shadows spirit-stained as Lena danced,
Her smile foreshadowing the warmth of spring.

He reached into the air to touch her hand.
He'd die, but didn't want to face her death.
She wasn't there. She danced, but wasn't there.

The Aftermath of Miracle

John didn't know if he would feel alive again.
The thought kept plaguing him: He'd slogged, with joy,
Through farmer's fields for twenty years collecting votes,
And now . . . the Rajah, Sitting Crow, Celest,
The Indian kids who'd foxed his deputies,
The light of angels as they danced in fires,
The wings of huge, black wraiths, the souls
Of ravers gaunt with death, mule guts, Thorn dead,
Face peeled from bloody skull, John's wife's bright eyes . . .
Inside the chapel he had yearned for proof of God.
Then proof had been presented while the Rajah raged,
And he had failed to feel the miracle
Until the moment when he'd let the Rajah coax
Him from the chapel's sanctuary, grace.

But now he wasn't at the church, O God,
          ". . . rat's feet over broken glass
          inside our dry cellar,"[38]
The words of Sitting Crow: "We'll die in here . . ."

What hell bedeviled him? When Paul[39] had seen
His vision going to Damascus, filled with hate,
He'd woken to glory. Then, exposed to grace,
He'd waited three dark days to see with reborn eyes.

The moon had risen white into the sky.
His breath puffed white into the night's cold dark.

John felt his burdens. God had shown Himself,
But that was not enough. John wasn't Job:
          "The Lord gave, and the Lord has taken away;
          Blessed be the name of the Lord . . ."[40]
His dreams were rising in a stream of smoke.

He'd spent his life pursuing dreams of tolerance
And Frank Lloyd Wright's Broadacre City,[41] homes
Across a landscape marked by peace, democracy.
Whites, Indians, blacks, and other races brought
Their heritage to songs of harmony.
He'd had the task of making order out

Of all the webs of passion in the nation's soul.

He faced unraveling, a demon loosed
By Satan's will, compliant God, a pestilence
Into a world that wanted order, peace,
Yet longed to know the sharpness of the edge.

What could he do?

> "Between the desire
> And the spasm . . .
> Between the essence
> And the descent
> Falls the Shadow . . ."[42]

He was no Paul[43]. He'd seen,
But he was not beside Skye Frays in church.
The cold was sharp enough to sting his hands.
He climbed Hard Maple Hill, looked at the world.

The world, ten years ago, was still the world.
Security, a good, clean life was possible.
The homeless didn't haunt the streets of towns,
Kids couldn't buy narcotics in their schools,
And men and women found a lifetime job
That helped them center family life in homes:

Until it all began unraveling,
The hours, the work, the Sunday sanity,
The villages and homes and farms that spread
Democracy and tolerance across the land . . .

> "There came gliding in the black night the walker in darkness
> . . . Then from the moor under the mist-hills Grendel came walking,
> Wearing God's anger."[44]

He had to find Celest. That was his job.
He had to find the wrong he felt around
The Rajah, chosen messenger of God.
He had to end the threat that Sitting Crow
Imposed upon the order John upheld.
He had to find Broadacre City[45], *citie on the hill*[46].

But why? For God's sake why? O Lord! O Lord!

He looked up at the stars and sighed. He needed sleep.
He walked toward the squad. Wings hovered, black.

The Shining

1

Sam stopped the truck and walked into the field.
The moonlight poured its silver on the snow.
Sam stood inside the shining filled with awe.
Around the field's edges black pines rose
Into the moonlit night alive with dark.

Sam was ablaze with words. Inside the light
Bill Winchell's madness raged so fierce with life
It seemed more beautiful than snow moon pines.
 "Will you submit your necks and bend your knees?"
The apparition roared. "I'll call you home!"

Sam saw the blood stained on the shining snow.
He felt the tempo of the madness sheathed
In Bill's wild spirit, rising wrath of God.
He felt the chaos in the dark, pines bathed
With moonlight, starlight, snowlight, shining peace.

Bill Winchell haunted him. What truth was worth
The blood portended by the words Bill spoke?
He saw the rapture in the faces of his friends
As Bill declared, "we must prepare ourselves.
The hour will come when we must stand as men . . ."
They felt a manic thunder in their chests
And sang the terrible, bright song of death
Bill wove spelled into their minds and hearts.

And Sam, in spite of who he was, a farmer born
Into an independence of the mind and soul,
Sat in the fire and felt the quickening.
He'd joined a crazy mob and felt the way
The leader, mad with eyes, expected him to feel.

2

The banker, Chad LeConne, looked sad enough.
He sat behind his gleaming maple desk.
Sam felt Chad's pain and saw how wrong he was

To force himself into the banker's world.
He didn't fit inside the sterile walls.
He was a farmer. Seasons came and went
And let him measure life by growing corn.
He lived in rhythms, swishing tails of cows
And scrapes of shovels shoveling manure.
He'd thought he represented something new,
A way of thinking modernizing the farm.

He looked at Chad LeConne and tried to understand.
Chad filled his plush gray office with a human grace
That didn't fit the heartless job he held.

"What can I do?" he asked. "The times are hard.
Nobody dreamed the interest rates would rise so high.
The board won't let me loan you money, Sam."

"You made those loans," Sam said. "You searched me out
And said expansion was the future's way.
I listened, took the loans, and farmed the land
And made it pay until you raised your interest rates."

Chad touched the papers on his desk impulsively.
"We're not to blame," Chad said. "You can't say that.
I'd give my arm to make things like they were.
The government, to fight inflation, changed the rules.
The board and I are trapped. Our hands our tied."

Sam didn't know the reason that he'd come.
Chad looked offended, put upon, a man
Who'd done his best in face of obstacles.

"We're friends," Sam said. "At least I thought we were.
You're wrong. Your board is wrong. That's all. You're wrong."

Chad opened up his mouth, then pursed his lips.
He didn't speak. Sam turned and walked away.

3

He'd seen how Bill had looked before he'd felt
The passion of Donn Truesdale's homosexual kiss.
The holy minister of God had known.

87

As Donn had woven through the crowded room,
Bill's eyes had shined, anticipating, filled
With calculation, burning with the need
To drive himself onto another plane
Of rage and leadership and destiny.
When Donn had leaned across the tabletop,
Bill's face had lifted to receive the kiss.

4

A cloud cut off the moonlight. In the field
The darkness came so fast Sam held his breath.

He felt his father in the field with him.
Sam senior walked the fields alive in death.
Sam saw his old grandfather walk, still young,
Beside his aging father, both of them
Alive to bird songs echoing in summer woods.
A double bladed ax bit deep into an oak,
The sound so sharp it echoed through the trees.
Sam's father smiled to see his father smile.

Sam felt his blood sing out to specters' dark.
He longed to touch their hands, see breaths puff white,
But death was death, and he was still alive,
Alone inside the living hell he had to face.

His father would have hated Winchell's hate.
His old grandfather would have laughed to think
There was a man with such phlegmatic bile
He couldn't see he had no chance to win
His way against the nation's government.

But still, there was the banker, Chad LeConne,
His black shoes shined and gray tie elegant.
There was the fire that Winchell stoked and brewed
Inside himself, the blood upon the shining snow.

How could a man like Sam, fourth-generation-proud,
Go borrow money from a bank and risk his land?
He was to blame. He knew he was to blame.
Commotion in the wind, frights, changes, horrors sang
Their songs into the dark, into the field.

He longed to see the shining once again,
But clouds had covered up the silver moon.

Legune

The steps were crumbling at the Legion Hall.
Above the steps, paint peeling, reservation pine
Boards, overlapping, went two stories high.
Behind the Hall dark maples hilled with black-eyed birch.

Two white men, bleary eyed, unshaven, stood,
Crossed rifle barrels, staring down into Legune.
Legune looked up into their eyes. Short, round
(She'd raised twelve children) eyes intense, she glared
Until they dropped their eyes. Resplendent with their heads
In morning light, surrounding Indians smiled.
Menominee controlled the media
And radicals, but hid inside the Hall.
They didn't want to face the elders furious
At seizing church owned land not theirs by law.
They didn't own Novitiate or Legion Hall,
Yet carried guns and brought white, Indian trash
Into the reservation home they claimed to love.

Legune walked up the steps into the Hall.
Inside, she stood still, waiting peacefully.
The radical Menominee elite stopped talking.
In rage she stared at them as silence spread.
She thought about the weddings, funerals,
And talk about Korea, the world wars, Viet Nam
That, through the years, had filled the Hall with life.

The young were taught to honor wisdom born
Out of the act of living life's experiences,
But then they took up arms, ignored their elder's words,
And tried to right the world by doing wrong.
Legune had gone to mass for sixty years.
She'd always felt a pride in serving God.

Without a word, Legune began to walk
Around the Hall. These were the kids she loved.
She went to one, and then another, eyes
Bored angrily into their eyes and hearts,
And backed each one against a wall. They didn't speak.
They were Menominee, the people of the Wolf.

She started naming names beneath her breath:
Beth, Wanda, Willy, Pete, Ben, Mary, Dan . . .
And each backed up against a wall, eyes black,
Defiance in their looks and bodies, hurt.

When she had finished, made the guns point down,
She looked at them once more, pride in her throat.
She turned and walked outside past Indians, whites.

She didn't speak; she didn't make a sound.

Healing

The moment that she knew that Dawn was living dead,
June left the corridor outside the emergency room.
She'd known Dawn White since they were kids,
Two quiet girls who'd sought their happiness
In woods behind the houses on their street.
Now Dawn, so full of life, intense, looked like
A nightmare come alive, eyes vacant, face
As white as baby powder, arms starvation thin,
Her body dragged behind the India Indian stiff.
June stood inside the corridor and watched.
The Indian guru, unrepentant, left.

When Doctor Rust had brought Dawn to her ward,
She'd slipped into the room and helped put Dawn in bed.
She didn't say her day and shift were done.
The doctor left. She sat beside the bed
And wondered where the India Indian was.
She'd heard the tales about the place he kept.
They said he beat and starved his followers.
Now, in the twilight of the room, she knew.

She woke up when she heard Pete Thorn's soft voice.

"You say Celest was kidnapped then?" he asked.
"That that's what caused Dawn White to lose her mind?"

He sounded skeptical, on edge. The Rajah's voice
Was filled with power, peace. "Dawn came to me
While I was teaching how creation shapes
Each nature to conformity with God's
Great Harmony," the India Indian said.
"She told me that she'd seen two men abduct
Celest by throwing her into their waiting car.
Dawn started shaking, palsied, crazy then,
And when she stopped, she'd gone into herself."

"Three hours ago," Thorn said. "You brought her here.
"And then you left. You want to tell me why?"

"I went to find John Israel," the Rajah said.

"I have to shield my followers from enemies."
"But why Celest?" Thorn pressed. "Why her? I've known
Her since she was a child. She doesn't have a dime."

The Indian's voice grew desperate, then calm.
Beneath the calmness June could hear his rage.
"You've got to find Celest," the Rajah said.
"You find her father, then you'll find Celest.
He's holding her against her wish to come back home."

"Jim Speltz?" Thorn asked, his voice incredulous.
"He's loony. Yet, Celest is flesh and blood . . ."

The Indian clasped his hands, eyes prayerful.
June looked at Dawn's pale face, its emptiness.

"He's after me," the Indian said. "He doesn't like
My teachings, so he's after ruining me.
He doesn't like to think his daughter's found
A truth more true than he can understand.
I'll find him if you won't, and then . . . we'll see . . ."

June got up from the chair beside Dawn's bed.
She'd never felt so horrified in all her life.
Thorn's skepticism died into his strength.

"Look Rajah," Thorn said. "If I hear you right
You just implied a threat. I'm warning you.
In Shawano County law still rules. If something bad
Has happened to Celest, I'll do my job.
I'll do it even though we've got our hands
As full as we can handle with the radicals,
But you won't take the law into your hands."

"Your Sheriff's going nuts," the Rajah said.
"He thinks he saw two angels dance in fire
Upon the altar at the Methodist's brick church."

June didn't want to hear the Indian speak.
Her heart was racing, making her feel faint.
Dawn slept inside a sleep too deep for dreams.

She walked out of the room and looked at Thorn.

He looked surprised. She seared him with her stare.
She turned and fled as fast as she could walk.

Out in the cold her Buick's engine whined.
She'd heard the promised rage against Jim Speltz.
She'd never liked Jim Speltz. He whined too much.
But still, she didn't want to see Celest like Dawn.
In spite of what the Rajah claimed, June knew
That Dawn had lost her mind because she'd faced
The Rajah when he had learned about Celest.
She didn't know just why she knew, but knew.

June drove out of the hospital's parking lot
And turned toward Bill Winchell's country bar.
The preacher was a mad man, but he kept
An army ready for the day when law broke down.
She'd heard the Rajah's rage and knew, down deep,
That neither Thorn nor Israel could stop his rage.

Bill Winchell saw conspiracies unfolding everywhere,
But he had guns and will enough to use his guns.
She wouldn't let the Rajah get Celest.
She wouldn't let a Shawano County girl
She knew sink down into inhuman death.

The Decision About the Drum

Pete Wilson felt Legune's bright anger push
Him back against the wall. His individuality
Seemed naked as he looked into her eyes.
He longed to slip out of the Legion Hall
So that he couldn't see or feel the shame
Of how his friends were lined against the wall.

He waited, shame a fireball in his gut,
Until, at last, the old, fierce woman left.
He felt her pride run hot inside his blood.

At last Beth Swan, enraged, moved from the wall.
"The white man's wrong," she said. "That woman's wrong!
She's old time, chained inside the Catholic Church.
We're on a journey through the spirit world
Our father's fathers knew was part of who they were.
Sitting Crow and Lena face the white man's guns.
I won't embrace a shame we shouldn't feel."

Pete's eyes began to shine. He put his hand
On Beth's arm, smiled, and stepped into the room.
He'd heard the fiery words of Sitting Crow
When Sitting Crow had spoken at the Rainbow Bar
Before he'd gone to seize the Novitiate.

"Our hearts begin to celebrate our elders' strength,"
He said. Beth grinned at him. He felt his psyche swell.
"But we, a tribe inside a tribe, are more.
We're one, a single, lupine, warrior's heart!"

He felt the fire that he and Beth had lit.
They all moved off the wall and started gesturing.

"We need to sing our courage home," Norm Davis said.

A thought struck Pete and caused his head to swirl.
They'd stood like children as Legune had shamed them.
They'd failed to use their heritage, their strength.
He turned and looked at Ben, his boyhood friend.
"We need a war drum, Ben," he said. "A drum."

Ben stared at Pete, eyes dark with incoherent rage.

"She shamed me!" Ben spit out. "And you and you,"
His finger pointed first at Pete, then Beth.
"We can't just laugh at how we felt, then drum
The poisoning we felt out of our lives . . ."

"He's right," Gwen Peaches said. "Legune reached out
And made us feel what we must feel about ourselves
Inside where none of us have looked before."

Beth's eyes flashed fire. "We'll end shame now,"
She said. "While Sitting Crow's alive we'll vanquish it
By facing those who've ruled our lives too long.
We'll make them feel ashamed for what they've done."

Ben looked at Beth. The room was silent. Wills
Confronted wills. Pete looked into Ben's eyes.
"Ben, Ben," he said so softly he barely spoke.

Ben turned. "Okay, we'll drum our shame away."
"Not drum," Beth said. Ben turned to look at her.
"We've got to do much more than speak with drums.
We'll make a strong War Bundle Feast and call
The *Wakanadja* for a blessing on our rage."

Pete felt the awful promise left unsaid.
"We need the drum," he said and smiled. He felt
The power that their songs would make, the fear.
The hair behind his neck stood up and bristled thought.

Ben stared at him, then turned and left the Legion Hall.

The Question

1

"What do you want from God?" a voice asked John.
The question echoed like a half remembered song.

Beside him, still asleep, Jane was comforting
Him just by being where she was at home.
His head was lanced with sharp, excruciating pain.
He got up, walked into the bathroom dazed.

What did he want from God? he asked himself.
The angels danced in flame upon the altar's wood.
When he had caught a glimpse of miracle,
Then lived inside the miracle, the world collapsed,

      "rat's feet over broken glass. . .[47]
      . . .spasmodic tricks of radiance miracles ..."[48]
What did he really want? What did he need?
          . . . . "a place
    where black granite rivers
    shine like obsidian in the sun . . ."? [49]

He looked into the mirror at his face.
His eyes were bloodshot from a lack of sleep.
In Schrodinger's dark box the cat is or never was[50].
The Wu Li masters[51] dance the dance of energy,
Enlightenment inside a world so small
That only mathematics has the elegance
To find the patterns woven by God's loom.
He longed for grace, but was afraid of God.

What did he want from God? He'd bathed in light —
Two angels dancing in an altar's fire.
Could he believe he'd seen what he had seen?
He'd lived without a hint of miracles,
And now he'd seen a miracle from God.
What burden had been placed upon his life?
His rationality had started crumbling
The moment when his phone had rung, and Thorn
Had told him Sitting Crow had seized the Novitiate.

He turned away from where he stared, got dressed,
Then walked into the early dawn depressed.

2

Thorn walked into the office looking grim.
His face was smoldering with anger half contained.
John stared at him in silence. Thorn's eyes flashed.
John stayed behind the ancient army desk
And didn't try to move his body or his eyes.

"I found Dawn White," Thorn said at last. "Alive,
But in a coma deep enough for death.
The Rajah brought her in half dead, then went for you."

John sighed. He felt the webbed complexity
Spin threads around the threads around his life.
"What made the coma start?" he asked, breath held.
He'd seen the bodies dead from holiness
At Jonestown deep in South America[52].
The Rajah ran a cult, and cults could kill.

"The Rajah isn't saying," Thorn said softly. "But . . ."

"But what?" John asked. He'd worn a badge too long.

"The Rajah made her lose her mind," Thorn said.
"He looks at her; you see the guilt he feels.
I don't know what he did, but she's so gone . . .
The doctors say she might not wake again."

Light filtered through his basement windowpane.

"You're mad as hell," John said.

                           Thorn looked away.
"This God-damned mess is stretching out," he said.
"My cousin's in the damned Novitiate
Proclaiming holy rage against you whites,
And now we have to face this man who wears
His holiness as if it's God-infallible.
I feel a storm so awful with its winds

———
98

I wonder who I'll be once hell has run its course."

"Celest was kidnapped," John said quietly.

Thorn shook his head. "But why?" he asked. "It's nuts."

John's eyes unfocused. Angels danced in fire.
Amidst the maple trees he tried to will
The voice of God into the dark surrounding him.

Thorn shifted in his chair. "We're friends," he said.

John focused quickly on his friend's black eyes.
Thorn wasn't done. He still had something else.
"I've got an Indian's blood," he said at last.
"They call me apple on the Rez." He laughed.

"I know," John said so softly that he wasn't sure
He'd made a sound.

                    Thorn got up to his feet.
John didn't move. He didn't want to move.

"Aunt Wilma's asked if I would lead a group
With food past roadblocks in to Sitting Crow,"
Thorn said. "The radicals are short of food.
Aunt Wilma thinks if she just makes the point,
And you won't let her past your deputies,
The media will make the Warriors look
Like heroes fighting hopeless odds against
Cold bureaucrats who hide behind a sheriff's badge."

"Aunt Wilma's got a point," John said. He paused. "And so?"

Thorn sat back down. "I just betrayed my Aunt," he said.
"I told her I . . . wouldn't tell you what she planned."
He shook his head. "What should I do? The media,
Menominee, all want a show, and I'm not white . . ."
His voice trailed off . . .

                    "You are American,"
John said, his voice so strong its force shocked him.

Thorn's rage flashed in his eyes. "Not you," he said. "Not you.
Your world's disintegrating in your head.
Don't tell me I'm American and that's enough.
I'm Indian. This country's not enough. No way!"

John looked into his head. The angels danced.
The Wu Li masters danced. The complications wove
On looms too large for human eyes to see.
Thorn stared. The rat's feet pranced on broken glass.

"How can we stop your Aunt? The Governor
Will chew us up if cameras show her waving bread
At men confronting her with loaded guns."

Thorn looked down at the ground. "You ask a lot,"
He said. "They'll say I sold my Indianness to you."

John sighed. "I know," he said.

                        Thorn looked at him.
"It isn't easy for the Indian or you whites.
My heart says Sitting Crow is wrong. He'll feel
That martyrdom and pain are gain enough."
He got up on his feet. "Aunt Wilma's bread
Will stay inside her cupboard growing stale."

He turned and walked into the hallway, grim.

John bent his head and buried it in hands.
He'd done his job, by God. He'd done his job.

3

That night John dreamed again. He saw his body cast
Into a fiery oven[53], heat his universe.
His pain was greater than the pain he'd felt
When he had burned his hand on charcoal coals
At eight years old out on his father's grill.
He lay inside the oven for an hour,
His horror lasting for eternity.

And then a mist rose up into the world
And covered up the moon's bright silver light.

The darkness spread and spread until the earth
Was clothed with darknesses that soaked up light.

He dreamed and dreamed. Beside him Jane woke up
And watched him struggle in his restless sleep.
He dreamed and dreamed — the dark so black it made
Him tremble as he felt its awful heat.

The Burial of the Machine in the Garden

1

Bill's dream — he knew it was a dream, quaked sleep.
He stood inside an ancient court, a rough,
Coarse man who had the task of feeding wood
Into a stonework fireplace near the King.
A poet stood before the King, his eyes as bright
With fire as Bill's eyes were when he preached war
Against the evils in the heart of modern man.
Small phrases chanted by the poet caught
Him as he stoked the fire:

> "Indifferent bards pretend," the poet sang.
> "They pretend a monstrous beast,
> With a hundred heads,
> And a grievous combat
> At the root of the tongue.
> And another fight there is
> At the back of the head."[54]

He shivered even though the fire was hot.
The poet's voice was deep, omnipotent.
Bill sweated from the power in the words.
The poet's voice went on and on, a sea
With waves that crashed and foamed on jagged rocks.

"If the Lord had answered," the poet sang.
> "Through charms and magic skill,
> Assumed the form of the principal trees . . ."[55]

Bill's heart began to pound. He dropped the wood
He held and stared toward the short, dark bard.

> "When the trees were enchanted,"
The bard sang.
> "There was hope for the trees,
> Of the nine kinds of faculties,
> Of fruit of fruits,
> Of fruit God made me,
> Of the blossom of the mountain primrose,

102

Of the buds of trees and shrubs . . ."[56]

A log cut from a redwood, whisper-sang at him.
"You hear?" it sang. "You hear? You hear? You hear?"

He jumped back from the log. The poet stopped
Turned, looked at him. Bill shivered with ecstatic fear.

2

Out in the woods, behind the bar, the trees
Wove mist and marched toward the town of Tigerton.
The poplars followed beech into the mist
And started singing songs so old the earth
Had long forgotten how ground stirred with marching trees.
Inside the moving trees Bill clung to maple bark
And felt the growling in the tree's dark heart.
Donn Truesdale, maddened with his lust, was armed,
His chainsaw slashing branches, trunks, and soil.
Black tractor wheels bit deep in moistened earth.

3

Bill tossed inside his sleep. The trees were joyous, crazed.
Their laughter rang into his stomach, heart.
Brain rhythms swept from hemisphere to hemisphere.
He felt the Presence loom into the maple tree.
He aimed his pistol with its useless paint
At darkness stained into the maple's upper limbs.

4

He woke up knowing what he had to do.
The edge of madness bubbled, unrestrained,
Into the greatness building through his life.
He got up, went downstairs, made coffee, watched
The sunrise break above tree canopies,
Put on his coat and gloves, then went outside.
A mile away he bulldozed frozen earth,
The blade a sacrilege against the meadow's purity.
He worked all day and deep into the night.
When he was done he left the yellow cat
Inside the meadow by the hole he'd dug

And walked back through the silent trees.
They did not sing to him or make a sound.
Moon spilled through winter branches on the snow.

5

Two hours before another dawn Bill left the bar
And drove to Tigerton and parked inside a copse
Two miles away from where Donn Truesdale farmed.
The morning air was biting cold, breath white.
He jogged two miles, slipped silently into the farm,
Then found the aging tractor in the barn.
Bill didn't stop to guarantee that Truesdale slept,
But used tinfoil to start the tractor up.
Its roaring in the morning silence startled him,
But then he drove it quickly off the farm.
He hid it in a wood with brush as camouflage.

6

That night he walked beneath the barn beams, farmer's mugs.
He wove his spell into his followers.
Donn Truesdale didn't show up at the bar.
The prophet rumbled through his voice. Eyes shined.
At three a.m. he closed the bar and drove
To where the Truesdale tractor had been stashed.

Behind the bar again, his hands were numb,
The drive so cold his feet stung, burned with pain.
He'd driven, hating what he felt compelled to do.
And now, inside the wood before the hole he'd dug,
His fears of madness danced inside his head.
What fool would steal a tractor just to bury it?

Bill drove the tractor down into the pit
And turned the engine off. Inside the walls
He felt the trees. He climbed out of the pit
And stood above the tractor, looking down.

"Machines defeat our sense of God," he said.
"Inside the Garden man was blessed.
Man knew himself, his wife, the angels, God.
But now we've fouled the Garden with our pride."

His voice rang out into the woods. He strained.
He felt like screaming out his pain, his dream,
But turned instead toward the hulking, dark
Bulldozer with its ugly, yellow mass.
It sat as stolid as an ancient beast.
Noise split apart the silence as the engine roared.
He laughed. The great, dark blade gnashed earth.
He jammed the gears into reverse, then pushed
Black earth onto the tractor in the hole.
He heard the trees. They called mist from the land.

The hole became a mound of dark, raw earth
Surrounded by the white of snow, a wound.
The moon poured silver light down on his head.
Trees celebrated with their deep tree songs.

Inside the Cadillacs
Where Mrs. High Makes Her Home

No peace, White Rabbit knew. He sat in Cadillacs
Whose roofs were sealed against the cold by tin.
Thoughts danced in fire that spiraled smoke
And warmed the two-car house. Beside him, on the seat
Before the fire and backed against the dash,
Face dark as winter bark, was Mrs. High.

White Rabbit knew he'd been a fool to come.
He'd left his house as aimlessly as leaves
Blown by the autumn winds and drove until beside
Plantation pine. He'd parked beside the road
And walked to where the Cadillacs stood sheltering
Against the winter cold. Each time he visited
The Cadillacs he came away unsettled, sad.

He turned to Mrs. High and asked her how she was.
Her face was lively. In the small, close place
She smelled unclean — of earth and plant decay.

"I'm always glad to have you come," she said.
"Your coming makes the winter easier to bear."

His memories were strong. Drums reached into the past
To make alive the dreams of all Menominee.
He saw the three of them beside the Wolf,
The water streaked with moonlight. Wanda laughed
And turned to hear the song of Matchapatow's laugh.
In light cast by the moon they'd been so beautiful.

"Your memories again?" asked Mrs. High.

"It hurts to see you here," White Rabbit said. "Legune
Said welfare could find you a place in Neopit."

"The old folks home?" she asked.

                              He looked at her.
"It's not so bad," he said. "It's warm and clean,

106

And when the winter wind howls cold,
The old folk sit and play their cards and talk
About how life was when we all were young."

She looked at him, her dark eyes fierce with pride.
"I am an Indian. In my blood the wind
Blows freedom to my bones. I am the trickster, wild.
The world provides my walls. My blood is cold.
In woods my voice weaves songs: of blue jays, hawks,
The whispering of mice in tunnels roofed with snow,
The silent trout beneath the river's skin of ice.
I am an Indian, strong enough to fall at Wounded Knee
And still live on, a woman-child of Mother Earth.
I am an Indian trickster bound by blood
And skin and bone to rocks and streams and sky.
I live outside where winds howl at the night
And stars shine brighter than the look inside
The eyes of Indian warriors making love.
I am an Indian, proud of who I am."

She was a woman mad from wilderness,
Her depths unruly, wild, the spirit in her eyes
As strong as that inside an eagle's eyes.

"You still write poetry," he said. "Out here."

She smiled. "I choose to live out here," she said.
"In summer I can take a bath by jumping in the Wolf,
But now I'm much too old to clean with snow.
I feel my life out here; I feel the way
Our great grandfathers felt before the white man came.
Blood pumped into our great grandfather's hearts
Is pumped into my heart. I feel I'm free."

White Rabbit looked into the fire again.
Smoke rose into the hole cut in the tin
That joined the Cadillacs. Smoke rose skyward
While leaving air for breath inside the cars.
No peace, he thought. The Indian youth
Were crazy from a pain long dead, afraid
To face their place inside the white man's world,
And Matchapatow ate the waste from garbage cans.

"You've heard about the Novitiate?" he asked.

She smiled. "I've heard," she said. "A young man stopped
By here to warm himself. He was a Warrior made alive . . ."

He didn't want to hear what she would say.
He tried to freeze his tongue inside his mouth.
He wanted freedom from responsibility.
He didn't want to look into dead rabbit eyes.
He was an Indian too, a ginseng gatherer,
An elder wanting more than Indians could achieve.

"What do you think?" he asked.

                          She didn't hesitate.
As feral as a screeching hawk, her voice
Was musical and strong; it sang as low
As wind sung hearts of great grandfather pines.

"I think you're joining them," she said. "You're old;
You'll run the risk of dying if you go.
Your skin is Indian skin, your heart an Indian heart.
You came to see if I would tell you what to do.
I won't, but you have heard the winds I've heard."

He looked up from the fire into her eyes.
His heart was pounding with the force of Pow Wow drums.
She had been beautiful when young, as beautiful
As Wanda, brighter than a sun ablaze with light.
They'd loved their tribe and all its ways.
And now? He looked away. What did he feel?
She looked as huddled as a rock upon a hill.

"I'll go," he said.

               "Good luck," she said. "And keep alive."

He looked at her again, turned, let himself
Outside into the winter's snow and ran.
The ancient water drum, so sacred true
It resonated with the spirit of the gods
Of Mother Earth and water, fire and sky,
Reverberated in his skin, his Indian blood.

———
108

Plagues and Portents

1

John walked into the barn. Affinity with dust,
Dim light. Plagues, portents shaking earth and mind.
The plastic yellow phone on bales of hay.

The conversation's liquid ran through thoughts:
"Come, Sitting Crow. It's done. You dissipate
In mist, a free man with your followers,
Or else we'll storm the walls, and you will die."

And Sitting Crow, invisible behind
The white stone walls, looked deep into his heart,
And, overwhelmed by vision, said, "okay, it's done."

John touched the phone. The ringing sound felt cold.
Time whorled in river eddies, unpredictable,
The past a future history spun dim.
The phone rang on and on, its ringing lost.
John felt his patience stretching out and thinning — dim.

At last he put the phone receiver down.
No Sitting Crow. No Lena. No relief
He didn't want to be the man he was.
He didn't want to hear the voice of God.

The ancient cry of Job assailed him:
        "I cry to Thee for help, but Thou dost not answer me;
        I stand up, and Thou dost turn Thy attention against me."[57]
The angel-light burned inside out into his head.
He'd asked for God, and God had answered. Job
Had longed for God, but John had turned away.

John turned. His men were huddled round a fire.
They looked like hunters from an age long past,
Their faces sere and gaunt from weeks of cold.
They'd lost the pace of living in the world
And found an older rhythm: fires that fought
Against the ravages of winter winds.

They looked expectantly at him. They longed
To go back to their homes and lives. He smiled.

2

The phone rang. In the hall John tried to calm
The fibrillating chaos in his heart.
His vision of a lucid Sitting Crow
Unwilling to continue in his march to death
Struck with redoubled force, hope strong. The ring
Turned sinister. What now? he thought. What now?
The Rajah? Sitting Crow? Celest Speltz? Thorn
With word that he had failed to stop his Aunt?

"John Israel," he said. "John Israel," he said again.

A voice, thin morning mists, spoke haltingly.
"I've been the victim of a robbery,"
It said. "A thief came to the farm at dawn
And drove my only tractor off." The voice
Paused, searching for its words. "I know the thief."

A drum began to beat inside John's head.
Why him? Of all the petty sheriffs in the world,
Why him?

   "Who's this?" he asked.

        The voice was faint.
"Donn Truesdale," said the voice. "Bill Winchell stole
My tractor while I watched him drive away."

"The preacher man?" John asked. "You saw him take . . ."

He didn't want to hear. He didn't want to know.
Bill Winchell had a following and guns.
John fell into his chair. The country was unraveling.
The drumbeats pounded endlessly inside his head.
"I'll be right out," he said. "I'll take your statement there."

He put the phone down, cupped his hand.
His breath ran through his fingers. Where was Thorn?

110

3

Outside the city, driving east to Tigerton,
John felt the tempo of events and felt
The climax building to a point of no return.
The waiting weighed him down. He had to act.
The squad tires hummed upon the road, their song
As steady as the beating of his heart.

Donn Truesdale's charge of tractor thievery
Against Bill Winchell wouldn't lead to good.

He tried to conjure up Bill Winchell's face,
But saw the Rajah's dark, thin face instead.

Cosmology[58]

At midnight Lena found the five of them.
The firelight flickered shadows on the walls.
They sat before the fireplace talking quietly.
In silence Lena moved into the room
And sat down on the floor, her back against the wall.
Her rage had died when she had talked to Israel,
And for the moment she was willing to forget
She soon might have to lead the kids away
From where she had to be if Sitting Crow
Would live beyond the crisis they had made.

Kim looked at Lena as she came into the room.
The murmuring beside the firelight stopped.
Kim placed tobacco in a dish and lit it with a match.
He let the kids, then Lena, cleanse themselves with smoke.

"We are Menominee," Kim sang, voice soft and young.
"Our earth is floating like an island washed
By waves that have no starting point and never end.
Above the living earth, below the earth,
Are regions where the supernatural live,
Benevolent above, malevolent below.
Each region is divided by four tiers.
As far away from earth as possible,
The Great White Spirit, burning, blinding sun,
Looks down upon the lives in all the tiers.
He is the power, song, of universe."

Kim's voice hushed, whispered. Marsha looked at him,
Eyes fiery from the power in the ancient song.
She looked at shadows leaping on the walls.
The four boys, wrapped into the ceremony,
Sat quietly, their hands beside their sides.

"The great Great Spirit saw his people, saw
The Indian being killed, the spirits killing him,
All kinds of animal destroying him,"
Sang Marsha. "Seeing, powerful, the Spirit thought:
'I will create a life to oversee my children's lives."
And then he made the shining Thunderbirds.

112

He made the Thunderbirds to watch the Indian, keep
Malevolent, dark spirits from his way.
The Thunderbirds would water everything
So that all life could flourish on the earth."

Todd didn't pause or look at Lena. Clear,
He picked the song up, made it grow and change.
"The White Bear lives inside the Underground,"
He sang. "He holds the earth up in his den
Below the tree's roots, down below the mountain's stone.
The Bear is whom the Spirit thinks about
While holding up the sky and all its tiers.
They tell each other all about the universe.
That's how they work, these two. They are alike.
They sing their power songs, and life and death
And spirit lives and songs go on and on . . ."

"The Hairy Serpent is not good," Sam sang.
"He sometimes swims as if he were a watersnake
And swings his serpent tail at a boat
Where Indians sit alive inside their lives.
And then the Serpent snares them in his coils.
And when men see the hairy night-dark snakes,
The Great Horned Serpents, black and golden scales,
Their spirits sing into the waving grass.

"The hairy snakes," Sam sang, voice powerful.
"Use holes to come into the sleeping earth.
They try to find and swallow frightened men.
They try to catch the Thunderbirds asleep.
They try to find a time when Thunderbirds
Are looking elsewhere in the universe.
The Thunderbirds are ever vigilant.
Their talons drive the Serpents underground.

"But if an Indian sees a hairy snake,
Death in the Indian's family follows swift.
The Great Horned Serpent seen inside a dream
Foretells a time of sorrow, time of woe.
When wizards keep a Great Horned Serpent's flesh
The witchcraft formed is powerful, malevolent."

"There is a wandering, wild man," Bob sang.

He didn't pause between Sam's song and his.
"He bears his burden ceaselessly about.
He sometimes settles down beside a town,
But then he disappears and won't be seen.
He never comes to tell a tale of peace,
But always tells of coming troubles, pain.
At night, alone, all travelers will hear
His rustling leaves and mournful passing songs.

"A gift of liquor or tobacco makes
Him go away, but if you anger him,
You must run like a deer and hide yourself.
He'll chase you like a hunter through the woods
And throw his sticks at you, and if he aims
Just right, then you will die. O yes, you'll die."

Bob's voice died down. The fireplace danced with flames.
Lena looked at Kim and felt their eyes.
They are Menominee, she thought. Like Sitting Crow.
They had to leave. She couldn't let them die.
She couldn't face the death of Sitting Crow.
She felt the wandering, wild man inside the walls.

"Each human being is possessed," she sang.
"Of two good souls. One has the width of shade . . ."
She paused. She felt a dark, bright stirring flow.
She felt her throbbing heart outside her chest.

"When death possesses us," she sang. "The intellect
Is loosed and wanders aimlessly about,
A lingering around the graveyard's peace.

"The soul, or *Tcebai*, lives inside the heart.
It is the soul that travels past the sun
And moon and stars to find its afterlife."

Her voice died down just as the other's voices had.
Kim looked at her. His eyes were bright with joy.
"You see?" he asked.

              As Lena looked into his eyes
She felt a cold wind whisper soft into her hair.
She didn't speak, but got up, left the room.

114

The Absorption of Hate

1

Legune woke. In her dream death was a stain
That started at the Legion Hall, then spread
Into Keshena, blackness loosed upon one house
And then another, death a creeping plague
That settled on those sleeping in their beds.
It slipped through windows, under doors, and crooned
Fuliginous death, spirits loosed as stains
Above the houses, up into the star-filled skies.

She couldn't take her eyes from streaming darknesses.
Their terpsichorean dance tugged at her heart.
She felt their terror at their metamorphosis.
She knew she had to make the dream evaporate,
But still it held her fast; the darkness spread.
The skies filled up with panicked souls. And then . . .

The dark inside her bedroom felt familiar, safe.
She sat up in the bed, the covers close.
She'd lived a long, long time. She'd learned that bogeymen
Were mostly self-doubts hidden in herself.

She forced herself from bed into the winter-cold.
She didn't want to face her dream again.
She missed her husband, Bruce, the gentle man.
The spirit of the bogeymen was strong.
She puttered in the kitchen for a while,
Then picked the laundry she had left undone
And went outside and got into her car.

She passed The Rainbow Bar, its lights turned off,
Then passed the black Wolf River Bridge, its river ice.
The Legion Hall loomed up in front of her.
She pulled into the park across the road.
The minute that she'd stopped a light turned on.
The bulb's white glare was eerie in the dark.
She tried to see the stain she'd seen in dream:

The darkness seemed to darken as she looked.

The light bulb dimmed. The night was rancorous.
Her heart began to hammer in her ears.
The stain seemed real, alive, not visible.
She tried to force her heart to beat like normal, tried
To make it slow into a rhythmic pulse.

And then she stopped her effort, got into the car.
By facing down the radicals she'd loosed
A spirit on the earth she'd never known.
She left Keshena chased by demon-dark.
She longed to see the glow of Shawano's lights.

2

Inside the Laundromat Legune collapsed.
The wall clock said the time was five a.m.
She looked toward the Kingdom Hall the Witnesses[59]
Maintained across the street and wondered why
The sect's intensity had not made poetry.
The terror, grained into her spirit, grasped her breath.
She'd found a bogeyman that wouldn't leave.

She turned and met another woman's eyes.
A load of clothes was tumbling in a dryer's heat.
The woman wasn't old, not more than twenty-four,
White, poor, her house dress plain as paper bags,
Yet pretty in a plastic, white man's way.
A poisoned hate poured from her blue-gray eyes.
Legune returned the woman's angry stare.

"You're Indian, aren't you?" Hate rang in her voice.

Legune leaned back into her chair, closed eyes.
She tried to feel how darkness felt before the dream.

"Oh yes," she sighed. "I'm Indian, born into a tribe
Who found a paradise of rivers, lakes,
And trees abundant in the fish and game
That made life possible in wilderness
Untouched by white men after whites had come."

The woman heard Legune's sharp tone of voice.
Her face turned ugly, livid red, with hate.

———
116

"Your people don't know God," she said, her voice
So powerful with hate Legune cringed, hot.
"God's place should be untouched by unclean scum
That crawl out of their reservation hole.
You shouldn't be allowed to trash a town
Of working, decent, God abiding folk."

The stain spread outward from the Legion Hall.
Her people's souls, clear, streamed into the sky.
The hate she'd fought against since she was old
Enough to think and know her worth welled up.
Rage made her tremble as she dreamed of striking out
And silencing this woman's pink-white tongue.
She'd told the radicals that they were wrong.
She felt their helplessness and mindless rage.
She hated whites. She hated all of them.

She opened up her eyes and forced herself
To look into the frightened woman's face.
The woman whirled around, disdainful of Legune,
And opened up the dryer. Clothes collapsed.

Legune closed eyes again and tried to free
Her spirit of the woman's hate. She struggled, wept.
She wouldn't let the hate engender hate in her.
She strained to drain the hate into herself.
The dark behind Legune moved inexorably.
Legune loosed love into the dark and soaked
The hate she felt into herself, her song,
Into the strength she'd spent a lifetime gathering.

> "The great sea
> Has sent me adrift, she sang.
> It moves me
> As the weed in a great river
> Earth and the great weather
> Move me
> Have carried me away
> And move my inward parts with joy."[60]

She felt the power kerneled in the song
The ancient Indian shaman woman sang.
She tried to send her spirit out to soothe

117

The whites and Indians threatened by the stain.

At last her heart calmed down. She opened up her eyes.

The woman wasn't in the Laundromat.
The first, faint smudge of light was in the sky.

The Dancing of Organic Energy

1

The Rajah, in his bedroom, felt the songs
Organic energy danced through the universe.
Light spread, diffuse upon the wood, that whirled
With energies coalesced into the shape
Of wood, the essence, heart, core, shape of chair.
The world, skies, empty space, suns, distant worlds
Danced like a river danced, slow, fast, light, strong,
As still and stationary as a stone,
Yet always flowing, never standing still.
And in their movement, stillness, were their songs,
The song, the heartbeat rising from the muscle dance
Inside the Rajah's beating, living heart.

The silence in the bedroom let him hold
The rage he'd felt inside his mind, its red,
Blind energy a madness pulsing hate
Into the world of dancing energies.
He saw it burn with flames that leaped and thrashed,
And as he watched it burn, he saw two lights,
Two tall, thin, graceful men, dance in the flames.
He felt the power of the Christian God
And felt the power of his Rajah's rage, the dance
Of flame against the dance of flame, a holocaust
Beginning, ending, flaring up again —
That spread, diffuse, upon the wooden chair.

2

Celest, caught in the nightmare, longed to feel
The peace of everyday routines inside
The compound: rising from her bed at dawn,
Then fixing breakfast as the sun's first light
Created morning shadows, hours of woman-talk.
But in her heart, beneath her consciousness,
She wove strength through the rage she felt.
She made herself relive her father's drunkenness
The night her mother died, his grief transformed
Into a vulgar rage at all life's petty wrongs.

She felt, again, his fumbling, drunken hands
Upon her teenaged breasts, the fear she'd felt
To see the nightmare of her Father's bulging pants.

"Jim Speltz." She spoke the curse beneath her breath.
"Jim Speltz," her father not a father: God
Cursed, angry, ineffective, evil man.

The nightmare was a test. Her father's will
Against her will, Trent Warren set between.
She didn't move, but glared with loathing hate.
She'd chosen Rajah for her father love.
He'd brought her freedom from the misery
Jim Speltz had always put into her life.

Trent Warren and her father had the look
Of men who knew they'd taken on too much.
She felt so tired she didn't know if she
Would ever feel refreshed by sleep again.

She shook her head and screamed and screamed. Her voice
Shook windows, made her father and Trent Warren jump.
Her father's rage boiled angrily into his face.
She cringed to feel the fear he'd always used
To force his male superiority.
She shut her mouth. The screaming stopped. She smiled.
The nightmare wouldn't end. The nightmare lived.

Trent Warren got up to his feet. "The Rajah's wrong."
Sincerity rang in his voice and words.
"In cults you have no will to call your own.
The only way you'll find to save yourself
Is by acknowledging your father's love."
She didn't speak, but stared into her father's face.

3

The Rajah, with a sigh, stopped meditating. Calm,
He left the bedroom, walked into the living room,
And sat before the fire. Ron Zukalov,
His first disciple, smiled to see him come.

"Your meditation done?" Ron asked. "We know

That Dawn is ill. The children said she told
You that Celest had been abducted by two men."

Fred Morrow, Gary Finney, Cindy Smaltz,
The others waited. He had taught them peace, life's core
Made powerful by wants that gnawed at flesh.
He felt a need to punish those who'd raped
Their peace and made them vulnerable to life.

He had to make them understand his need
Was more than discipline could heal.
"Celest was kidnapped by her father. That I know,"
He said, the calm from meditation in his voice.
"He's hired deprogrammers to steal mind
And heart from us, her family and friends."

They waited. Panic, fear, and hatred filled their eyes.
Their silence flowed as river waters, light.

The Rajah didn't speak, but waited patiently.
Fred Morrow looked toward the fireplace fire.
"We've got to free Celest," he said. "She left
Her father years ago. She's part of us."

"But how?" Ron asked. "Our violence only harms our selves.
We can't become a pack of mindless wolves."

The anger sparked by Fred danced in the room.
A harsh, gaunt Cindy burned with inner fires
As bright as angel-fire upon an altar's wood.
"Celest is one of us," she said. "We have the right
To take our own back from the pack of thieves
Who hated her enough to take her from her own."

The Rajah held his hand up, called for peace.
"The Christian God is powerful," he said.
"His legions march and threaten all our lives."
He stood up suddenly. He was aflame.
"We have to plan. We have to free to Celest.
She can't be held against her own free will."

The hate inside the room intensified.
He felt their anger build. He was the focal point.

121

"It's simple," Gary said. "We'll watch Jim Speltz's place,
Then move the minute that he drops his guard.
He can't keep watch all day and every night."

Ron stood as thin as figures wreathed in flame.
His face was sharp from years of discipline.
"We aren't a pack of wolves," he said again.
"We can't debase ourselves with violence born
From hate, destruction, love, heroics, fear . . .
We can't let instincts dominate our lives.
We have to keep our peace and trust our gods."
He paused. "We have to say our prayers for Dawn."

The Rajah felt the river waters shift.
They eddied, whorled, and flowed against the light.
He wouldn't be denied. Celest would join
Community again, her spirit fierce
With joyous celebration, joyous song.
He'd light a conflagration that would spread
Its light into the Methodist's brick church
And end God's angels dancing; quench the altar's flame.
And when they'd freed Celest, Celest would go
To Dawn and heal the awful emptiness he'd caused.
He looked into Ron's eyes. He loved this man.
He'd always loved this fierce, strong, loyal man.

"We'll find Celest!" his voice rang out. "We'll free
Her from her bonds and challenge Christianity!"

Ron looked down at the floor, obedience
Etched on his thin, sad face. The others' flames
Flared up into their eyes, a light so bright
The Rajah felt as if he'd fallen up
Into the fires inside the morning's sun.

Lena and Sitting Crow

The warmth of Lena's breasts against his chest,
Their bodies matched and feverish with rhythms born
Before they'd been conceived in mothers' wombs.
He stepped back, looked at shining, naked flesh,
Her nipples dark against her darkened skin.

The grandeur of the dining hall was ruined.
The place where once the brothers ate
Amidst the marble pillars burned with cold.
Lena smiled to see him smile and lifted arms.
He shed the contemplation bothering his nights.
He felt alive, a man whose death was lost.
He ached and longed for all the love he felt
Before him in the dining hall's half dark.

"You're life beginning," Sitting Crow said, stirred
To feel the strength of beauty's full display.
He sobered. "Death can't touch you. You are life."

Lena slowly turned toward the fire, then back
To face the burning lust of Sitting Crow.
"And I am yours," she mocked. "And you are mine."

The shadows from the firelight flickering dark
Across her legs and breasts, the woman curves.
His hands reached out to touch her warm, smooth flesh.
She smiled and put her hand upon his chest.
Wild, Sitting Crow stared past her at the fire.

"In old times people said the stars could speak,"
He said. "They said they spoke of fate, the future's weave."

His words made Lena stare at him. She dropped her arms.
"What's wrong? You talk like that, and something's wrong."

He fought the sudden sense of doom assailing him.
"You're life," he said. "I wear the blanket of my death.
The white man's waiting patiently right now.
John Israel is not our enemy.
But we aren't holding to his laws, and soon he'll break,

123

And then I'll face my history, my death."

"So what?" she asked. "You're not alone. I'm here.
There's Superstar and Johnny, Carla, Major, Horse . . ."
She thought about the kids inside the basement room,
Creation's song affirming, celebrating life.
"We'll face the consequences of our acts."

He smiled and looked at her, his body lean.
"But you are life, and life can't marry death.
Just look at you, so beautiful you take . . ."
He paused, his insides flinching from his thoughts.
"I can't imagine you inside a casket's box."

Lena glared into his eyes. "What do you want?"
She asked so softly that he had to strain to hear.

"Somebody's got to take the kids out through the swamp."

He didn't want to say the words. He wanted time
To stop, to live his life beside her as the fire's
Light danced upon her shoulders, down into the curve
Where love and life made life and love newborn.

She shook her head. "They're just like you," she said.
"They feel as if their hero's let them down.
They've got free will; they are Menominee;
They want to live or die just like you live or die."

Her words stung, made him fell inadequate.
"They're young," he said. "We're charged to keep the young
Alive and well. They'll keep our dreams alive."

The bitterness she felt rose in her voice.
"And I'm the one who's got to turn her tail and run."

He looked at her. He threw his eyes away from her.

"I'm not the hero type," he said. "Death frightens me.
You stay; I'll choose to live instead of die,
And everything we've done will end up meaningless."

The tension wrung into his body disappeared

124

As Lena grabbed her shirt and slipped it on.

"I don't believe we'll have to die," she said.
"John Israel's no fool. He's not the man
To make a martyr for a cause he feels
Has justice hidden in its history."

Sitting Crow reached out and touched her arm.
"We've got to pass beyond our history.
We've got to stand in cold of winter suns
And carve a spirit Indians everywhere
Can know as fires of martyrdom and death."

"You sound like some crazed maniac," she said.
"The Christians like to talk about their martyrdom.
Our Mother Earth speaks words of life, not death."

Her words struck hard into his stomach, wounding him.
He was a Warrior made to make a stand
Against the wrongs the white man forced upon the tribe.
"Perhaps I am a maniac," he answered.

                              Lena turned.
"You are the man I love," she said. "The warrior chief
Who knows no fear, who loves me fiercely with his life."

Sitting Crow faced the anger in her eyes.
"Injustice rules the world the Indian's forced
To live his poverty inside," he said. "If death
Will lead a little way toward a juster day,
Then martyrdom is what we have to face."

Lena slipped out of her shirt again.
The way she held herself burned through the dark.
We've got the guts," she said. "Both you and I.
We'll live or die together, not apart."

He stood his ground, his stirring passion wild . . .
"You've got to take the kids. We can't risk kids
Too young to know how final death can be."

Then Lena stood and pressed her body into him.
Unwillingly, he put his arms around her waist.

———
125

He drove his hips against her hips and nearly cried.
She took his ear inside the hardness of her teeth.
He sucked breath, felt the pulsing-beat of universe.
He wanted life and love, not death, not death.
She pulled him down beside her on the rug.
The fire inside the fireplace burned and burned.

The War Bundle Ceremony

The cooking for the feast went on and on
As people, Indians, whites, Menominee,
Moved from the outside in, the inside out.

Ben brought the drum and set it at room-median.
Five other drums were placed around Ben's drum.
By dusk both drums and song rang through the hall.
Old ways were half remembered, dim, but drums still beat.
Menominee invited other Indians, whites inside.
The straggly white men stared at living ritual.

At last, the feasting done, night soft against the sky,
Pete left the drum and waited. Silence spread.
"As host," he said. "I'll say a prayer in our way:

"Grandfathers, we have been remiss in what we've done,
But do not hold our failures in your hearts.
We greet grandfathers, great war-bundle braves.
We cannot live the lives of those who went before,
Or sing songs how you sung them on this earth
When white men were a dream no one had dreamed.
In our relationship with you, we want to do our best.
No song, nor prayer, will provoke you from the songs
You've sung since you embraced our Mother Earth.
But we have had this feast, and we will sing these songs."

As Pete sat down, Ben stroked the drum and laughed.
He stood up, smiled. Storms grew in eyes and hearts.
"Ay yie!" he said. "You make the prayer long.
I'll sing a Trickster song.[61] Ay yie! Ay yie!
The Trickster is not man nor beast nor anything!

"One day he walked into a wood, a pack
Upon his back, and someone called to him:
'Say you! We want to hear you sing.' "All right,"
He said. "I'm carrying my songs inside my pack,
And if you wish to dance, you first must build
A lodge that has a small hole for a door."

"The people wanting songs were quick to build.

127

They made the great lodge circular, a hole
Left in the roof to honor Father Sun
And Father Sky. And when it rose, its top
Above the topmost branches of the trees,
The people went inside, the Trickster following.
The people that had asked for songs were birds.

"The Trickster told them that his songs were powerful,
And if they didn't want long hours of pain,
They had to dance shut-eyed, controlled by song.
He took the songs out of his pack and sang . . .

"The birds all danced, eyes shut, but when a fat,
Sweet bird danced near ecstatic Trickster's hands,
He grabbed the bird and choked it dead. And if
The bird cried out, he laughed and said, "that's it!
That's it! A whoop! A whoop!" And so the birds
Kept dancing, caught into the music of the song.

But then one bird became suspicious. Crazed
With dance, he still cracked open just one eye
And saw the Trickster choking all the birds.
"He's killing us!" the bird cried out. "Let all
Who can fly for their lives!" And with a squawk
He flew out of the hole atop the lodge.
The Trickster took the birds that he had killed
And roasted them.

                    "But then," Ben said, his voice
As dark as night, as cold as winter winds.
"Night Spirits cloaked the sky and stole the birds.
The Trickster failed to get a single bite. Hai yie!"

Beth Swan stood up, dressed in a buckskin dress.
Pete stared at her and felt her fearlessness.

"The war has come," she said. "We've lost the chants
That made us warriors, but I've seen the Thunderbirds.
They have no hair, but wear their arbor vitae wreathes.
I walked inside their village in the west and saw
Night Spirits, those who have ascendancy in war.
They've heard our drum and celebrate our songs!"

The drumbeat deepened, lengthened out its song.
The women moved onto the floor and linked
Their arms to Beth's arms, started dancing, birds.
The men let feet dissolve into the songs.
The singers sang with great war-bundle-lives.

Pete stood beside the drum and made an offering
To Thunderbirds and dark Night Spirits, war.
"Accept tobacco from our lives to yours," he sang.
"Let smoke draw you to earth so that our songs
Will reassure you as you contemplate our aims.
We've suffered much within this modern world.
Our people live in poverty and want
While white men live with bellies full of meat.
We plan address to this inequity.
We are a single, lupine heart, a soul.
Drink deep tobacco smoke and feed our bravery!"

He held the ceremonial wood pipe
And filled his lungs with smoke. Another singer took
The long, black pipe, inhaled, and passed it on.
The drums were strong. Their power filled Pete's head.
The pipe went round. Eyes glazed. The dancers danced,
The singer's voices starlight, sunlight, moon.

"If you, the spirits, accept our offerings,"
Pete prayed. "Then grant us blessings, goodness, strength . . ."

A dancer stopped his dancing, fell down on the floor.
He started ripping off his clothes. He danced.
The drums beat as another man took off his clothes.
He'd found his way into the spirit's world —

Beth Swam began to rip her clothes . . .
This wasn't like the old times when the men
Were warriors and the women councilors.
The wildness entered Pete. The world dissolved.
He saw the *Wakandja* greeting him with smiles,
Their bald heads gleaming in the spirit-sun.
They mimicked all his movements, laughed
To see inside their village, not a spirit, man.

"Dance on, dance on," they said. "We see Beth Swan.

You want to touch her, be her lover now?"
They laughed. He laughed to hear them laugh. He drooled
Into the spirit-earth their village sat upon.

"Go on, go on," they said. "We like you here.
We'll watch you go to war. Legune was wrong.
You've got a warrior's heart and lover's loins."

He laughed at how they laughed and stared at eyes
So bright they seemed to burn into his head.
He looked around to see Beth's nakedness,
But saw instead a darkness growing on the earth.
He heard the drum and felt the songs and dance.
Clouds rumbled warning drums as lightning flashed.
He reached toward the darkness of the clouds.
The spirits laughed. He tried to tear away.
The spirits danced possessed as no mere man
Could ever dance, their clothing rainbows arced,
Eyes suns that flared and pooled with rainbow light.

"We'll grant you what you prayed for," laughed the Thunderbirds.
"We'll make you brave enough for war . . . for war."

Pete laughed, fell down upon the pinewood floor.
He rolled inside the dance that was no dance.
Floors bruised his all too human flesh. He laughed.
He loved Beth Swan, he thought. He laughed. He rolled.
He'd make his warrior-woman his for life.

The Tree Goddess

The tractor buried, earth above, below
Its smelted metal soul, Bill left his seat.
Tree singing hummed vibrations into bones.
He felt confused. The holiness of woods
Surrounded him when frostbit feet touched ground.
The trees were celebrating tractor death?

The tree's song changed. He strained to hear the words.

>*"Bum Twrch ym Mynydd*
>*Bum cyff mewn rhaw*
>*Bum bwall yn llaw. . ."*[62]

He turned toward the great bulldozer, numb.
The dark woods stirred. Songs turned rumbling chants.
His body hummed at earth-deep, trembling sounds.

He was awake; still, in the snow wrapped woods,
A woman dressed in white, hair wild as winds,
Stood like a queen, her living wooden staff,
Her scepter, beckoning to him. Her three hearts sang.
Her woman's warmth enveloped him with life.
Her face, as glittering as ice, was beautiful —
Beyond what he could stand and still remain a man.
Her hair was raven-black, her eyes dark earth.
Peace flowed through veins into his heart.
The woman brought alive a wild desire.
He daydreamed nights of passion in the grass,
Her breasts and nipples brown as earth, taut, young.
His hips drove forward like the blade
When metal gnashed into the frozen earth.
He stepped toward her, felt her holiness,
Felt passion in the sperm he longed to drive
Into her folds and realized (he paused in shock)
That now he knew a force that was not his.

The woman smiled to feel his coming. Bill stood still,
The cold so cold it made him want to weep.
The woman drew her warmth from magma's fires.
She'd wash his feet in fire and take away the cold.

131

He'd leave his petty fears and hates behind
And revel in the ageless life of earth.
He'd lose himself and start a dialogue with stars.

He muttered incantations to himself.
Who was he? Master? Puppet? Prophet? Thrall?
The Celtic King and poet in his dream
Had stared at him, his death a promise in their eyes.
He'd whisked himself away into his bed
And then woke up the goddess in her woods.
He wrapped the self he'd always been into this self
That longed to leave his life behind and clasp
The woman's beauty glittering with cold.

The Goddess smiled and made his heart beat wild.
He looked at her and stepped toward the trees,
Her woman-fire and woman-ice, her song.
He stopped, aflame with pain perpetual.
He longed to touch the perfect breasts, her skin.
He was a man. He was a man. A man

      "Get behind me Satan!"
he said.
      "You are an offense to me,
        For you are not mindful of the things of God,
        But the things of men!"[63]

His words struck at the spirits of the trees.
The trees cried out! Their chants became a scream.
Sweat beaded on his forehead, chest, and arms.
The woman's painful smile knifed through his heart.
He felt remorseful for his anguished words.
The woman sank into the frozen earth.

Bill cried out like the trees had cried. Death, death!
His rage, more powerful than ever, stopped.
His shaking made him powerful again.

He stumbled forward on his frostbit feet.
He wouldn't hear the trees or drive the cat.
He felt the burning if he touched machinery
Touched by the tree's destruction-weaving spells.

He passed the elm that first had sung to him.
Its song of loss surged rhythms through his heart.
It beat into the song that made him live.
He ground his teeth and forced his heart to stop.
Blind, boiling pain raced through his arms and chest.
The elm tree's song was cut off, drowned. His search
For rhythm, life, forced him to pass the elm.

       "If anyone worships the beast and his image,"
he told himself.
       "and receives his mark on his forehead or on his hand,
       he himself shall also drink of the wine of the wrath of God. . ."[64]

The woman beckoned him through memory.
Her thighs were slender rivulets of rain.
He would forget. He was American.
He knew the prophecy he had to speak
And knew that he was more than prophet-fire.
A warrior's pain was armor on a battlefield.
He'd use his pain to stir the winds to war.
He'd just destroyed Donn Truesdale's farm.
He was a prophet warrior blessed by God.
He wouldn't fail like Gordon Call had failed.
He'd had a sign, and other signs would come.

He stumbled from the woods. Smoke spiraled up
Into the heavens from the bar's sweet warmth.
He forced himself to stumble over snow.
He lashed out at the hell he felt. He smiled.

       "I will extol You, my God, O King:
       And I will bless Your name forever and ever . . ."[65]
He threw the song, defiant, back into the woods.

Lifesap From the Sun

White Rabbit had no thoughts. He took his gun
And drove his Oldsmobile down logging roads.
Great pines slid past, their branches threatening.

"All creatures draw their lifesap from the sun
Like men draw sugar from the sap of maple trees,"
His voice sang. "Without the sun the dark will grow,
And night will end all life on Mother Earth.
The sun is sterile fire. If sun alone
Burns down upon the earth, its heat will kill.
But clouds bring rain, and sun and Mother Earth
Supply a world where life can know itself,
Where life derives its lifesap from the sun."

He didn't know exactly why he'd chose
To brave the dark and cold and snow-packed roads
To reach a place the white man ringed with guns.
He wasn't young, and even though he had the strength
To face the cold and hardships of the run,
He wasn't sure the radicals were right.
At missionary school Menominee
Were beaten if they spoke their natural tongue
Or violated what the priests called, God's own laws.
Now schools encouraged Indian heritage.
Fights flared between the whites and Indian kids,
But white authority held back its hand.
In need to right the wrongs their race had done,
They sometimes even gave a college scholarship
To Indians disciplined enough to face
The loneliness of universities.

The white man still had evil in his heart.
He didn't try to understand the earth,
And every fall he'd kill, in orgied hunts,
Both bear and deer without a need for meat.
Their prejudice at times made raw a wound
Created when Tecumseh, Sitting Bull, were forced
To bend to white man law and government.

But hate had never served the Indian well.

134

Its harsh impatience flared into the light;
The white man lost what peacefulness he had
And used his power as a lightning bolt.

"All living creatures and all plants derive
Their lifesap from the sun," his voice sang. "Hate
Destroys the world while patience eats away
At rottenness until its sap decays
Into the spirit and the body of the Earth."

He stopped the car and turned its engine off.
The silent cold surrounded him. I'm old,
A fool, he told himself. He thought about
The rabbit he had seen hung still alive.

THE ONLY GOOD INDIAN'S A DEAD INDIAN.

He picked his 30-30^{66} up and walked.
He felt the darkness fanged into the light.
Snow crunched. He started running, forcing miles behind.
He was a bear, a creature part of earth.

At last, breath painful as it knifed into his lungs,
He stood across the river from the Novitiate.
He stopped and looked at rough-hewn limestone walls.
He wondered how the Indians in the building felt,
Guns taken up against an enemy
Too powerful to ever win against.

He felt exalted, tree and snow and beast
A part of him, the dark an ancient promise made
To guarantee eternities of rising suns.
He didn't think about the men with guns.

He ran out on the river ice. He failed to hear
The lead pierce through his coat into his flesh
Before he heard the sound that echoed down
The river's course into the cold and dark.

He felt the black snake twist inside him, writhe
Toward his lifesap.

Then, face down, he died.

As Superstar Looked Out Upon the World

As Superstar looked out upon the world,
He felt his loneliness, impenetrable night.
Three stories high, he watched the outside world,
Snow shining silver, stone walls wrapped by snow,
The riverbanks against the blackened pine.
He held his rifle tight against his chest.
He felt his enemies surrounding him.

Below him, dark, a man slipped from the pines
Onto the snow above the river ice.
Instinctively he slammed his rifle to his arm.
He waited as the old man, tired from miles he'd run,
Kept shuffling steadily on river ice.
Superstar felt tenseness as the old man ran.
The moonlight and the loneliness webbed fire
Into the silence as the old man ran.

And then the pure, bright, ringing sound of death.
A single rifle flashed death out of pines.
The old man fell, face down, into the snow.
Superstar began to tremble. In the room
Behind him darkness lurked alive and sinister.
He was alone inside Novitiate's white walls.
White Rabbit's dead, he thought. His gun fell down.
He'd let the old man live, and now he'd died.

You're not a man, dark said. You're not a man!
He shrugged and forced himself toward the door.
In dark he had a rabbit's fearful heart.

Outside the room he started running. Sitting Crow
Would have to know. White Rabbit's dead, he thought.
We'll all be dead before the white man's done.

He felt his panic running with him down the stairs
Past floors of darkened hallways, to the rooms
Where all his brothers sat, eyes fierce with light.

Rationale For Murder

1

Jim Speltz escaped the house. He looked at Trent.
Celest's screams blotted out his rationality.
What could he do? He couldn't face the pain
Celest had brought with her into the house.
He fumbled in his pocket for a cigarette
And thought about the death of Violet.
He closed his eyes, inhaled the day's first smoke,
And saw the three of them, Celest's blond hair
Outside McDonalds', hands linked into hands,
Lives plain as swallows flitting through dusked barns.
The memory was sharp enough to make
Him wince — to feel a pain he'd long since killed.
It made habitual bitterness the only guard
He had against a life too hard to bear.
He'd loved his wife. Why had she had to die?
What fate had made him face his life alone?
What evil in him made him try to rape Celest?
What weakness made him what he didn't want to be?

He cussed beneath his breath, looked at the house.
Trent Warren waited patiently for him.
The man sat in the storm and watched Celest
Shake from its wracking hell and didn't flinch.
Hour after hour he tried to reach Celest,
To make her understand the Rajah's chains
And how he'd shackled her and all his followers.
Trent Warren was a saint. But Jim? He laughed.

He slid behind the Plymouth's steering wheel.
He'd only buy one fortifying drink and leave.

2

He parked outside Pete's Bar. The rope they'd used
To hang the rabbit hanging from its branch.
He hesitated, wondering about Celest.

Inside the bar Gene Roth turned round and laughed.

137

Escaped from storm, Jim grinned. He'd left the hell behind.

"The Indian hunter!" Gene barked out. "My man!"

"We showed the bastard, didn't we?" Jim asked.
He felt the hollowness of empty words.

Gene looked at Pete. "Our friend needs beer," he said.
"Ambrosia of the gods! Sweet manna sent by God!"

Pete pulled the silver tap and filled the mug.
"We celebrate our heroes while they live."

Jim sobered. Hero? Him? The group of them?

"We should have killed the buck," he said.
"He came in here and mocked us to our face.
I should have sent him to his happy hunting ground."

Pete shoved the mug at Jim. "A man that old
Will meet his maker soon enough," he said.
"I don't need Indian blood stained on my floor."

"You let a drop of blood fall on your floor," Gene whooped.
"We'll let you starve before we buy another beer!"

Jim shook his head. "The country's gone to hell,"
He said. "The Reservation doesn't keep
Their bucks at home; that crazy freak who's got
My daughter's head all disarranged crows blasphemy,
And liberals make a bedlam of the world."

"Our Indian killer!" Gene exclaimed again.

Jim looked at Gene, a promise in his eyes.
"You'll see someday," he said. Celest smiled, screamed.
The vision danced inside the quiet bar.
He looked at Gene again. He couldn't stay.
He couldn't let Trent Warren face Celest alone.
He threw his head back, drained the mug, and frowned.
"I got to go," he said.

"So soon?" Pete asked.

"You've never had a single beer before."

Jim scowled. "I got to go," he said again.
"I said what should be said. I've got to go."

He turned and slowly walked toward the door.
Jim slipped a noose around the Indian's head and hanged
Him just like Pete had hung the rabbit, still alive.

3

He sat inside the Plymouth in the cold.
Trent, in the house, wild with his endless faith,
Stared at Celest, his will against her fear
Of Daddy, father, shaper of her soul,
The man who'd driven her into the Rajah's arms.

What kind of man would sit inside his living room
Beside his child and listen to her scream
In pain and never try to stop her pain?

The questions drove themselves into the self
That raged against the greasy Indian buck,
The Pollacks, niggers, wops, and crazy spics.
He'd dreamed for years about a night
Of ecstasy, black breasts above him in his bed.
He'd touched his daughter's breasts and felt . . .
A shame so great he'd never loose its vice?

He jerked the car in gear. The Indian stared.
Jim moved his hand toward the pistol strapped
Into his ancient leather cowboy belt.
I am an Indian, said the old man, pride
A power in his voice. Jim's hands ungripped
And gripped the steering wheel as cleared land interspersed
With wooded lots into the snowy countryside.

He saw the farmhouse down the road, the barn
He hadn't used for years dull red against house white.
He'd face the hell, he told himself. He'd face the hell.

Celest would thank him when she'd found herself.
She'd praise what he and Trent, the saint, had done.

He couldn't question who and what he was.
He was Jim Speltz, the Gresham radical,
The man the village loved to rail against.

He said the incantations in his mind.
He fled the consciousness of questions, thought . . .

He wished the Rajah dead, the Indian dead.
He wished the law would let him kill them both.

Inside the Darkness of Herself

1

"You've got to leave," he'd said. "You can't die here.
"You've got to take the kids away from here."

And when she'd stared at him, her eyes stone hard,
His eyes had flashed with love, the song of love now gone.

"I can't face death if you're where you can die!"
He'd raged. "I can't become the martyr that we need
To shake away the white man's cultural yoke!
I need to face my death away from you!"

And she had listened with her rage and love.
She'd thought of Kim inside the basement room,
His voice as sweet as summer wind, eyes warm.
She'd seen a vision of a dying Sitting Crow
Who sat beside the fireplace dreaming nights
He'd spent beside the fire inside the trap
That they had shaped together from their love.

And then she'd turned away and walked into the halls.
She wouldn't leave him. He was love and life.
She'd followed him into the Novitiate.
In dark she'd flinched to see the tongue-fired guns
As white men shot at Indians; Indians shot
At white men, death a promise barked at night.
Now Sitting Crow, her lover, warrior chief,
Had told her that she had to leave so he
Could have his chance at death and martyrdom.
He had to mold the spirit of the tribes
Into a rage against the white man's wrongs.

She wouldn't leave. She wouldn't die. She'd stay.

She stormed down one long hall, then flung her hair . . .
Upstairs, downstairs, moving, cursing, crazed
With worry, fear, and blinding, blinding rage.

Inside the chapel Lena stopped. Last light
Was slanting through the stained glass monk who looked
Into the chapel's well of maple pews.
Upon the balcony, the monk below
In darkness, Lena felt the racing of her heart,
The brilliance of the light that slanted red,
Brown, blue, white, dark into the empty pews.
And standing there, alone, away from Sitting Crow,
Her rage congealed into detachment, cold.
She shivered, neither physical nor spiritual.
She felt life evanescent, burned like morning mist.
She floated in the air above the balcony,
Her body lost, her spirit lost, her heart
Made comatose, slow beating, near to death.

She fixed her eyes upon the altar's emptiness.
She wasn't Christian. If she had a faith
It was a faith in Mother Earth, the womb.
In Christianity nails struck through Christ
Had been the nails used to subjugate the tribes
To all the crosses crucifying Indian life.

She forced herself to look beyond the pews,
Past dust-caked symbols of the Christian faith
To where the chapel's wall soared to an arch.
Fire licked the wall. It burned, but did not burn.
Inside flames Lena's mother, dead for thirteen years,
Was kneeling down before St. Anthony,
Worshipping the God that Lena loathed.
Lena's mother's face was radiant with love.
Her hair was still a raven-black, touched gray,
And in her dark, dark eyes she smiled to see
Her daughter locked inside a dangerous
Religious building now besieged by violent death.

As Lena looked at flames, her mother's eyes,
She felt her self, her body, head, sides, legs,
Arms, breasts, and lean, hard thighs come back to her.
She trembled, feeling all her wars inside.
She wrenched her eyes, by force, away from where
Her mother knelt inside God's flames, then turned.

She felt the burden of her mother's faith.
She'd die before she walked from Sitting Crow.
The kids would die before she walked away.
She'd hold a gun inside her hands and fight
Until the white man's death had greeted her.

She touched Novitiate walls. Mother's eyes embraced
Her in the dark and followed her down empty halls.
Outside a shot rang out, a hollowness.
In anguish Lena tried to make her mother leave.
Her mother wanted back a child long lost.

3

The sound of footsteps on the stairs that led
Into the tower startled Lena. In her head
A mourning chant was pounding at her sanity.
A dozen warriors, dressed in full regalia, wailed.
She stopped inside the stairwell, drawn to see
The ghost she knew was crashing down the stairs.
The footsteps echoed in the silence, clangorous.
Lena huddled, backed against the stairwell wall,
Alive inside a universe of ghosts.

Then Superstar, face drained by fear,
Came leaping down the stairs, his face afloat
Above the noise his legs were making, eyes white, wide.
Lena smiled relief. She pushed off from the wall
And reached toward the rushing Superstar.
She brushed him with her hand. He didn't stop.
He rushed into the halls toward the dining hall.

In panic Lena stayed right where she was,
Her hand extended, smile half formed, relief
An aftertaste transmuted to despair.
He hadn't seen her. She had touched his arm,
And Superstar had kept on running, caught
Inside his own reality, oblivious.
Loose from the substance of the walls, the dark
Intensifying, darkening about her head,
The altar standing firm before the flames
That framed her mother's face. Lena tried
To find the courage felt while kneeling down

Beside spring's mist before the eyes of men with guns.

All history trailed blood behind its march.
Her mother stared at her. The darkness swam
With almost-ghosts, her fear alive and crazed.

She felt the madness burned in Superstar.
She didn't want to climb the stairs, wanted Sitting Crow.
She longed to hold him tight inside her arms,
To feel his hands alive upon her breasts,
The hardness, softness of his pressing love.

She put her foot upon the first dark stair.
Her mother climbed beside her, filled with faith.

4

The night was murmuring with distant words.
The moonlight burned soft light on river's snow.
The pine trees stood, tall, silent sentinels.
The shaman's fresh spilled blood was dark on snow,
His body skewed in death, his arm thrown out
Toward the softly gleaming, bright Novitiate.
Around the body white men clustered, gesturing.

As Lena tried to comprehend White Rabbit's death,
She felt cold twitching through her arms and legs.
She reached to walls around her, desperate
To find solidity within the world.

Her life was evanescent, burned away,
Exploded by the homing of the lead
Thrown from a gun into an old man's heart.

Her lover, Sitting Crow, was desperate
To know she wouldn't die if he faced death.
The children had to live. There was no way
The wild, courageous, foolish children ought
To walk the path of death. They had to live.

Beside her, Lena's mother wept, the dark
So black it whirled with dancing, coal-black flames.
What Sitting Crow was after was a life

Unburdened by the white man's good and bad.
He wanted wind to blow through Indian hearts
And eagle's wings to carry Indian braves
Into the clean, bright freedom of a summer sky.
He wanted Indian glory burned in bones.
He wanted Indian dreams to spread through worlds.

Above his blackened blood, White Rabbit smiled.
Inside the tower Lena couldn't see his face.
She knew he smiled. She turned. Her mother smiled.
To Lena death was more than she could face.
She had to live. But life was not, alone, enough.
Her warrior had to live, the children too.
The mist inside her head seeped through her past,
The self she was, into the awful core
Of fear she felt at being who she was:
An Indian woman in a world where white men ruled.

She reached out to the darkness, tried to touch
Her mother, touch her mother's peace and faith.
She gasped to feel the pain she felt when all
She felt was darkness, emptiness, cold air.

She turned toward the stairwell. Sitting Crow
Would hear about death from a frightened Superstar.
She wouldn't fold into herself. She had to live.

She stumbled down the ghost-filled, darkened stairs.

Like A Serpent Poised To Strike
A Poison Into His Spirit Heart

1

Donn Truesdale shook his head. "He called me queer,"
He said. "I tell you that? I worshipped him
Until I saw how much he hated me."

His voice trailed off. John looked into his eyes,
But didn't smile to ease Donn's hesitance.
The man was wrong inside. He couldn't bear
The cross of misery Bill Winchell had imposed.

"There's not a law against your sexuality,
And frankly, how you are is good with me.
A man can be the man he is inside,"
John said. "The only question is, did Winchell steal
Your tractor. If he did he broke the law."

"I'm Christian," Truesdale said. "I'm not a queer."

John felt the power Winchell had and frowned.
In Truesdale's clear blue eyes the brooding fire
Bill Winchell cultivated shined dark, powerful.
The young man hated Winchell while still loving him.
The idea Christianity denied
A human being human being rights was wrong.

John looked into his eyes and asked again:
"You saw Bill Winchell steal your tractor, yes or no."
He waited. Truesdale shifted restlessly.
He'd called John, made him come out to the farm.
He quelled his nervousness. His yellow hair hid sweat.

"I saw him come at dawn," he said at last.
"He took the tractor from the barn and drove it off."

"Okay," John said. He glanced from Truesdale's eyes.
"You didn't let him take the tractor then?"

Donn, twenty-four, stared hatefully at John.
"A man can't give his tools away," he said.

John looked into the young man's brooding eyes.
Inside the blue eyes, black eyes stared at him
As Sitting Crow considered how he'd set
The world afire with passions strong enough
To change the substance of America.

2

Bill felt John Israel before he'd turned
Into the driveway leading to the bar.
For hours he'd sat beside the window looking out
Toward the road as darkness faded into light.
His toes and hands were numb from frostbite now,
But painless as his flesh began to heal.
His spirit felt half fey, as if he'd dipped
Both heart and mind into a forest well.
To keep his sanity he kept repeating to himself:
      "O Lord
        my Rock: Do not be silent to me . . ."[67]
He felt the stirrings of his power shift
From darkness into light as dawn spread light.
The Goddess, who had made the trees alive,
Was dead. He'd sent her back to earth, her bed.
He'd faced the Devil's power, found God's will.

John Israel was a threat to quench the flame.
The Sheriff was the only government
Bill recognized since government derived
Legality from people, not from ads
That flitted, ghosts on television screens,
Or from the voices camouflaged by dollar bills
That alchemized themselves to votes.
John Israel was twisted from the path
Bill saw, envisioned, for America.

Bill smiled to see the squad turn off the road.
Time spun, a precipice of destiny and truth.
He'd weave a tapestry of swift events
Into a chaos built of chaos wrought by Sitting Crow.
He'd build, at last, his *citie* on the hill[68].

He wouldn't let the Goddess, skulking, terrible,
Impose herself into the world he'd made.

3

John walked into the bar. He didn't look
At Winchell. In his head he felt his emptiness.

Bill sat behind a table, measuring
His enemy, a man without a soul.
He smiled to think about the Sheriff's shock
The moment that he came to realize
His insignificance.

        John waited for his eyes
To grow accustomed to the twilit bar,
Then looked at Winchell, Winchell's black, bright eyes.

"I hate to bring bad news," John said, voice soft.
"But someone stole Donn Truesdale's tractor from his farm.
He says he's lost if he can't work the farm."

Bill didn't blink or let his face reveal
The thought that buried Israel into a hole
Beside the tractor in the frozen ground.
"Donn never seems to find a bit of luck,"
He said. "The boys tell me his other tractor's down."

"Donn says that you're the thief," John said. "He says
You think he's queer; you've got it in for him;
You've got yourself convinced he is the Antichrist."

Bill laughed sarcastically. "You swallow that,
And I'll predict the ending of the world."

"You're not the thief?" John asked.

        "I've stolen hearts,"
Bill said. "I'll let you search the place. No tractor's here."

John felt the insolence inside the room,
The building hate that wouldn't be denied,
The conflagration born of God-like pride.

"Perhaps I ought to check for guns instead,"
He said. "They say you've built an arsenal."

The Sheriff was a fool who'd earned the right to die.

"You shouldn't listen to the rumors spread
By those who think I'm nuts," Bill said. "I'll need
A warrant if you want to search my land,
And if you can't find what you're looking for,
I'll sue until I own your house and soul."

"I thought you said that I could look around," John said.
"What I don't understand is why you'd take
A tractor when you knew Donn needed it
To plant his crops. I always thought you preached
That you're the savior of the family farm."

A whispering swept like a breeze into the bar.
Bill didn't move. He couldn't move. The trees
Were singing songs foretelling his destruction, death.
They were alive; the Goddess was alive.
John Israel was their instrument of death.

Outside, the Goddess moved around the woods
So deep with her awareness and her cold
That even Christianity was young
Beside the power in her womanhood,
And Bill had somehow made himself aware of her,
And in awareness was a siren song.

He forced himself onto his feet. He spit his words.
"I am a Christian man," he said. "God's man.
I am a warrior for the jubilee of God.
If you appreciate your life, repent
And join your brothers as they stand in light
As angels fight the dragon's fire. Repent!"

John didn't move, but saw the angels dance
Upon the altar wreathed by light and fire.
The Preacher's words rang like a gorgon's song.
He felt the Preacher coil, a serpent poised.

"You threaten me, and I'll run you in," he said.

"You'd make the law your personal preserve,
But it's not happened yet. The law's still here."

Bill saw the trees appear behind John's back.
The Goddess stood between the trees. Bill ached
To see her, felt like groveling before her feet.
She stood, somehow, inside the windowpane,
Upon the windowpane, reflected light.

        "Get behind me Satan," he said.
     "You are an offense to me . . ."[69]

John winced. The angels in the fire were bright.
They walked with him and moved about the bar.

"You nuts?" he asked. "What's wrong with you?"

                      Bill frowned.
He had to make the Goddess go away.
"Get out!" he said. "You need a warrant that you haven't got."

John looked at Winchell's eyes and shivered, cold.
The man was mad, possessed. John shook his head.
"Are you all right?" he asked.

                    Bill waved his hand.
"You've got to go," he said. "The tractor isn't here.
Go tell Donn Truesdale that his tractor isn't here."

He lurched toward John like a sodden drunk.
John backed away. The man was driven by a fire
That burned him inside out. John shouldn't leave.
He had his job to do, a thief to catch.
But still, the Preacher's madness was too close,
A mirror of the madness plaguing him.

Bill Winchell looked at him again. "Get out,"
He croaked. "Get out. His voice was pleading, mad.

Across the barn beams, evil flew inside the dusk.
The light in bat eyes blinked and seized John's chest.
John tried to stop his fear, then turned and walked
Out of the bar and climbed into the squad.

He saw Bill Winchell's face inside a grave.
Rain fell in sheets of water on his head.
The Lord again had loosed the torrents of a flood.

John looked into the bar's front window. Trees
Reflected off the glass. They seemed alive.
Bill Winchell sat before the windowpane,
His face contorted as he screamed his rage.

John tried to find the courage that would let
Him leave the squad and go inside again.
But nothing came. No courage. No resolve.
He turned; the engine caught; he drove away.

The Meeting of the Elders

Wrapped in a blanket looking at the ice
On Legend Lake, Moon sat beneath the pine.
His wife of fifty years stood heron-wrapped
In feather-white beside him, back against the tree.
Four, Mabel Sams, Tree Hope, Joe Davis, Snuffy Dodge,
Stood in the snow beside a campfire wisping smoke.
Legune came last. She wore her mother's blanket made
When she was still in school. Its blues and reds
Contrasted brightly against the tree and snow.

The minute Legune had stopped beside
The fire and put her hands out to its warmth,
Moon stood and turned to look at all of them.
Flesh folds surrounded shining in his eyes.

"They've used the Winnebago's old War Bundle Feast."

"But they're Menominee!" Tree said.

          Moon smiled.
"You think they know?" he asked. "Pete Wilson's leading them.
His Dad was Winnebago. Does it matter anyway?
The point is five of them became entranced.
They spoke with Thunderbirds who blessed their war."

"How blessed?" asked Snuffy Dodge. "The Sheriff still has guns.
The army's big enough to put a man
On every inch of Reservation soil."

"It's Sitting Crow," Legune said softly. "They believe
Tecumseh's come to life. He's merged the Prophet's heart
Into Tecumseh's warrior heart and can't be killed."

"They're nuts!" Tree Hope exclaimed.

         Moon's wife, June Oh,
Looked at the old man with her angry eyes.
Tree Hope stepped back. She'd talked him down for years.
"They may be nuts," she snarled. "They're still our kids.
We have to face that they believe they're led

By those who've talked with spirit Thunderbirds.
The war is boiling in their brains and hearts.
We end the madness or the snow will run with blood."

"Has anybody seen White Rabbit?" Snuffy asked.

"He visited Pete's Bar in Gresham ten days past,"
Moon said. "His daughter told me he has roamed
The woods since then. I've heard he's visited
With Mrs. High."

       "What will he do?" Joe Davis asked.

Black pain struck through Legune into her arms.
"I've had a dream," she said. "Death started as a stain
Upon the Legion Hall, then sent dark streams
Of spirits up into a moonless, starless sky."

June Oh moved round the fire and touched Legune.
Moon looked into his wife's black eyes and saw
Her worry at the way Legune had paled.
Perhaps their talk beneath the Council Tree was bad.
"The Tribe's entrusted to our care," he said.

"White Rabbit ought to be with us," Tree said.
"He's oldest of the shamans."

       "But he's not,"
June pointed out. "And time is short. We need to act."

"You think he's joined with Sitting Crow?" Tree asked.

The thought reached deep into their individual fears.
They milled around the fire, their feet a dance.
They didn't speak. Each looked into the others' eyes.
White Rabbit owned a courage born of spirit worlds.
If he and Sitting Crow had merged their purposes . . .

"What if Pete Wilson's right?" Tree asked. "What if
He's talked to Thunderbirds. We had our warriors once."

Legune stared angrily into the old man's eyes.
"I've got white friends," she said. "They aren't our enemies.

I've earned a university degree.
The whites can be our friends."

           "I won't accept
That suicide can lead to good," June said.

"The elders should be honored," Mabel said.
"Young people ought to know that every year
You live you learn."

        Moon stared into the fire.
He thought about the schools the government
Had run, and how the teachers had removed
Their language and their culture from their lives.
At home, away from supervising eyes,
Grandparents, parents, relatives had passed
Old ways along through ceremonies, songs.
And now the youngsters tried to find the faith,
The spirits, which the tribe had barely kept.

The white man was a symbol for their pain.
The white man wasn't evil, wasn't good, just numerous.
Moon looked at how the pine tree's branches swept
Into the sky above the snowy ground.

"I'm standing up to them," Legune said quietly.
"They'll have to trample me into the ground.
They want good things, but I can't let the stain
That's bled into their spirits loose in us."

Moon looked at her and shivered uncontrollably.
She'd put her death mask on. He'd never thought
Legune would ever bend her will to death.
"Nobody can command another's will," he said.

June looked at him, disgusted, shook her head,
Then turned and walked toward the frozen road.

The Red Serpent

The great red serpent, with its ten dark horns
And seven heads and seven diadems
Thrashed with its tail of stars into the universe[70]
Toward the woman white who sang to Bill.
The serpent made her shine with living light.
She was the glory of the gods, the woman clothed
With sun, the ancient moon beneath her feet.

The fiery serpent writhed again, eyes red,
And as it writhed in fire, the woman changed.
Adorned with pearls, she'd put on silken clothes
Of scarlet, blood-rich purple, royal gold.

Bill saw the whiteness of the Goddess blaze
Inside her eyes and heard the tree songs thrum
Their power past the serpent's scales into its heart.
His waking dream was stronger than the songs
That made the serpent tremble as the woman sang.
It trembled light along its strung out tail of stars.
The need Bill felt was terrible. He longed to feel
The woman's hands upon his chest, his thighs.
He longed to touch her breasts and put his tongue
Inside her hot, moist folds, their rhythms matched.

Bill didn't see the serpent fade, but saw
Instead the woman's beauty blazing with a joy
That made him ache to feel her legs about his legs.
He felt the tree roots growing down in earth,
The darkened soil and hardness of the rock
That formed her spine and welded her to him.

He thought of Israel and laughed to live again
The Sheriff's fear, his madness stoked by serpent fires.
He felt triumphant, scared, a man unleashed.

      "My God! My God!" he cried. "You have delivered me
        to the ungodly, and turned me over to the hand of the wicked."[71]
The woman smiled. The serpent thrashed and writhed
And spouted fire from all its seven heads.
The stars swung wildly in the night dark sky.

155

My God, my God, why have you forsaken me?[72]
He cried. The woman looked at him and smiled again.
She was as beautiful as dawn, as love.
Bill tried to turn the woman's force away.
His words writhed like a serpent's slashing tail.
She cursed, her beauty withering with pain.

"I'm free!" Bill thought. "I'm free!"

                               The woman shook.
"Not yet," she said. "You'll see the signs, then act,
Then face the truth of what you've done in pride."

The trees receded from the bar. The woman stood.
Leaves, bark were clothes that covered nakedness.
Bill clutched a chair and tried to call her back,
To bring alive the senses he had lost
The moment he had called for God, but she
And all the trees were gone. He was alone.

He looked at how the barroom looked. The beams
Dark, hand-hewn, beer taps polished brass, the bar.

"I've lived to worship God another day,"
He thought. "She's tried, but I'm still here, alive
To God and all the miracles of God."

He didn't want to die into the woman's arms.
He didn't want to fall into the serpent's eyes.
He was a man of God. He'd stay a man of God.
He'd smite the fools who'd stand against his truths
That roared like dragon breath out of his mouth.
He'd force his will upon his fellow men.

He tried to stand, but sat back down. Too weak.
The woman was a foe who sapped his strength.

He bowed his head in hands. What could he do?
John Israel would gain control of fear —
And if he looked he'd find the tractor's grave.
The Goddess hadn't left. She'd gone to woods.
She'd come back beautiful beyond what he could stand.
He'd fall from grace as surely as the sun brought day.

———

156

Bill tried to find the fires he'd built inside his self.
He knew he'd find them when he needed them.
But now he sat inside the bar and stared at dreams.
How long before the woman spoke her spell
And made trees march in rows of battle ranks?
How long would Israel wait, finding strength
To face the fear Bill used to drive him from the bar?

He felt his power building in his guts.
It sang its serpent song into his mind.

He'd build his revolution now. He'd crack
The unity that made the country whole
And follow Sitting Crow's rebellion with his own.
He'd take the ten-horned dragon's fires, spread flames.
He'd rave until the country's evil died
And saints came down from heaven dressed in robes.

The shopping centers with their opulent
Displays of garish wealth would all decay,
The buildings falling down in rubble heaps.
The banks would fail from lack of trade, and government
Would center on the small town church and home.

He'd stand a pinnacle of faith and hope
Within his God inspired theocracy.
He'd oversee the separation of the blacks
From white society and guarantee
The purity of every race forevermore.

Inside the fortress God had sanctified
He'd deal the fruits of justice out. God's voice
Would speak to him, and in its strength he'd face
John Israel, the Goddess, and her trees.

A Vision of Ghosts

1

The ghosts had come alive. They streamed down halls
And entered rooms with hair blown back and eyes
Burned silver-dark by light cast by the moon.
They made the darkened halls shine luminous
With coming, going, coming . . . In the dark
The sound of horses whispered on a wind
That didn't stir the stillness of the air,
And campfires glimmered, died, and sparked again
And died again between the spaces of a breath.
The cold intensified each time a dark,
Bright warrior sighed, their ghost-born breath a mist
That exhaled out into dark, empty rooms.

They all were there: Tecumseh, Sitting Bull,
Chief Luther Standing Bear, Chief Joseph, Curly Chief,
Smoholla, Black Hawk, Crazy Horse, Black Elk,
Chief Oshkosh, Neopit, Seattle, Roman Nose,
Powhaton, Chief Red Jacket, Flying Hawk,
Geronimo, Blue Jacket, Plenty Coups,
The warriors, wizards, chiefs, and orators
Who'd fought the white man, won, lost, given up,
And stirred inside their rotted burial shrouds
Alive, but dead, a host in spectral winds.

When Sitting Crow first felt their chilling breaths
Inside the dining hall, he stood up from his chair.
He strained to hear the breathing that he felt.
He looked at Superstar, his friend's face flushed
With anger at White Rabbit's bloody death.
The coldness of the dead benumbed his hands.
Beside him Superstar stopped talking, grabbed
His rifle, swung around, and looked about the hall.
The others, lounged around the fireplace, froze,
The feeling emanating from the ghosts
Containing all the laughter, weeping, hatred, love,
Religion, terror, hope, and memories
Of all the tribes from all the times tribes lived.

And then they came in force into the hall:
Not ghostly like the ghosts they were, nor firm
Like living men, but stable as they moved.
Their braids hung down before their chests.
Their skin was creased by ravages of time.
Their eyes were hollow from the strain they felt
At leaving earth to join the unfelt wind.
But still, each one of them stood tall and proud,
Their pupils black, lips grim, hair white with age,
Determination, sadness in their stance.
Each one was separate, but still a part of light.
They chilled the hall and made it quieter,
And emptier, than it had ever been before,
Their emptiness more empty than the years
The halls had spent without community.
They didn't speak, or move, but stood and stared
At Indian braves with eyes that didn't see.

As Sitting Crow looked close at faces, eyes,
He breathed. Not human, but humanity
Was in their eyes and in the way they stood.
He swallowed at the dryness in his mouth
And tried to think beyond his pounding fear.
He glanced at Superstar who'd dropped his gun
And stood unmanned before the warrior ghosts.

With trepidation Sitting Crow looked for his strength.
All Indians knew the dead returned to earth.
These weren't real ghosts, but strong, a potent dream.
"What do you want?" he asked the waiting host.

Chief Joseph parted from the spirit group.
His hair was darker than the others' hair.
It flared up from his forehead, then swept down.
Behind his ears he'd hooked medallions in his braids.
Below his neck, upon his woven shirt,
A dozen white stone necklaces were hung,
Each ring below another ring, the force
Of circle strengthening the brightness of his face.
He looked at Sitting Crow, his sadness lined
Into the fierceness of his frown. He waved.

"Your shaman's dead. Your quest for death has been fulfilled."

He sighed, his breath so cold it burned its mist
Into the breathing making Sitting Crow alive.
There was a quiet rustling of unfelt winds.
The light from campfires sparked behind the ghosts,
Then died to darkness. Sitting Crow held back
His breath, his body trembling at the sounds
Of dying, living, loving, dying, death.

A mist that showed a woman and her child,
Emaciated, wounded in the midst of death
At Wounded Knee, solidified, then faded dark.
A coyote yipped its love song to a desert moon.

The firmness of the ghosts began to waver, change.
Chief Oshkosh, stove-pipe hat askew, his eyes
As mocking as the songs of mocking birds,
Saluted Sitting Crow and Superstar
And faded upward into mist and smoke,
A blood red shining stained upon the dark.
Chief Joseph smiled his sad, long smile and whirled.
His body's brightness thinned into a line
As silver as the stars, the flow of mercury.

The other ghosts, each face and body filled with light,
An individual for a moment only, Chiefs
Keshena, Neopit, Seattle, Sitting Bull,
And shamans Chased-By-Bears, Black Elk, Short Bull,
Smoholla, Chief Tecumseh, focused, then
Joined with the stream of ghosts riding the wind
That was no wind. Each one intensified,
Became so bright they hurt the eyes, dissolved.
No sound was made. Menominee stood still.
Each ghost grew radiant, then streamed to light.

Outside the dining hall cold chilled to temperatures
Below the thresholds felt by human flesh.
Sounds that were no sounds reverberated, hushed
Into the silence of the halls. And then . . .

There were no ghosts. The only sounds were those
Made by the breaths exhaled by those alive.

2

Sitting Crow stared at the fireplace fire.
The warrior, orator, and shaman! Visions birthed,
But he was small, a man inside a wind.
He turned to Superstar. His friend was staring hard,
Fear burned into his body, face, and eyes.
"White Rabbit's dead," he said. "He's dead; you're chief.
The ghosts stirred from their graves to speak to you."

Tom Waters, Sylva Matchapatow, Horse,
Clean River, Sampson, Turtle, Sam, Bill, Eve,
The rest were facing him with Superstar —
Afraid of him, afraid of what they'd seen.
He longed to run from how they looked at him.
He knew he wasn't who they thought he was.
He longed to know where Kim and Lena were.

"I was afraid. They made my blood run cold."

"No," Superstar said. "You had the guts to speak.
You are a shaman. Chiefs and shamans came to you."
He smiled, fanatic, crazed from all he'd seen.
"I'd follow you to hell and back," he said.

"To death," Eve whispered. "Even there, with ghosts."

"You told John Israel we'd made a pact,"
Tom Waters said. "You said we'd die to ratify
Our bonds to history. We're yours," he said.

When Lena walked into the hall, face pale,
She looked at Sitting Crow and shook her head.
"He's dead. White Rabbit's dead," she said. "He's dead.
They killed him like they'd kill a dog or pig."

Dazed, Superstar knelt down, eyes locked with Sitting Crow's.
"He was our brother," he declared. "The ghosts
Appeared to tell us that. He was our soul."

As Sitting Crow looked at the rage surrounding him,
He felt inside himself and found despair.

He turned his head away from Superstar
And looked at Lena: beauty, sex, and love.
She had to die, but shouldn't die. She had to live.

Chief Joseph, breathing ice-cold mist, had said,
"Your quest for death has been fulfilled."
What had he meant? White Rabbit, ginseng gatherer,
The heart and soul of all Menominee, shot dead?

The damned white man! The damned white man! The damned . . .
His laws and wealth and crass society
And cancers eating at the Indian's soul.
He looked at Lena, frightened her, and turned
Toward the door the ghosts had used to leave the hall.
They hadn't gone through walls. They'd streamed through doors.
He strode across the hall. Damned the ghosts!

A black, harsh mood descended, weight of death.
He didn't know the reason ghosts had come.

The Song That Rose Like Smoke Toward The Stars

Kim felt the ghosts the minute they appeared.
He woke from dreamless sleep and slipped his arm
From Marsha. Silent as a cat, he left
The room and stood inside the basement's dark
Elated, shivering to feel cold winds.
Novitiate tension/boredom shattered. Light,
Glory walked the halls as campfires burned
Through years of Indian life, sent wisps of smoke Toward
stars blinked like eyes that watched the earth. Great treks
through prairie grass and endless woods Were undertaken;
stories, legends, spun
Into the breath of men and women born
Into the prairies, woods, and mountains, lives
Inspired from beat of drums, the heart of songs.

Kim felt the ghosts and felt the limestone walls Dissolved
into the openness of history.
Time shifted, moved, and twisted from the force
Of gravities that made the ghosts alive.
Kim tried to spread his falcon wings and soar
Into the specter winds. He longed to see
The Thunderbirds, the White Bear holding earth,
The Trickster scheming as the people's songs evolved

But, as Kim dreamed of flying through the tiers
Of universe, as time kept shifting back
Into itself, he felt the moment of his birth,
The coldness of the world, the straining need
For breath that made him twist and turn inside
Song wailed as breath calmed pounding heart.

And then he saw a crouching Sitting Crow
Wrapped deep in vortex. Crow's legs. Human bones.
Death whorled about the Warrior leader's head.
Life pulsed and ebbed inside the vortex-storm,
Its rhythms flaring like the campfires born,
Then left behind as Indians moved in waves
Across the forests, prairies, deserts, hills.
Kim heard the death-song, life-song Sitting Crow

Sang out into the limestone walls. He felt
The restlessness of ghosts riding a wind
That was no wind and saw the white man's world
Aflame with passions born of Indian rage.

And in the basement's dark, alone, he saw
The song that rose like smoke toward the stars.
A song of growing, blending, separate,
Yet part of melodies that wove through tiers
Where Thunderbirds and spirits danced the heart
That was no heart, but was a living song.

He heard the white man's dissonance, saw dance
The white man made from metals, chemicals
Inside, outside, the song the Indian sang,
The white man's heart a multitude of hearts,
Each fused, unfused, into the drumbeats' whole.

"I'm like a crazy man, a macho man,"
Kim thought. "I'm like a river's deep-cut bed,
The waters flowing through me, over me,
My falcon wings the banks of earth and trees
That feather life into the winter sky."

He felt the ghosts. What should he do? He felt
The fear the Warriors felt inside the cold.

The white men, huddled in the cold with guns
Laid on the snowy ground, surrounded him.
The falcon longed for wind beneath its wings.
The walls, the guns . . .

        The ghosts were glorious.
He felt their eyes. He saw their villages
Built on the wind, the bark *wakinikans*,
The teepees, snug longhouses, lodges filled
With throngs of people living from the past.
He saw them talking, making love, live feasts
Of movement, dancing, songs, smoked fields of stars,
A conversation of the universe.

What should he do? He saw the Warriors' eyes
As hour passed hour, the boredom making them

Like ghosts, alive but dead, emotions edged with fear.
What had he thought before he came inside?
That glory was a benefit of death?

He longed to live. He longed to feel his life
Continuing until it reached its natural end.
Death whorled inside a dancing Sitting Crow.
Kim felt the ghosts of Sitting Crow and death.
If Sam, Bob, Todd, or Marsha died . . . Kim turned.

If Lena died . . .

              He looked at Marsha: beautiful. . .
Why had they come? he thought. What had they thought?

They'd live. He made the promise to himself.
He knelt upon the sleeping bag and felt
Time thrash and move and shift inside the dark.
He felt the ghosts. The ghosts were telling them
That time was short and changing. Death was near.

Pete Wilson's Message

A hand touched Pete's right arm. He smiled at Beth.
They'd drummed and sung for days, and he was tired.
Her eyes were anxious with the news she had.
Foreboding made him leave the pounding drum.

A white man, Johnny Orr, was waiting, dressed
Against the outside cold, eyes feverish.
He was a runner moving back and forth
Between the Legion Hall and swampland bordering
The lands controlled by Israel's police.
The white man looked as if he'd run a dozen miles.

Pete looked into the white man's eyes, but didn't speak.
He waited for the news upsetting Beth.
As Johnny searched for words, he slumped into a chair.

"White Rabbit's dead," he said at last. "Just that."
He sighed. "The cops have shot your shaman dead."

Beth wailed.

    "The Ginseng gatherer?" Pete asked.

"I heard them on their radios," the white man said.
"He died last night when sneaking through the woods
To join with Sitting Crow. They said a cop
Had shot him even with an order not to fire.
The cops are nervous now. They know about the drums.
They know that you've declared a holy war.
Some woman's been snatched from a parking lot.
They're faced with trouble from a fascist group.
They've got a case of nerves like I have never seen."

Pete tried to handle Johnny's rush of words.
Beth's body heaved with silent sobs. Pete stared.
Confused thoughts jangled, jumbled, in his head.
"White Rabbit's dead?" he said again. "The cops?"

His feelings coalesced into triumphant rage.
The *Hokawasmanina* and *Wakanadja* had foreseen

166

This hour, this government in disarray.
He felt tears on his cheeks, war in his heart.
The time had come! He looked at Beth and grinned.
He felt as if he'd found the *Wakanadja* once again,
Was dancing wild upon their spirit-earth.
His grief obliterated humanness.
He was a beast, a beast of death and war.

Beth looked at him and caught the rage he felt.
She slammed her fist into the wall and wailed,
"Ay yie! Ay yie! Ay yie! Ay yie! Ay yie!"
Her keening echoed through the Legion Hall.
The drums stopped beating. Singers stopped.
The dancers turned and tried to find the sound.

When Johnny heard Beth's cry he stood,
Then crouched into a fetal crouch. He was afraid,
Pete realized. He'd been a radical
Without the sense to know the costs of war.
"White Rabbit's dead!" Pete screeched. "Our shaman's dead!"

He left the room and ran into the singing room.
He grabbed his shirt and ripped it as he sang.
Beth's keening stopped. The silence echoed universe.
Pete looked at them, his brothers, sisters, friends,
The white men, black men, Zuni, Chippewa,
And Navajo. The Potawatomi,
Oneida, Winnebago, Blackfeet, Souix,
Chinese, Menominee, Arapahoe,
Osage, and other people from across the land.

"White Rabbit's dead," he said again with rage.
"The cops have murdered him. He tried to join
His voice to Sitting Crow's Novitiate."

He keened like Beth had keened. She came into the room
Disheveled, wild with rage and grief, hair wet.
"We've formed!" she raved. "My enemies are weak!
I am a beast of war! A burning, killing beast!"

Pete picked his drum stick up and struck the drum.
The grief and rage spread wildly through the room.
Beth wailed her feet into an angry dance.

We are the *Wakanadja*-mad," she sang.
"We'll count our coup upon our enemies
And match their murder with a host of men
And women killed by war, the awful dance . . ."

The other women, crying, beautiful
As songs, joined Beth and danced out on the floor;
The men, both white and Indian, rose and danced.
The drums beat strong. Pete lost himself and felt
The wolf-heart pounding underneath his skin.
He felt the other hearts inside the room.
They danced and danced. They sang and sang. They wept.

Peace

1

The demons flew into the squad. John parked.
Wings black and luminous, like smoky quartz,
Eyes bright as suns in space beyond the moon . . .
John tried to ward them off with deadened hands.
Their small black wings kept beating, beating . . . soft
And sibilant inside the squad's closed space.

The winter glittered in the sun, the snow
So bright it made stars dance through sightlessness.
Bright colors washed, intense, into the stars,
As fiery as the northern lights or lava flows.

The images of Indian children, sprawled,
Eyes dulled by death, assailed him. He blanched.
Their blood had frozen red on chests and legs.
Behind their lifeless bodies fire licked hot.
Stone turned to molten rock. Burned flesh smelled sweet.

"My God," he thought. "Forgive my human pride!"

The Rajah sat inside the squad an emptiness.
Strange dreams were swimming dark inside his eyes.
The demon wings were black and luminous,
A whir of hummingbirds, a hurricane.

Two angels blazed before John as he walked
Toward the Red Owl Store. He couldn't see.
He walked in light, a blaze of body parts.
He felt the goodness, holiness, of God

The darkness swirled and swirled inside the squad.
The demon wings kept whispering of flight
And freedom from life's disciplines and pain.
He longed to lose his spirit at a feast
Where men and women raped each other, laughed,
And sang, and murdered law and order, peace.
He melded hot into the blending stars.
He hummed at dark depravity that held

Him captive to the wing songs woven deep
Into the demons' dark, bright, endless flight.

Black eyes of Sitting Crow stared angrily at him.
John Israel was white, the Conestoga wagons, land,
Blood, sinew, bone of tribes and Indian lives.
He was a soldier uniformed by destiny
Made manifest by guns that seized the land
And penned the Indians in their Reservation cage.

"My God," John whispered to himself. "My God."

The angels danced inside the altar's flames.
Wings white, they smiled and sang and danced.
Wings black kept beating counterpoint to angel light.
In Sitting Crow's grim smile the truth was plain.

John shook his head, and groaned. He grabbed the mike.
"Thorn, Thorn," he croaked. "Come in. For God's sake, please. . ."

2

Thorn watched his Aunt and nineteen others march.
The cold was harsh enough to freeze their feet.
Aunt Wilma was a warrior woman, waving bread
Into the cameras, shouting out her chants:
"Let all our people go! Let all our people go!"
Ben Whitehorse beat his drum and sang a song
That gave the people bravery and peace.
The others shuffled through the snow, cloaks bright,
A portrait of the people's great nobility.
The cameras beamed the march to towns worldwide.

Thorn smiled to see their angry posturing.
He'd argued for a half a day, voice hoarse,
To keep his Aunt in Neopit, but then
She'd looked at him with eyes and left her house.

Yet, as he watched her brave the cold, he sang.
He was an Indian. They were relatives.
They'd filled the white man's camera with a show.
He'd failed, but they had triumphed. He had failed,
But still, he felt the drum as people marched.

170

The radio squawked angrily at him.

"Thorn, Thorn," John croaked, pain in his voice.

Thorn grabbed the mike. "What now?" he thought. "Thorn here,"
He said. John didn't speak. He heard Thorn's voice,
But demons danced and flew away from angel-light.

"What now?" Thorn thought again and said, "Thorn here."
He felt the wrongness, shuddered, panicky.

"I need you . . . here," John said. "I need your . . . help."

"Where's here?" Thorn asked.

                                    His Aunt had disappeared.
They'd walked into a grove of maple trees.
Thorn knew he had to find John Israel
Before the man had lost his sanity.

"Near G on 29," [73] John said. "Before the church."
He dropped his mike. His head rolled back against the seat.
He'd side with angels any day, he thought.
He smiled and looked into a face-bright light.

"Come. Talk to me," Thorn said. "I'm on my way."

The pavement ran before the squad car's wheels.
Thorn thought about his Aunt, John Israel.
His Aunt would tear apart the universe,
But John would give his life to keep her free.
The Sheriff had his goodness. Still, his Aunt
Had goodness too. She was an Indian, born
Despairing at the world, and yet, she'd persevered.

Thorn shook his head, his siren wailing loud.
He didn't think John fit the white man's world.
He'd been successful in his way, at odds
With whom he thought he was or ought to be.
Thorn understood his Aunt, not John, not whites.
John fought his demons, tried to save his world.
His Aunt was fighting for her race, her pride.
She wouldn't fall apart with ghosts and angel light.

She'd lost what she had lost a score of years ago.

He saw the church and John's parked squad in front.
John wasn't in his car. The road was empty, gray.

3

John walked up to the church's double doors
The sheriff of a county wracked by flame:

A heap of broken visions, where the sun beats,
And the dead tree gives no shelter, the cricket no relief,
And the dry stone no sound of water . . .
A man still reaching out for miracles.

The foyer's plainness, with its coat racks, registry —
He walked inside the unlocked door, then walked
Into the small, dark chapel. Where was peace?
His demons, fears, were stronger than the light.
He'd lived his life a man embraced by manly strengths:
A good provider blessed with good position, family man . . .
And then the call from young Joe Stims. Late night:
Rebellion, television cameras, newsmen, hate . . .

He'd spent the first night driven by events:
The wild ride through the dark, the frantic calls,
Alexian brothers in Chicago stunned,
The gunshots when he'd tried to walk the grounds.

But then exhaustion as the phone rang endlessly.
The politicians, lawyers, deputies,
And Indian leaders clamored for his time
Inside the maelstrom of the great event.
And now this country church. The demons warred
With angels as he knelt before the altar rail.

He clasped his hands before him. Nothing came.
He'd walked with angels, but he'd not found faith.
He had no words, no prayers, no forgiveness, hope.
He'd failed to keep the peace. He'd failed his oaths.
The war drums wailed with grief and mindless rage
And pounded news of death and loss into the earth,

"He longed to linger in the chambers of the sea
By sea-girls wreathed with seaweed red and brown."[74]

But, in his head, he felt a nothingness.

"Our dried voices, when
We whisper together
Are quiet and meaningless . . ."[75]

The silence of the altar gathered, grew.
He didn't comprehend. He didn't want a miracle.
He didn't want to see an angel wreathed in flame.
He didn't want to face the failures in his life.

He didn't move. He felt the sound the silence made
And waited. Then

                    His wife stood dressed in white
Before the altar, shining in her love for him.
Her face soft, eyes as bright as morning sun,
She turned, the veil before her face, and smiled.
He touched white lace then lifted up the veil
To see the woman he had pledged to love.
Her lips were warm against his lips, alive
With promises and faith in all the years
They'd spent together wrapped into the web
Of small and great events that fashioned lives.

The vision's brightness grew. He held his breath:
The altar, radiance in Jane's green eyes.
She smiled, then faded, growing thin like mist.

He sighed. Bill Winchell, Sitting Crow, the Rajah, dark,
Cold demons swirling like a band of dervishes.
What did they mean? How could he really fail?
He'd done his part for more than thirty years.

He got up from the altar rail and turned around.
He smiled to see Thorn sitting in the pews.
He'd be okay. He had a wife who'd loved
Him all the years he'd made a life with her.

Death Chant

The drums reverberated in the earth.
Inside the Legion Hall the men sat down
And looked into their hands as women wailed.

White Rabbit's dead, the drums said. Dead.
The white man's guns have silenced him, his voice.
The earth has known his bloodstains on its snows.
The words he's spent a lifetime gathering
Have been extinguished, lost. The flakes of flesh
That made him whole have started loosening.
The earth waits now. She calls his flesh and bones to life.
Spring rains will drive grass roots toward his flesh.
Blood gone, White Rabbit's dead, the drums said. Dead.

Beneath the sound of pounding drums, inside
The wailing grief and rage, men raised their eyes.

The white man took our land; he desecrates our graves;
He's brought the past alive by murdering
A warrior old enough to have white hair.
This is our time, they told themselves. Our time.
Find courage now, or find a place where shame
And degradation dance as specters clothed
With all the cowardice inside dead souls.

White Rabbit's dead, they told themselves. We'll make
Our vow of blood. A white man shot him in the back.
We'll make our lives a present to the past.
We'll make the white man lose flesh meshed to bones.
And as we die, the drums will shake the earth.
Against the sound of drums our mothers wail.

We've got our guns, they said. We've got our lives.
We'll wait until the darkness comes, they said.
And then we'll take our guns and lives and make
Them rage against the white man's ancient guilt.
We'll fashion justice out of blood and death.

White Rabbit's dead, the drums said. Dead. His heritage
Is death. Our heritage is death. He's dead.

The Dance of the Crow

He didn't feel the difference in the halls.
He paced through darkness full of fear, bereft.
He felt the feather-like extensions pierced
Into his arms and felt the sharpness of a beak
Below the coal-black brightness of his eyes.
He stopped, spread wings, and danced a bird's dance, legs
As thin and leathery as cattail reeds.

And then he felt the halls. He felt the wind
That was no wind brush through his hair, felt warmth
Of campfires filled with flames, black flickering.
The ghosts were singing, too, their voices mute.

He shivered. In a rush he felt a straining jump.
Great darknesses intensified and grew.
The wind died down as dark whorled into dark,
A hurricane of death and living death,
The walls and winter-cold and earth unbound
From universal laws of time and space.
Death grew, became a vortex shaping universe.

He was a crow, the Sitting Crow, who longed
For death and courted death, but hated death.
Inside his heart the darknesses whorled out
Toward his mind, a hunger ravenous.
He dropped onto the floor that was no floor
And curled into his mother's womb, his life
A seed decaying back into inception's pulse.
In fear he scratched his bird-legs at the air
And danced inside his fetal crouch, a man,
No man, alive, but dead, a visitor to death.

And then a pale light shimmered at the dark.
It wavered, faded, then intensified.
It hung between existence, nullity.
The light solidified. White Rabbit, black eyes,
Gray hair behind his bowing back, took form.
The outline of his body wavered, firmed.
He struggled to become a ghost, died out,
Then forced himself to form a shape again,

Dark potent with the darkness of his death.

At last he spoke. "I tried to come to you," he said.
His voice was thin and whispery, a breath.

A devastating horror washed through Sitting Crow.
He felt the death inside his spirit stir with life.
He reached out of the womb toward the dark.
In harsh, bird's croak he cawed out at the ghost:
"You're scaring me!" he cried. "You understand?"

He tried to move himself away from where
White Rabbit shimmered darkness, but he couldn't move.

"Your quest for death has been fulfilled," White Rabbit said,
His eyes as sad as all the sorrows caused by death.

There was no Sitting Crow. He fought against
The darkness overwhelming him, his fear.
He tried to picture Lena's face, her courage strong.

"I just don't understand," he said. "I don't . . ."

White Rabbit touched his chest. "I'm dead," he said.
"Your quest for death has been fulfilled." He paused.
"You're in the ancient fields of death right now."

A blinding anger staggered Sitting Crow.
He rose out of his crouch and slammed his fist
Into the wall. Pain jolted up his arm.
"I'll battle on my terms, not yours!" he screamed.

White Rabbit dissipated, swallowed up
Into the darknesses. A wolf howled hungrily.
Surrounding Sitting Crow war's carnage flashed
Past untamed winds, trees bent toward the ground,
Rain driven angrily into the earth.

Smoke rose above a mournful battleground.
An ancient woman, crying, tried to leave
A burning teepee. With a bloody yell
A white man pushed her back into the fire.
An old man, dressed in cavalry's blue clothes,

A funny hat upon his head, eyes glazed,
Collapsed when two stray bullets thunked into his back.
A beautiful young woman, blinded by the blood
That streamed into her weeping eyes, sat down
Before a horse's hooves and smiled to feel
Her chest cave in beneath the horse's weight.
A round-faced child ran screaming from a bayonet.
The soldier stopped, cocked back his arm, and threw
His rifle, spearing steel into the child's small back.
An Indian brave, eyes manic, grabbed a man
And sliced skin off his bloodied, white-bone skull.
Two Indian children squirmed inside a soldier's grasp.
A Colonel rode up to the soldier, looked
At children's eyes, and said: "These nits grow into lice."
The soldier let the children go, aimed, shot them both.[76]

The death storm howled and raved; the lightning danced;
The Indians killing, dying, white men mad
With killing, dying, all the universe
A battleground deluged with nightmare agonies.

And then the earth became, again, a void,
And darkness was the face of universe,
And in the darkness Sitting Crow was left alone,
A shaman filled with truths he couldn't comprehend.

What now? he asked. He tried to find his fear,
But there was nothing: Only dark and winter cold
That led to where the white men clutched their guns.

He wouldn't run away. He'd died, but lived,
And now he had to face his quest for death.
It was fulfilled, but unfulfilled. He was a mask.
He had to make the white man see the white man's wrong.
He didn't trust the ghosts. He was a shaman now.
He held his future burning in his hands.

He shuddered at White Rabbit's shining eyes.
He turned and walked toward the dining hall.

Measuring

Sam walked between the barn stalls, measuring
His life against the life inside the barn:
The Holsteins, swallows, cats, and unseen mice
Inhabiting the stalls, the rafters, rooms,
And secret places made by beams and bales.
He wondered how a man could measure life
Without a place that made him who he was.
Such thoughts were morbid, though. Closed eyes:
The vision of a smiling Chad LeConne
Ensconced behind his maple banker's desk,
The auction when his friends would come to see
The measure of a lifetime lost and sold.
His heart ached in his chest. He left the barn.

Fred Darrow, Lawrence Staub, Pat Duncan and his wife,
Steve Newt, and Franklin Timmers and his wife, Simone,
Were parked beside the tractor shed. Sam frowned.

Inside the house he shed his coat and gloves.
Her hand upon the handle of the coffee pot,
Rose went from guest to guest, the worry lines
Etched deep into her face forgotten, pushed
Away so that habitual hospitality
Could flow as freely as the coffee pot.
Sam looked at Lawrence Staub, the old man's eyes
Red, rheumy, weeping from the winter's cold.

"You're here," Sam said, voice non-committal, flat
The wives and Rose all quieted and looked
At Lawrence, waiting for the old man's words.

"No use in mincing words," the old man said
"Bill Winchell's going mad. He's bound to try
And capture Tigerton and make it free.
The question is, especially after Gordon Call,
Are we prepared to follow Bill? Or should we face
His madness down before it kills us all?"

Pat smiled. "Bill's never let us down," he said.
"We've followed him, and he's been right each time.

I say we stick with him and make our point.
Just look at Sitting Crow. He's trapped inside
That monk's tomb thirty miles from here, and half
The newsmen in the world are clamoring.
We take a stand, like Bill intends, and men
Will take a side: the government or us,
The ones who've got the guts to stand up tall."

"But Gordon Call is dead," Simone said quietly.
"And Franklin's got a mortgage, wife, and kids.
I'm not for widowhood, and neither Rose
Nor other women want to see you old fools dead.
I feel for Mrs. Call. Her husband's dead;
One son is dead. Her other sons have prison terms.
The world can go to hell as long as I
Have Franklin when the kids are grown and gone."

Pat laughed. "Just like a loyal wife," he snarled.
"Who doesn't have to face the real world."

"I've shot a gun before," Jan said. "Bill Winchell's right.
This country's gone to hell. I want our country back."

"The country's good enough," Rose said. Words cut
The room like knives designed to slice up human flesh.
Sam flinched to hear the rage inside his wife.
"Just look around," she said. "We're suffering.
The country's changed. The big farms flourish while we fail.
But life is more than farming, more than minds
Locked in a past that never truly was.
My father's father fled the wars that made
The Europe of his time a living hell.
Sam's father's father wanted land and dignity.
They came because democracy was strong
Enough to sweep away the evils that they knew,
And now you men are sick because democracy
Has left the few of us behind." She stared at Pat.
"Sam joins this madness if he wants to lose his wife."

"You nigger-lover, you!" Jan-May declared.

Rose looked at Sam, a pleading in her eyes.
Sam, lost, kept staring at the place she'd left.

She'd lived with him for over thirty years.
Simone got up and followed Rose outside.

"We've got to take our stands now," Lawrence said.
"We follow Bill or stop him in his tracks."

"What's your opinion?" Steve Newt asked. "Seems like
You ought to be the wisest in this room."

"I am a true believer," Lawrence said.
"I see what Bill sees in my own weird way,
But then I'm old. Sweet sister death
Seems like she has some sweet-limbed charms to me.
The trick is, will we stick together when
It gets so rough our insides stink from fear.
I said Bill's mad, and I believe he's mad.
From where I sit, the real question is,
What's Sam about to do? He sticks, we'll stick.
He isn't mad, but everything we hate
Is crashing down upon his head."

The rheumy eyes bore fiercely into Sam.
The others at the table also stared.
What should he do? Go in to Rose? The hurt
She felt was plain. She wanted him alive.

He thought about the field the night his father walked
With him through snow so deep it pushed his knees.
He felt, again, the ghost's eyes in the dark.
His father would have never given him the farm
If he had thought that Sam would lose the land.
He would have raged if he had known that Sam
Would follow men against the government
Old Werner Ludwig loved with all his soul.

But Chad LeConne, the banker, ran the bank,
And Sam had borrowed, of his own free will,
With greed, the money that destroyed his life,
His father's farm, his father's father's farm,
His farm, the farm to which he'd brought his bride.
Grant Tobin, auctioneer, would gavel strike
The lectern's wood and spiel Sam's life as cows,
Tools, tractors, implements, chairs, tables, crops

Were brought into the snow-white yard and sold.

He looked at Lawrence, sighed. Rose wouldn't leave.
She'd stuck through good times, bad times, foolishness.
"A man has got to stand up like a man
And let conviction rule someday," he said.
"The banks are wrong. If Gordon Call can face
His death with equanimity, I'll stand
Beside Bill Winchell with a steadfast soul."

The old man smiled.

    "I'm in," Steve Newt said. "Nuts and all."

"Simone thinks that I'm crazy," Franklin said.
"But I won't let you fellows down. I'm in."

Sam glanced toward the living room and tried
To think about the words he'd use with Rose.

Death Sat Upon The Ground, Head Buried In His Hands

1

When Sitting Crow first turned toward the halls,
Time freed itself from entropy and moved
Toward the past and future, wild, chaotic, smoke
Long cold with ash inside the dining hall —
And what would be had been, the death of Sitting Crow,
Hands touching Lena, eyes bright from the drums.

As Lena felt time thrash about, a beast,
She tried to turn and grab at Sitting Crow
As he ran out into the darkened halls,
To stop his craziness before it bent
Both time and gravity into a universe
Not meant for human beings, but she couldn't move.
Her mother, from another time and place,
Had wrapped her arms about her daughter's heart.
About the dining hall were flowers, trees, a spring
Made bright with summer birds and endless songs.
The dining hall's great fireplace and the endless cold
Hung like a memory inside the warmth of spring,
And Lena couldn't move. Her mother's love
Fused with her love for Sitting Crow. She turned
To save her lover, longing for her mother's love.

Death shifted, turned inside the universe.
Death could not find where he could feel secure.
He sighed, and men and women died, but lived,
Their bodies marching backward, forward as their souls
And spirits rose out of their earth-bound graves.

2

Out of the mist, inside her head, a dark,
Cold figure, large and indistinct, solidified.
His huge, black hood was thrown back from his head.
His eyes, aglitter, dulled into an earthen brown,
Their seeing shrunk from athanasia down

182

To small horizons seen by those of earth.
He scratched his crotch, rubbed hands on trousers patched
With cloth as black as coal, glanced down at hands,
Then looked up at a sky unsullied by the light of stars.
He grinned, his white teeth dark, and seized a pick.

He swung the pick, eyes anthracite, and sang:

> "In youth when I did love, did love,
> Methought it was very sweet,
> To contract; oh, the time, for a-behoove,
> Oh, methought, there-a was nothing-a meet.
> But age, with his stealing steps,
> Hath clawed me in his clutch,
> And hath shipped me intil the land
> As if I had never been such."[77]

"Why are you talking like an Englishman?" she asked.

He stopped, and looked at her, then grinned again.
He threw the pick down, kneeled, reached down into his hole,
And pulled a skull out of the grave's grim dark.

"Each skull once had a tongue and sang," he said.

He tossed the skull into the air, and with a whoop
Began to juggle one, then two, then three
Decaying skulls. He seemed to grow each time
A skull fell to his hands and then was tossed again.

But then she felt the shift inside the universe.
He shrank, became a clown who dug up graves.

One skull arced up toward the sky, smiled joyously,
And was alive, a woman bright outside her bones,
So perfectly alive she stirred men's blood with lust.
The woman's foot touched ground. She laughed, ran into mist.

The second skull went up into the air.
Death grimaced, eyes confused and wary, filled with fear.
An old man came to ground, blue eyes, bright life,
Hair white as frost beneath a silver moon.
The third skull rose, and Death stood still, breath held.

183

A child touched earth, his eyes filled with the juggler's black.
Sad laughter, sweet with mourning, dead, alive,
He too turned from Death and walked to mist.

"What's going on?" she asked.

                              Death smiled, sad eyed.
"Death's dead, but still alive," he said.

                              She twitched.
Her vision brightened, failed. The water drum
Began to beat, its sacred sound alive with holiness.
She twitched again and turned to feel the universe
As it began to turn and shift and shift and turn.

3

The naked child splashed out into the river's flow.
The rocks and sand beneath her feet, she felt
The way the water flowed its life around her legs.
She dived into the water, came up sputtering,
Then reached out for the grassy bank. She smiled.

Her mother, dressed in beaded buckskin, laughed.
"A muskrat child," she sang. "All brown and slickery!"

Delighted with the image of a muskrat child,
Lena leaped into the air, the river water caught by sun.
She reached to seize the sky into her fists.

Her mother laughed. Her mother was alive again!

And then the shift, the turn . . .

                              The night was murmuring.
The moonlight burned. Pines stood, tall sentinels . . .
She felt the mist, turned to her mother's eyes.

Her mother, darker than the dark about her, smiled.
"I came to say that you can choose to live," she said.

As Lena tried to touch her mother's peace
Inside the life her mother once had lived,

She gasped to feel the pain she felt, the cold.

4

Death sat upon the ground, head buried in his hands,
Tears running down his pale, wan cheeks.

5

She slapped at mist. It had to go away!
It couldn't hold her. In a dream she saw his face,
Her love, the Warrior chief, abandoned, filled with pain.
She touched mist, gathered wetness in her hands.
It turned and thrashed inside her grip, alive.
She tried to yank it from her mind. It breathed.
She didn't scream. She shook it, radiating rage.

Above her Superstar was looking down.
He looked as tired as any man she'd ever seen.
Tom Waters stood behind him looking stressed.
Beside Tom Waters, Horse stood still as death,
The ghost-light still a haunting presence in his eyes.

"He's dead," she whispered.

                    Superstar looked stunned.
"I know. I saw," he said.

                    She shook her head.
"You know White Rabbit's dead," she said. "Not Sitting Crow.
I saw his eyes lost in the chaos of the ghosts."

Tom Waters touched her forehead. Horse looked down.

"Hush now," Horse said. "You fainted. Try to rest."

"He's dead," she said. "I looked into his eyes."

Spirit Woman/Spirit Man

1

Thorn saw the vision John had brought alive.
Diffuse, soft light, and then John's wife at twenty-one,
Brown hair in braids, eyes shining hazel-green,
A womanhood of promises and song.

Thorn sat down in a pew and tried to feel
His way into the truth of what he saw.
John's face grew softer as his wife stood, dressed
In wedding white, before him. When she smiled
The demons in John's head began to fade,
His flesh translucent, filled with spirit-light.
Thorn hadn't thought John's visions were alive.
He'd thought his friend was going mad, the drum
Of swift disasters stronger than his sanity.
He'd thought that white men didn't have a world
Where spirits danced between their sacred earth
And Mother Earth, alive with meanings born
Beyond the reach of individual souls.

But now? The vision faded. John was motionless.
Before the altar angel's wings brushed soft
Against the silence, tearing down and building up
The substance of their lives with ceaseless work.
Thorn heard their laughter, saw the worlds that shaped
Into their hands and then went spinning blue
Into the void that surged in waves against reality.
John smiled at him, then walked into the cold.
He didn't say a word. He saw the visions bright
In Thorn's dark face, then walked away from him.
Thorn couldn't, wouldn't, didn't understand
The white man's spirit-world alive like shaman's dreams
Inside a world Thorn had thought was spirit-dead.

2

The dream was of his Aunt before the camera eyes.
She held the loaf of bread she'd brought from home.
She waved it, like a power stick, at eyes

186

She couldn't see and smiled to feel their shock
At seeing how an old, round woman stood
Defiant as she faced the lawmen's guns.

But then, she changed. Her years and roundness dimmed
Into a darkness that surrounded her.
She, not his Aunt, stood small upon a cliff
Above rocks overlooking hills and streams.
She wore a living heron cloak, bird's eyes
Above her shoulder, looking up into the sky.
Her breasts, with nipples small, hard, dark, were round,
The heron cloak revealing them, her belly, legs,
As it swept down from shoulders to the ground.

A silken lynx, with fiery yellow eyes,
Its spotted hide a celebration of the dawn,
Stared stoically at Thorn. Its life arose,
Somehow, out of the feathery heron cloak.
Its spots spilled off its hide onto the woman's flesh.

The lynx looked up into the sky. The totem born
Inside the white man flowed from empty air.
The man was powerful and nude, his arms
And legs alive with muscles moving as he moved.
His long, white beard flowed, wind into his flesh.
His flesh kept moving, blending with the sky
And separating from the sky, joy's song.
He reached his hand toward the woman's bird.
The woman lifted up her arms, the bird,
The silent, waiting lynx, into the sky.
The rock and soil of earth moved as she moved,
The high cliff growing higher still, dark rock
Thrown up in chants into the moving sky.

The woman-spirit laughed, her naked glory bright.
The sky-man sang his triumph at the earth.
The woman's laughter sang into the sky-man's song.
Earth rose, heaved, slammed into the rhythmic sky,
The sky-man, woman-earth alive with songs
Made from the song the other sang, the life
The other lived, the joy the other felt.

And then, the woman's laughter slipped away

Into a pregnancy so powerful
It stilled the sky and forced the air to swallow up
The man who flowed back to the nothingness of air.

The cliffs shrank backward, down toward the grass,
Toward the roots that anchored Mother Earth.
The woman, shining, more than beautiful,
Sighed, whispered to the bird and waiting lynx.
The lynx looked steadily at Thorn, eyes glittering.

Thorn groaned and tossed inside his bed.
The woman disappeared. She hadn't lived.

3

He heard the drums. They sang of war and death.
He saw John's grief and knew his pain and fear.
He saw a woman's bones cleaned white by worms and time.
He shuddered in his sleep. He heard the drums.

Responsibility

John parked the squad. Trish Harmon came outside.
Her coat unbuttoned, cold eyes terrified.
The wondrous feeling bathing John since he had seen
His vision of his wife began to dissipate.
"What's wrong?" he asked when Trish had reached the squad.

She'd been a veteran of the force for twenty years.
She'd seen it all: The robberies, wife beatings, murders, frauds . . .

"There's been an accident," she said, face hard.

"What kind of accident?" John asked, eyes closed.

She didn't flinch, but looked him in the eyes.
He halfway wished she had a softer side.
"An Indian's dead," she said. "An officer's
Responsible. He shot him in the back."
She paused, reluctant to reveal the rest.
"White Rabbit was about to link with Sitting Crow."

John looked at Trish's eyes in disbelief.
The demons in the universe began to sing,
Their wings a whispering inside his head.
The peaceful chapel was a dream without a place
Inside a world of rat's feet, hollow men,
Spasmodic tricks of radiance and miracle. [78]

The nation was a promise to the world,
A beacon shining freedom, hope, democracy
To peoples torn apart by chaos born
Of harsh dictators, famines, terrorists,
And wars on endless death-strewn battlefields.

But here in Shawano County, heartland of democracy,
Kidnapping, maybe rape, rank prejudice,
The Rajah's fierce fanaticism, rage,
The madness of Bill Winchell and his followers,
Rebellion of Menominee who'd lived
Too long near white man's pride, John's bouts with miracles,
And now White Rabbit's death, raged like a storm.

"How long ago?" he asked.

"Three hours," Trish said.

"I wasn't told . . ." He let the question hang.

"We tried," Trish said. "You didn't answer when we called."

He tried to see the chapel's simple altar rail,
The dimness of the holy room, the clean,
Bright whiteness of Jane's wondrous wedding dress,
But all he saw was Edvard Munch's lithograph,
A fluid human, mouth agape, hands clasped
In terror on its skull-bare head, upon a bridge.[79]

He sat back down into the squad, drums in his head.
White Rabbit's dead? Reality snarled, mean.
He saw the old man, hair as white as snow,
Walk through a crowd of men and women, blessing all
Who saw him as he smiled and talked and touched
His way around the grassy Woodland Bowl.

"I've got to go," he said. "I've got to go."

He shut the door. Trish looked at him. She frowned.

The vision of his wedding day was gone.
The child's skull, with its empty sockets, sang.
The soldier lifted up his rifle, threw
The bayonet into the fleeing child's small back.
The wings inside the squad sang songs of death.

John drove from town into the countryside.
White Rabbit's dead, he thought. White Rabbit's dead.
A cop had killed a reservation holy man.

Sitting Crow's Invisible Dance

1

He felt the feather's quills inside his skin.
He felt the power of the mask he wore,
The yellow beak, the black-hole eyes, the ebony
Of feathers covering his humanness.
He felt the wing joints fused into his shoulder blades,
The huge, invisible, black wings that pushed
Against dawn air and tried to tempt him into skies.

The firelight leapt about the dining hall,
Beast ghosts alive inside the shadow's venery.
Beside the fireplace Lena sat, head in her hands,
Her spirit wrapped into the death-storm's cloak
As time rent after he had met White Rabbit's ghost.

He felt the throbbing drums. We'll make our vow,
They said. The white man took ancestral land;
He desecrates our graves; he's brought the past alive
By murdering a warrior with white hair.
A white man lifted up his arms into the skies.
Time shifted. Ghosts began to weave their flesh
From substances webbed from their perished lives.
A white man brought his outspread arms together, sang.
His left hand gripped the knife his right hand held.
The death song, death dance whorled through universe.

He was the Sitting Crow, a shaman past the past,
A martyr to a future time when Indians stepped
Into the beating drums and celebrated lives
As bustles shivered bright with dance, and shawls
Swept wings that strained against his shoulder blades.

He stared at Lena, locked in shadow dance.
In wracking grief and pain she turned toward
The shadows where he stood, the feather's quills in skin,
Eyes bright with bird-life he had put into his face.

His eyes burned holes into his yellow beak.
The question burned his spirit once again.

He loved her. He was Sitting Crow – the man,
The warrior, wizard, martyr, history.
He felt blood pulse inside his veins, heart drum.
How could he live? He saw the Colonel's eyes
And how they shined to see the fear in children's eyes.
"These nits grow into lice," he'd said. But still,
He felt the feathers quiver on his face.
As Lena stared, not knowing that he was the dark,
The mask that was his face began to break apart.

A chant began to throb inside his chest.

     "Medicine man relent, restore —
     Lie to us — dance us back to the tribal morn!"[80]

The song wove out of him into the world,
Its dancing chant as dark as lightless caves,
A creeping plague that settled, silently,
Upon those sleeping in their warm, safe beds.

He shook to feel his power. Trembling, eyes
Wild in his head, he moved his feet and arms.
He sang a white man's song and felt hands shake.
In ecstasy he chortled at his warriors, laughed
And wept to see unseeing, sightless eyes.

2

When Lena heard his voice and saw him move
The fear depressing her dissolved to joy.
He stood before her, eyes entranced by songs.
She felt as if she were a garden filled
With pomegranates, apples, peaches, grapes;
She felt as if she were a honeycomb.
She was the living water, wine, the chant and song
That made him shake and dance. He was alive!
He wore the mask of death. She saw the mask,
But still, she knew. Behind the mask he was a man.

3

He saw her see him in the shadow's craze.
He grinned a death's-head-grin, became invisible.

Her eyes, so bright with hope, kept tattering
The veil of shadows woven by his hands.
He was a warrior shaman, powerful.
He laughed. Her eyes kept following and following . . .

4

When Lena started staring at the dark
Where Sitting Crow was dancing, Superstar
Sat back against the fireplace hearth and tried
To see what magic was entrancing her.
The night had been too long. He'd seen White Rabbit die,
And then the ghosts had streamed through darkened halls.
He'd stood amazed as Sitting Crow ran out
To haunted halls, and then he'd dealt with Lena's shock
When Sitting Crow had ran past her to face
The horror he had faced alone. And now?

As Sitting Crow congealed from shadows, Superstar
Drew in his breath. He had a rabbit's heart.
He tried to blind himself to shadow-fire
About the dancing, swirling Sitting Crow.
The specter didn't go away. It danced
As if the universe was wrapped in dance.

"My God," he whispered. "Sitting Crow's invisible."

He felt afraid, half faint. Tom Waters gasped,
And Wanda Matchapatow touched her face
As Sitting Crow, omnivorous, black, carrion fed,
Without a human name, kept dancing, legs
And arms and head alive with shadows, dark.

5

He tried to stop. There wasn't any need
To be invisible when he'd been seen.
He'd been awake all night. His life was tired.
The shadows of his dance kept flitting, beasts
That shrunk, then lunged at light. But still,
He felt the death-storm raving, clouds like buffalo,
Long streaks of lightning flashed in angry skies,
The carnage of the white man/Indian wars.

He danced inside the shadows:

"Medicine man relent, restore —
Lie to us — dance us back to the tribal morn!"

                             The white man's song
Kept mocking him. He moved his shaking hands.
He wanted Lena's arms around his waist.
He tried to feel her warmth fused with his warmth,
But all he felt were winds that howled like wolves
And sent their freezing fangs into his flesh.
He felt the feather's quills inside his flesh.
He felt the power of the mask he wore,
The yellow beak, the black-hole eyes, the ebony.
He was alive! The drums kept beating . . . beat.

6

Rage flowed from Lena. Sitting Crow would live.
He danced.

"Come home," she said aloud. "Come home."

Her fierceness burned the shadows of his dance.
He was alive. He wore the mask of death,
But it was just a mask. He was alive.
She wouldn't let the ghoul who'd wept to see
The dead alive possess his spirit or her love.

"Come home," she said. "Come home. Come home."

7

Tom Waters shook his head, then shook again.
The apparition wasn't real, he told himself.
The ghosts he'd seen were false. He was no fool.
His eyes denied the shadows that he saw.

8

He'd die, he told himself. He had to fight
The white men camped around the Novitiate.

———
194

He had to fight John Israel. But still he danced
And felt the gouging quills mask deep into his face.
He wept inside himself, but still he danced,
Whirled, chanted songs that married songs
The drums kept sending out into the night.

"Death," said the drums. "We sing the song of death.
The white man's death. There is no ending to our song."

He danced.

9

      She saw him fall. He hesitated, fell.
She crossed the floor and knelt beside his shroud.
He was alive. She said it to herself: "Alive."

He slept so deeply he looked as if he'd died.

Bill Winchell's Sacrificial Calf

1

He'd seen the signs for days: The Judas kiss,
The death of Gordon Call, the dream about
The mead hall where the poet and the King
Became aware of him, the elm tree's touch
Inside his mind, the madness when he stole
Donn Truesdale's tractor from his farm and then
Heaped earth upon its metal angst, the heat
The Goddess caused each time he saw her ice,
The vision of the great red serpent's scales,
The coming of John Israel into the bar . . .

Bill sat up in his bed. The madness crept
So silently in him it frightened him.
He'd struggled for his faith in God while all
His body longed to touch the goddess flesh.

A group from Tennessee kept struggling
To learn of firing anti-tank guns accurately.
An osprey, wings outspread, appeared above his head,
Its hovering white, speckled brown against the sky.
That evening, as he drove toward the bar,
An eagle winged a dozen feet above
The pine trees bordering the road. And then,
That night, a little woozy from the beers he'd drunk,
He'd listened as a Shawano nurse had told
About her friend hospitalized a vegetable.
The India Indian Rajah had destroyed
Her friend, the nurse had said, a non-American.

First eagles, then the evidence of rot
Inside the country's heart. The signs were there.
The Goddess in the trees reflected real
Into the bar upon the windowpanes,
The Goddess singing as he lost his mind
And longed to join her in the bower she had made
Beneath the earth inside the roots of trees.

And now the news that at the Novitiate

An Indian medicine man had died. He'd watched
The television news and saw the way
The Indian drummers looked outside the Legion Hall.
Inside the Novitiate, surrounded by the guns
Of white men guilty of White Rabbit's death,
Revenge a blood song, Sitting Crow would be aflame.

Bill looked toward the Bible on the shelf
Above his bed and turned its pages aimlessly.
His sleep had puzzled out the meaning of the signs.
He reached out for the phone. He felt alive
Beyond his body. Fate pursued his days.

Sam Ludwig answered from his ancient barn.

"You got a calf?" Bill asked. "A fatted calf?"

                              "A what?"
Sam asked, his heartbeat pounding in his chest.

"A fatted calf," Bill said. "I need a fatted calf."

"Right now?" Sam's stupefaction in his voice.

"Right now," Bill said, his voice commanding. "Get
The boys together. Have them bring their guns.
We'll call for help. We'll need men, lots of men.
White Rabbit's dead!" he shouted. "Dead! He's dead!
We're gonna have to move so fast and hard
The Sheriff and the Governor will get confused.
We've got a chance to realize our dreams!"

"Yes . . .sir . . ." Sam said.

2

                    Sam held the phone and looked
At Holsteins stanchioned in against the cold.
He wasn't mad, he told himself. He wasn't mad.
His father's time was gone. His life had changed.
His eyes fell on the bull-calf pens and shook his head.
A newborn bull was awkward yet from birth.

"Deliver me from my enemies, O my God:"[81]
Sam quoted to himself. He swallowed hard.
"Defend me from those who rise up against me.
Deliver me from the workers of iniquity,
And save me from bloodthirsty men."[82]

What should he do? A fatted calf? Sam shook his head.
Small mounds of milky ice encrusted doors.
Bill Winchell's mad, he told himself. He's mad.
"And what will Rose do now?" he asked himself.
He loved his wife. He'd always loved his wife.

He turned toward the milk shed-door and longed
To walk away from all the madness that he felt.
He'd promised Lawrence Staub, the men . . . He cursed
The god damned bankers and the government
And grabbed a rope from off the brown board wall.
The bull calf bawled, eyes white with terror at the rope.
He touched its trembling, birth-wet hide. It tried
To get away. It bumped against the rail.
Sam shuddered deep inside his beating heart.

3

The phone clicked dead. Bill sat up, dressed, and went
Downstairs and sat upon a bar stool, quiet, waiting, filled
With feelings much too powerful to name.
Time flared out from the sun and scorched the towns
Of Shawano County. Heat poured out from the bar.
The people that it touched began to gnaw black tongues.
Bill wondered if he'd lost his mind. Time crawled.

Sam brought the calf into the bar and stood,
His scratchy rope in hand, eyes skeptical.
The calf was bawling loud enough to wake the dead.
The Goddess stirred inside the woods, eyes bright.
Bill felt triumph at his coming victory.

"The Bible says to sacrifice a fatted calf
To please the Lord," Bill said. "We need the Lord
Behind us in our battle with the infidels."
He blinked his eyes. "You've called the men? We'll build
A bonfire big enough to char your calf to ash."

198

Sam hesitated. "These ain't Bible times," he said.
Bill hadn't noticed that he'd brought a calf new born.

Bill frowned. "Read Revelations: Blessed are
        The men that do commandments. They may have
        Right to the tree of life, and they may enter in
        Through gates into the city of the Lord."[83]

Sam stared at Bill. What should he do? He frowned.
Momentum, building through the years, was now
A freight train moving much too fast to stop.
"I'll build the fire," he said at last, eyes closed.

"With wood felled naturally," Bill said. Relief.
He wasn't mad. "Green wood won't do the job."

Sam shrugged and went outside. The calf, now calm
Inside the bar's snug warmth, had quieted.

Bill didn't move. He watched Sam go and felt
The Goddess as she tried to understand
The import of his madness to the earth.
He listened. Cars drove to the parking lot
And car doors slammed. Men said hello and talked.
Nobody came into the bar. He was alone,
Caught in a vortex void of everything
But light and woman-spirit presences.

At last Sam came into the bar, face red, cold.
The Goddess sang her panic at the world.
She felt his purpose, saw the hand of God.
Bill laughed and startled Sam. He'd beat the bitch!

"We're ready, Bill," Sam said. "We jury-rigged
A table for the slaughter of the calf.
The wood is all dead wood just like you said."

Bill felt the tremulous nature of the earth.
All things must change, he thought. Our people need
To start out fresh. They need to leave the rot
So that at least a few can live for God.
The Goddess wouldn't die. She'd lived too long.
But, with his offering accepted by the Lord,

She wouldn't, couldn't trouble him again.

He walked out in the cold. Sam handed him
A butcher knife. Gil Straubmuller, face red,
Face practical as any face surrounding him,
Stared curiously at Bill.

                "You ready for the calf?" Sam asked.

"I'll be the supplicant who kills the calf," Bill said.

Sam looked at Lawrence Staub. He struck a match
And threw the tiny flame onto the wood.
The smell of gasoline. Sam led the calf,
Now docile, through the crowd of milling men.
Their eyes were bright with all the power sung
Into the crazy spectacle they'd joined.
Flame raced toward the woodpile's top and licked at skies.
Bill felt fire lick at lovely Goddess bones.
John Israel would have to fight another front.
The nation was afire with passion's flames.
He motioned, smiled. Gil grabbed the calf
And threw it on the homemade tabletop.
The calf bawled terror at the men and fire.

Bill loomed above the calf. He lifted up
His arms into the cold, blue winter sky.
He slowly brought his outspread arms together, smiled.
His left hand gripped the knife his right hand held.
He cast his eyes into the sky. The men
Were hushed, hearts racing as they tried to understand.

"Our Father, please accept this sacrifice,"
Bill said, his voice as deep as tolling bells.
"We need your grace to face the dangers faced
Before this day and coming night bring dawn."

Strength flowed into his arms. He plunged the knife
Into the calf. The calf bawled out its pain.
Blood stained Bill's shirt. He lifted up the knife
And plunged again. He felt life leave the calf.
He felt the Goddess sink into the healing earth.
The calf's sides, red, stopped heaving. Struggle stopped,

A mucus dulled the wild, white terror in its eyes.

Bill grimly looked up at his followers,
His bloody shirt a testament to God.
"Tonight's the night we've waited for," he said,
Voice gentle as a freshet's early spring.
"We've called for justice for a long, long time.
The government has answered with disdain.
We're Constitution, Bible-swearing citizens.
But evil stalks this land we love, and now
We've killed a sacrificial calf to seal a vow
So deep inside our hearts and minds grim hell
Itself would quail before Beelzebub
Would find the guts to try and cut it out.
"We've got our guns. We've got our courage. We
Declare our freedom from these once United States.
Tomorrow dawn we're taking over Tigerton.
By dawn three thousand men will heed our call,
Will hear the trumpet we are sounding now,
Tomorrow night this county will be free!"

The fire was roaring at the sky so loud
It nearly drowned the ragged, hoarse voiced cheers.
Bill motioned for the men to throw the calf
Into the fire. The pungent smell of burning hide
Surrounded them. He looked up at the sky.

Smoke billowed black in columns straight toward
The heavens, stretching to eternity.
A nation fit for man and God, he thought,
The light of slaughter burned in shining eyes.

We only want this little bit of land,
He thought. This country's too damned big to rule.

The Crow's Heart

1

The crow's heart, hot and fibrillating, throbbed
Inside crow's skeleton. He touched bones, felt
How tight they knit to flesh, put hands to face.
The heart-heat pulsed against his human skin.
The membrane of his dream surrounded him.
As thin as gauze, it was a jail that wrapped
His heart, his bones, his heat, his human heart.
His crow-eye blinked. He shifted in his sleep.
The crow inside him stirred and spread its wings.
The crow-heart jumped toward him, growing powerful.
He tried to move, but felt the crow's blood freeze his heart.
He strained to cleanse himself of blood. The crow's wings spread.
It cawed; he cawed; it cawed. The dream collapsed.
The heart touched bone, then leaped at bone again.
He was the crow-man! Not a man! A heart!
A pounding, frightened, fibrillating crow-
Black, ebony dark, membrane-smothered heart!

2

The morning light was empty of the hope
That once had Lena celebrating dawn.
Beside her Sitting Crow's lieutenants slept.
They'd lived to see another dawn, but none
Were ready for the aftermath of ghosts.
She looked at Sitting Crow, his face devoid of life.
There was no future. That she knew. The white men's guns
Had never faced a spirit or a ghost,
But still would screw their courage up and come.
She'd die or go to prison. Dawns would pass,
And she and Sitting Crow would be apart.
Despair clamped down on her. Her eyes wept tears,
The morning light as vile as bone afire.

Why had they thought that they could change the way things were?

They'd mostly spent their evenings at the Rainbow Bar.
At first they'd been the "Eight Menominee,"

Her, Sitting Crow, Tom Waters, Superstar,
Beth Thunder, Wanda Matchapatow, Horse,
And Sylva Crane, Neopit Warriors, wolves.
All summer long they'd laughed and joked a lot,
And she and Sitting Crow had passionately
Made love out in the woods beneath starred skies.
They'd got their kicks with dope and thievery
And dancing to the music of the Grateful Dead.[84]

But then the jokes took on a bitter edge
As Sitting Crow, intense, smile devil-proud,
So handsome he had made her ache inside,
Began to change. One day he'd been as wild
As them — and then . . . once funnier than Horse,
He stopped his joking, started brooding over how
Menominee were forced to live in pain
When once they'd been the guardians of earth.
And then he'd started mocking them, his voice
So powerful it made them shake inside their guts.

>"Tecumseh said 'to kill their stock. They owned the land.
>War now. War forever. War upon the living. War
>Upon the dead; dig corpses from their graves;
>Our land must give no rest to white man's bones!'"[85]

"And here we sit," he'd said, his voice a song.
"Our people doomed to live a life of poverty
While whites in Shawano dine on china white.
We spend our nights carousing at a bar
While Indian children wake up crying in the night.

"We're not true warriors sworn to right the wrong
The white man's greed has visited upon our race.
We're children doomed to whine away our lives
While stealing tires and numbing pain with booze . . ."

And, as he'd spun his spell about the eight of them,
They'd spread the word until, at last, in winter cold,
They'd sat inside the bar four dozen strong,
Their faces rapt with wonders as he dreamed
Of conquest, martyrdom, and Indian pride.

"We'll die a glorious victory," he'd said.

She'd loved him like she'd never dreamed she'd love.
"And from our bones our voices will cry out
For justice, causing justice, long deferred, to come."

And so they'd come into this place, she thought,
The white men armed with death, the ghosts alive.
They'd come ablaze with dreams of glory, rage.
They'd change the world, they'd thought. She'd thought her love
For Sitting Crow could make a fire that burned
Away the miseries of Indians everywhere.

She touched the fever on his face. He was alive.
She still had that. She laughed. What had they thought?
She didn't know if she could keep on going on.

3

He woke in Lena's arms. She watched him stir.
He looked into her face. Her eyes were tired.
"You've got to leave this place," he said, voice soft.
"You have to take the kids out through the swamps."

Tears welled into her red, sore eyes. She looked
About the dining hall, the mess hall tables, chairs.
"You too," she said. "I couldn't live if you were dead."

He sighed and sat up. Everyone had left the room.

"They're all afraid of you," she said. "Horse thinks
You've gone through metamorphosis. He thinks you're dead."

He smiled, the smile so grim it made her shake.
"Why did they leave?" he asked.

                              "I asked them to,"
She said. "We saw you waking up. They're all afraid.
I didn't think you'd want to face them yet."
She paused. "Not of the white men. They're afraid of you."

"I'm shaman now," he said. "White Rabbit came
Out of his death. I sent him back into his grave."

She stared at him so steadily he met her eyes.

"I want to live," she said. "Together. You and I."

"There's life and life," he said. He frowned.
He jabbed his hand into the air. "There's death
And death; I choose to live the death I choose."

She held herself inviolate. She wouldn't let
His words and meanings bring the cold, white mist.

"I'm still in love with you," she said.

                      "And love, sweet love
Is stronger than resplendent death," he mocked.
"That's what you want to hear, but now you see . . ."

He lifted both his arms above his head.
He felt the death-storm stirring deep in memory
And felt the crow's heart's pounding cadence match
The rhythms beating in his human heart.

"I've been inside the realm of death," he said,
His voice an echo of the voice she loved.
"I didn't bring a ram or ewe for sacrifice,
Or dig a pit to hold black blood for ghosts.
I'm neither cursed nor blessed with prophecy,
But still, I've been where men don't dare to go."

He felt the panic felt inside the crow's hot heart.

His eyes, first fiery with a shaman's potency,
Then filled with pain. The anxious, cold despair
She'd felt at dawn engulfed her in a rush.
"I'm scared," she said. "I didn't follow you
In here so we could die."

                    He looked at her.
He looked all shriveled, tired. She looked at him.
She had to understand. He loved her still
No matter how the death-storm drove him mad.
No matter how the death-song wove from him
Into the world poised now upon war's brink.

"The children have to live full lives," he said.

"The white men have no patience. Soon they'll start
To think that we might win a victory,
And then they'll spill our blood on marble floors,
And every soul behind these walls will move to where
I've been and never see the light of day.
I hear the drums. They talk of death to come.
They've sung White Rabbit's death all night and day."

She tried to see beyond the moving mists.
She tried to tell herself that he was Sitting Crow,
But in her ears, so soft it wasn't real,
She heard the crow's heart sing its drum-wild song.

"I'm still in love with you!" she raged, voice soft.

He turned away to look into the fireplace flames.
"Love's not what makes our history," he said.

What made them mad enough to think that they
Could change the way things were? she thought.
She wouldn't let him die. He couldn't die.
She felt the mist inside him, felt the certainty
That made him more than he could ever be.
She didn't want to die. She knelt down in the snow
And threw her hair into the hotness of the spring.
The cold was fire that blazed toward her heart.

He looked at her. She looked at him. Each stood
Without the heart to really understand.

At last, he looked away from Lena at the floor.
His eyes were ebony, his skin crow-black.
He wore the crow-mask's eyes, the yellow beak.
"They're warriors. I have brought them war," he said.

"I still love you," she said again.

                              He looked into her eyes.
He'd won. She'd take the children out of death.
He felt exultant, sad. She made him ache.
He tried to shake the crow-mask from his face,
To look at her with his old human eyes.

"You have to understand," he said. "White Rabbit showed Why we are how we are . . ."

She looked at him.

4

The crow's heart, fibrillating, hot, throbbed ceaselessly.

Death and John Israel's Contemplation Of Suicide

John took the body to St. Joseph's in his squad.
He'd called the priest, young Father Holdman, first.
His voice as soft as rain, the priest had asked
To send a nun to bring the body to the church.

"The radicals will kill you if you're seen,"
He said. "They'll blame you for White Rabbit's death.
They won't care if your orders weren't obeyed."

John's eyes had misted unexpectedly.
"I know," he'd said. "I've been the law a long, long time."

Then, moments later, as his white-faced men
Wrapped up the old man's body in a shroud,
He'd faced Pete Thorn, his friend for thirty years.

"White Rabbit was my uncle," Thorn had said.

The dawn was still an hour away. The only light
Was shadowed light cast by the waning moon.
"No Thorn, please," John had said. "No."

                              "These aren't normal times,"
Thorn answered. "You're a white man. You're the law.
I had a dream." He paused. "A waking dream,
A vision like my people's holy men
Have always seen. I saw the spirit earth . . ."
The words he wanted said escaped the night.

The moment etched itself into John's brain.
Thorn hugged John quickly, fiercely, let John go,
And ran toward the Novitiate. John watched him go.
He dared his men to put hands on their guns.
He'd murder them, he swore. Right there. No trial.

The men about him stood in place and watched
As Thorn braved Indian guns to join his gun
To radicals who could have shot him down.

He'd been a cop, an Indian living white,
And now he'd turned his back on what he'd been.

In rage John blocked White Rabbit from his sight,
Then got into the squad and drove as mad
As Satan to the brown brick Catholic church.
He didn't think. He didn't watch the road.
He drove until he'd parked before the church,
Then stood beside the squad to listen to the drums.

Young Father Holdman met him in the parking lot
And helped him move White Rabbit to the church.
Inside the foyer two young nuns helped put
The body in a coffin as John prayed
To God to find a way to exculpate his sins.
He should have been there when the old man ran
Across the river's shining snow and ice.
He should have left the Lutheran church alone
And never seen the vision of his wife.
The wraiths had known. They'd forced him off the road.

A little later, after dawn had spilled red light,
He called the Governor and asked to be relieved.
The Governor was eloquent. He argued, hot:
The National Guard was unprepared to walk
A tightrope through the minefields revolution set.
No one wanted death exploding in the North.
John knew what words would make a lasting peace.
Another man might light a powder keg of hate.

John listened, cold, then hung the phone up, blank.
He sat behind his desk and thought about
White Rabbit's face, the old man's eyes death-glazed.
Why did he want to live? He'd lost the dream
Of strong communities made whole by law
And lived the consequences of his dream:
White Rabbit, mad Bill Winchell, Sitting Crow,
The Rajah, crazy Indian kids . . . and Thorn.

The early morning light inside the room was dim.
He pulled his pistol out and put it on his desk.
He stared at it. He was a cowboy still, inheritor
Of wrongs and rights he only dimly understood.

He'd had his years of glory: victory at polls,
Which meant that he was still the man behind the badge;
The summer days when he and Thorn had lounged
Beside the Wolf below the reservation line,
Two friends who'd left race differences behind.

The pistol stared at him. It was alive.
He touched the trigger lightly, carefully.
The touch stirred deep inside his groin, a shock
As powerful as sex or, even, life at birth.
He put the pistol on his desk and stared.
He loved his country, loved the dream that said
All men were equal under God and law.
He couldn't see the death of all he loved
Inside the county where he'd made his life.
He couldn't face his failure as a man
Who'd sworn to make the law a fair, just judge.
The rat's feet whispered on the cellar floor.
The hollow men stared sightlessly into his eyes.

At last he moved his chair back, stood,
And put the pistol in its holster at his side.

He drove home then. Jane met him at the kitchen door
Dressed in a nightgown similar in style
To nightgowns she had worn for thirty years:
Pink, slightly clinging, something, like his wife,
Familiar in the reeling of his world.

She didn't speak or try to make him speak.
She made a pot of coffee, poured two cups,
And stood behind him as he stared at air.
He wanted life. He wanted death. What else?
He wondered how he'd feel if suddenly
He pulled his pistol from his holster, stuck
The barrel in his mouth, and pulled the trigger, death.
He wondered if he had the guts for suicide . . .

And then he found himself in bed with Jane,
The woman that had made his marriage bed.
He didn't know what she had done to get him there.
"It's been too long," he said. "We're getting old."

Her fingers moved. He felt so distant, lost.

He moved his hand. Jane's breasts sloped down from age,
But still were firm and smooth. He touched her flesh,
Made nipples harden, looked at her, her light.
Her pubic hair was still as black as coal.
She moaned, her nipples dark against her skin.

He slid between her legs and rolled on top of her,
His hardness driving down into her heat.
The spasms ached inside his teeth and groin,
Her love/his love the meaning given life.

She held him, forcing him to feel she still was there.

He wondered what the Governor would do.
If Thorn had joined the radicals, he wouldn't fight.
Laws didn't recognize a friendship, but he did.

Jane kissed him. Unexpectedly
She forced her tongue into his mouth. He rose.
He felt her glory, wondered why he'd thought
That she would let him give himself to death.

Benevolence

1

Ron came into the Rajah's room and kneeled.
In meditations about the universe,
The Rajah had to force himself to face the world.
He knew why Ron had come. He felt in touch with tides
That linked the moon with rising, falling waves.
He'd known the news since he had sat entranced
Inside the squad car in the Red Owl parking lot.

He slowly ceased his chanting. Ron, distressed,
Stared steadily into his eyes. "She's there."

The Rajah sighed, the tension in his stomach quelled.
"We'll meet," he said. The time of truth was near.
Celest would know her freedom once again.

Ron didn't move, but waited patiently.
Surprised, the Rajah looked at how he kneeled,
His back as rigid as a hissing cat's hunched back.
"There's more?" he asked.

                    Ron's eyes were steady, calm.
"I need to understand," he said. He gathered thoughts.
 "I've been with you for more than twenty years.
We've moved from New York City to this place.
We've tried to meditate and fast away
The violent evil loose inside the world.
But now you want to violate our peace.
You'll justify those men who hate our ways."

The Rajah shook his head, his god-head filled
With fire, light sparking from his burning eyes.
"Celest is one of us," he said. "She chose
Our way. We didn't take her from the world.
We can't just sit around while evil plots
Destruction of our truth and way of life."

"But you have always taught non-violence, peace,
The need for meditation, fasting, faith . . ."

"I've taught obedience," the Rajah said.
"To god encoded in the dance of energies
That form the stuff of matter, spirit, flesh!"

He felt the rage he'd always fought against
Rise like a tide into his chest and arms.
He held his breath and looked at Ron's long face,
His oldest, dearest, most loved follower.

Ron didn't look convinced. "What now?" he asked.
"Where will your anger lead? Where is your peace?"

"You want to question me?" the Rajah asked.

Ron eyes were calculating, cold. "You've always said
We had to act in peace to find our peace.
You've always said we didn't need the world."

"Celest is wracked with pain," the Rajah said. "She's here!"
He thumped his chest. "No follower of mine
Or yours should ever feel unrighteous pain!"

"You talk about Celest, not Dawn," Ron said, his voice
A whisper Rajah had to strain to hear.

The Rajah felt Dawn's catatonic shock
Shock through his shoulders down into his legs.
He fought the boiling turbulence inside his mind.
He was a man of god; the god was him,
His body, heart, and spirit wild with fire.

"You've always said," Ron said. "That willingness
To face the pain of fasting is the only way
To find the truth we hold inside ourselves."
"We must protect ourselves," the Rajah said.
"We cannot let our faith destroy our truth."

"Okay," Ron said. "But if this turns out bad, I'll leave."

Ron's words struck at the Rajah's breath. He didn't gasp.
He didn't move. He kept himself as still as stone.
He felt a cold, hard fear grow outward from his gut.
Rage boiled into his chest. Calm, calm, he told himself.

Organic energy danced through the universe.
Light spread, diffuse, upon the wood that danced
With energies coalesced into the wood.
He saw the angels dance inside the fire
Upon the Christian altar, and he knew they danced
For him, the infidel, the Antichrist.

"We'll meet inside the living room," he said.

Ron dropped his eyes and looked down at the floor.
"Your wish," he said.

        He moved so swiftly, silently,
The Rajah didn't see him go. Ron Zukalov
Would leave the faith they'd built together? Leave the light?

2

The laughter and the talking stopped when, fierce,
He walked into the silent living room.
He stood amidst them, teacher, leader, god-
Inspired, and gathered all his feelings, thoughts.

"Ron's found Celest," the Rajah told his followers.
"She's at her father's house. The man she left
To join our family has taken her against her will.
Our oneness with the universe conflicts
With what we ought to do when violence strikes.
I've meditated, as you've seen, for days,
And what I see is that we have the right
To take our sister back into our midst.
I don't believe we have the right to use
A force of arms to bring her back, but still,
I think we are enjoined to find relief
For any brother, sister, child who's forced
To face the pain Celest has faced. This is my will."

"But what if all we do is stir up hate
Against the rest of us?" Fred Morrow asked.

The Rajah bowed his head. "I came from lands
Where men were cast into a prison by their caste.
Caught in a darkness of my spirit, light

Danced as I dreamed about this nation's shores.
I am a holy man, and holy men walk rocky paths.
I chose this land. This snowy place. Our home."
His rage was building like a roaring fire.
"I spit upon those fools who'd try to ruin our home!
Inside these walls light burns its shining hope.
My being — yours! — must never flinch aside.
These walls will last until our children take our place."
He slumped into a homemade straight-backed chair.
"We'll raid the Speltz's farm before day's light."

"Jim Speltz is known to carry guns in town,"
Ron said. "What happens when he shoots at us?"

The Rajah smiled benevolence at Ron.
"I've seen the truth," he said. "No one will die.
I saw where Speltz had hid Celest before
You saw her walking in his living room."

Ron bowed his head. The trouble hadn't left his eyes.
The Rajah stared at Ron — at them — and smiled.

The Start of White Rabbit's War

1

The drums were silenced as the sun rose red
Above trees. Shadows stretched into the light of day.

"Sleep now," Pete said. "At twilight Thunderbirds,
Night Spirits, hearts filled with the power of this feast
Will loose the fires of war. Sleep now," he said.

As sleeping bags and blankets spread on floors,
Beth came and took his hand. He felt tired, worn
From singing to the spirits he had seen.
His legs felt heavy from a need for sleep.
But still, Beth's hand clasped tight about his hand
Sang through his blood and made him praise the times
When love would burn amidst the fires of war.

They slipped into the warmth of blankets, held
Each other, went to sleep, too tired for making love.

"I love Pete Wilson," whispered Beth before sleep came.

Pete smiled. He'd known this woman since their high school years,
But not until she'd stood to vanquish shame
Had he discovered all the fires of love.

"I love Beth Swan," he softly whispered back.
The sweet, dark waters of his sleep were swift.

2

Norm Davis woke Pete up. He touched Pete's hand,
Then moved on, whispering and touching, groans
And grumbling behind him as he moved.
Pete's hand touched Beth's round breast. He groaned.
She woke and smiled, then stood up suddenly,
The cold replacing warmth a shock against his flesh.

"It's time," she said. She stood above him wonderful.
Her presence made him feel the power of this day.

This was a war of life and love, not death.

He laughed and threw himself into the cold.
"It's time," he nodded. "Time."

                              The gathering
Created mass confusion as the clothes
And sleeping bags and blankets, food and guns
Were piled upon the Legion Hall's pine floor.
The early winter night was gathering,
The half full moon a glittering upon the snow.

At last, Pete called the Warriors, women, men,
To circle round the drums. The singers threw
Their heads back, let the drums talk, sang their songs.
The others knelt and sprawled upon the floor,
The Indians, whites, Hispanics, blacks danced, sang
To make an Indian War, White Rabbit's War.

"We are a beast," Pete said to them. The singers stopped.
"One heart, one spirit, many arms and many heads.
We go to war. The *wakanadja* dance
Above the clouds, above the breathing sky.
They watch us as we set the white man's earth aflame!"

The Warriors stood and cheered. They heard his words.
He shined to feel the power they imbued in him.
"But, as we face this time of war and hate,
Of fires we scorch in white men's hearts, remember this!
We are an Indian tribe, each one of us.
We brandish guns; we're fighting for a peace
Where justice for all peoples flourishes.
Our cause is for the life of everyone who lives.
We'll make the white man homeless with the aim
Of building homes for every people pressed by need."
He waved his thirty-thirty overhead.
"We've brought alive the Thunderbird's great wrath.
We bring destruction, like a raging beast.
The light of triumph burns the brightest for the soul
Who's given up his life to make a life
For everything he loves and cherishes!"

The beast stirred in the dark. Pete looked at Beth,

At yellow eyes gleamed from the beast's mad heart.
He smiled, his grimness promising a reckoning.
He moved into the beast and touched its arms
And brushed its shoulders as it turned with him.
The beast was silent as it moved toward the door.
The stain spread outward from the Legion Hall,
And in its heart the drum song beat and beat.

3

Legune, Moon, Mabel Sams, June Oh,
Tree Hope, Joe Davis, Snuffy Dodge, and, ranged
Behind them, half a dozen others stood.
The group of them could feel the moods that spilled
Out from the Hall, the drum beat harsh with rage,
The voices shouting out for ancient war.

Legune felt myriads of sadnesses and rage.
 As chants grew more prolonged, she wondered why
The Indian people always fought and raged
Toward a vision of a future wrapped
Into the bindings of a mythic past.
She mourned White Rabbit's death. He'd been a friend.
She didn't understand what need had driven him
To join the Warriors in the Novitiate.
She didn't understand what need had made
The white man pull the trigger on his gun.

She knew that only sorrow emanated from revenge.
The cycle was an ancient one: A death
Caused death, and in that second death, death raged
Unbound by law, or common sense, or decency.

A young life taken is a wasted life,
She thought. The old will die into their peace,
But when a youngster dies their spirit haunts,
A wailing curse above unquiet graves.

She knew she couldn't stop them. When the chant
Was done they'd come outside, their guns in hand.
They wanted shamans powerful enough
To change the circumstances of the past.
They wanted lives unwed to poverty.

They wanted glory wrapped about their lives.

They'd fail. The white man knew the ways of death.
He'd brought his death onto their continent.
He'd lit the holocaust above Japan
And made the world look at its poisonous face.
They'd fail, and then she'd have to mourn their lives,
The Indian guilt a thread inside the white man's guilt.
The Indian always failed. The white man always won.
In failure, winning, there was too much shame.

She shivered from the cold and looked at Moon.
Wrapped in his Indian blanket, calm, just like
The other elders standing with her in the cold.
Beside him, in the dark, his wife kept touching him
As if he anchored her to both the dark and life.

At last the drums were silent. Stars spoke tongues so cold
Their ancient silence couldn't be undone.
The men and women in the Hall came out to night.
She stepped in front of them, their bravado and guns.
She tried to make them individual,
But all that she could see was darkness massed.

"You've got to stop. You'll only kill yourselves."

The mass of darkness shifted. Restless, filled
With warrior chants and ancient rage, it stared
At her, each pair of eyes a single eye.

"War's been declared," a voice said. "You can't stop us now."

The mass divided. In the dark and cold
It moved toward the waiting cars and trucks.
Legune began to sob. She felt her vulnerability.
She raged against the ancient rage, which boiled
Beneath the landscape, festering with sores.

Then she collapsed, her breathing ragged, pained.
She sighed so softly it seemed as if
She'd breathed a benediction on the night.
A death caused by a death: The second death
A rage against the rage that poured toward

The houses near the Reservation line.

The elders bent beside her in the dark
In agony at knowing age and death.

4

They passed the elders as a beast and poured
Into the trucks and cars that came from dark
Into the Legion Hall's dim front door light.
A mile down 47, Pete pulled in the drive
Of Manion's Place, the ranch style house that stood
The closest to the Reservation's borderline.
Heart wild, he hugged Beth, opened up the door,
And stood in snow as car doors slammed and men
And women gathered in the Manion's yard.
The lights went on inside the house. Pete waved.
Norm Davis then moved purposely toward the house.
He didn't knock, but shrieked, then kicked the door.
Young Farley Manion's face was pale with fear.

"You've got to get the wife and kids outside,"
Pete said, the door unhinged. "Or else they'll die."

The white man stared at him dumbfounded, stunned.
"You can't . . ." he started.

                    Beth moved angrily.
"Right now!" she said, her voice intense. "Or else you'll die!"

"It's cold outside," protested Farley, angry-brave.

"Then get into your car and drive downtown,"
Pete raged. "You've got to tell the Sheriff war's begun."

The white man turned. "Jill, Jill!" he called, voice shrill.

A pale, slim woman came into the living room,
Two bundled youngsters circled by her arms.
She handed Farley his down jacket, looked
At Beth with loathing, fear. The kids began to cry.

"Right now!" Pete threatened. "Hurry up or die!"

The small, white family stumbled through the door.

Pete turned to Norm. "The gasoline," he said.

Norm splashed the smelly gas around the room.
Pete tried to feel the spirits' hovering.
He wasn't sane, he knew. Their talk had made him mad.

He reached into his pocket, found a match. "Get out," he said.

Beth, Norm, the others turned. Pete heard the drums
Of Thunderbirds sing flame. They smiled at him.
He backed toward the door and threw the match.
The fire whooshed flames around the room. It licked
Toward the ceiling, popping, cracking, filled with song.

Pete turned his back on flames and ran outside.
His followers were cheering in the dark and cold.
"The war!" they sang. The truck backed up toward the road,
Red light reflecting on the white, cold snow.

Defeat of The Goddess

1

They came in groups all day: from Michigan,
Wisconsin, Minnesota, Illinois . . .
In trucks, cars, vans, jeeps, semis, every man
A white man victimized by government,
Their eyes all haunted, trapped, still bright with hope
Sent through the phone lines: "come to Tigerton.
Bill Winchell's gathering men armed against
The government, the banks, unfairness, men
Who represent the government, the banks
Who've stolen all our dreams, America."
"We'll make a stand," they said. "We'll wake America.
If Indians up in Gresham have the guts,
We white men have the guts. Come on to Tigerton."

At noon Bill opened up the cellars dug
A dozen years before and started handing out the guns
He'd bought from West Virginian thugs who'd stolen them.
As Sam helped move an anti-aircraft gun,
The horror of the weapons brought to light
Amazed his sense of what could really be.
How had the government allowed so many guns
To come into Bill Winchell's crazy hands?
What would the next dawn bring? The weapons made
Their enterprise more dangerous, Sam knew.
The FBI had shot it out with Gordon Call
For causes pale beside what Bill had planned.

All day tents, dirt latrines, and paths were built.
By dusk six hundred men had come to Tigerton.
Bill, Sam, and Lawrence kept on making calls.

"North Idaho will rise if we're attacked," Bill said.
"Then Maine, Nebraska, Florida, and Arkansas."
His eyes were bright with all he'd brought about.
"We'll rise, then fade away, then rise again."

The FBI seemed impotent. They had to know.
And still men came, by twos and threes, in trucks

And cars, a dozen at a time, an angry storm.

2

At midnight, tired, triumphant, Bill climbed stairs,
The hubbub of the army left behind.
He'd made his offering to God and watched
As smoke from wood and burning flesh rose straight,
Unwavering, into the winter sky.
He'd called for men with guts enough to build
An army; men had come; he'd given guns
To patriots he'd never known or met.
He knew he had to get some precious sleep.
He wouldn't get another chance — perhaps for days.
At dawn they'd move on Tigerton, declare
Their independence from America
And start the task of building heaven's earth.
God's Aryan nation would be born. The world
Would see the Christian goodness of the Lord.

He opened up his bedroom door and paused.
His room had disappeared. The outside trees,
Snow on their boughs, had come inside his room,
His walls, bed, clock, and chester-drawers gone.
Beneath a huge white pine, its branches thrown
Into a moonlit sky, stars large and bright,
The Goddess stood undressed, three feet from Bill,
Her eyes and womanhood bright promises.

Bill lost his dreams, his army, guns, and men,
The passion driving him toward his God.
Beside the Goddess, on the snow-cloaked earth,
Eight other women, dressed in smoky silks,
Sat watching Bill, each one so beautiful
She took Bill's breath away and made him faint.

"We meet at last," the Goddess said. She smiled.
Her voice sang of the earth, trees, flowers, early spring.

Bill felt the laughter deep inside his heart,
The days of joy renewing life as years turned past.
He saw a simpler life as men and women loved
Each other, kept the beauty, balance, living earth

223

And lived inside the limits of their lives,
Fertility entwined with nights of frenzied warmth
Engendered by two lovers in their bed.

Bill looked the Goddess up and down, his flesh
Aflame with wild desires and promises.
He longed to melt into the woman's arms.

But all the madness he had felt before was gone.
The smoke had risen straight and black to sky.
His years of talking, planning, dreaming neared
A climax powerful enough to shake the government
With men inspired by God's great mightiness.

"I've pledged myself to God," Bill said. "Not you."

The Goddess smiled. "You choose to sacrifice
A life upon the altar, celebrating death
Instead of life," she said. She opened arms
And stepped toward him, promising him joy.

"Why me?" he asked. "An advocate for God?"

She stopped and brushed her hand across her breasts.
Small nipples were as hard as passion's fire.
"You think you are an advocate of God?" she laughed.
"You think you'll die into your Jesse's arms?"

Bill found the anger he had lost and stoked
It as he fought against desire and need.
"I am a prophet of the Lord," he said.
"You're nothing but a hag, illusion dressed
In woman's flesh, the enemy of God!"

She shook her head, her ice-white hair, earth-eyes
So bright they made Bill flinch toward the door.

"I'll die again," she said. "Just like before, I'll die."

The women on the ground began to laugh.
The Goddess smiled. Mists, brown and heavy, rose
As all the seated women rose and swirled their silks,
Diaphanous, and started dancing dances long

Forgotten by the women of the earth.
In Viet Nam the soldiers, women, children died
As Bill watched Agent Orange drift down on trees.
In South Korea soldiers died as women wept.
And in Japan, the trees, men, women, children died
As light exploded on the earth, and death
Swept on the winds swirled from the great, white cloud,
The Father, God of progress, Western man.
Wars drifted past Bill's eyes, an endless march;
The women, then the Goddess danced, their arms
And legs, earth-eyes, alive amidst man's pain.
The earth's trees died, renewed themselves, then died
As axes, dynamite, machines denuded earth.

And then the dance was done; the Goddess gone.
Bill stood alone inside his room, the bed
Against the wall beside the elm nightstand.
At dawn he'd lead the move on Tigerton.
He wasn't mad. He'd made the Goddess die.
He'd never hear the trees again or see them march.
He wouldn't fail like Gordon Call had failed.
He'd killed a fatted calf, and God had drawn
The smoke straight up into the winter sky.

Kim's Vision

Kim saw the ghosts and felt the pounding drums
And saw and felt the universe on edge,
A shimmering between what was, was not,
The past and future intermixed, alive.

He'd slipped out from the basement when he'd felt
The coldness of ghost-ridden winds across his skin.
He'd moved away from Marsha's warmth, alive
To rhythms he had never felt, and went upstairs.
And then he'd seen them in the halls, magnificent,
As soft and bright as sun before the dawn.
They moved through darkness tall and proud, eyes glittering,
Hair streaming backward in the unfelt wind,
With knowledge born of star-stuff, afterlife.

And then he saw a stumbling Sitting Crow
Rush through them, blind, cold terror in his heart.
The ghosts kept struggling with human speech.
Their lips kept moving soundlessly. Hands moved,
But every word and gesture swept away
Into the soundless wind, the ghostly light.

And then he heard the drums. Not ghostly drums,
But real drums, their song a wailing scream
Against the white man and his endless wrongs,
Against the Indian and his failures to adjust
And change enough to meet the white man's threat.

Kim walked into the stream of ghosts and light.
One ghost perceived his presence as they streamed
Toward the spirit-starved, emaciated Sitting Crow.
Kim didn't feel afraid. He felt the drums
And felt their power as they spoke of war
And dreams of new beginnings on the earth.

Then, as the drums sang deep with bitterness,
He stopped. White Rabbit's dead, he told himself.
And as the knowledge froze into his brain,
At just fourteen, a wild man brave as Sitting Bull,
He saw a Thunderbird, bald head, eyes night,

As powerful and beautiful as dawn
That's broken red above the great white pines.
Kim stopped, saw eyes that knew the history
Of all the varied peoples on the earth,
And let the ghost wind flow away from him.
The Thunderbird was dressed with northern lights
Which ebbed and surged in endless pulses rocked
Into the ecstasy of human love.

And then the universe was split apart.
The terror raved and howled inside the death storm.
The Indians killed and died; the white men killed and died,
And all the universe of time became a battleground.

The Thunderbird looked deep through Kim's scared eyes.
"Your brothers and your sisters dance," he said.

Kim tried to find a thread of sanity
Inside the howling, in the Thunderbird's night eyes.
He felt unkeeled. I am the macho man,
He told himself, the fool who'll run so fast
He'll cross Wolf rapids free from water's touch.
I am the macho man, the macho man.

"Look here," the Thunderbird said reasonably.
"You got a handicap? I spoke to you."

A wolf howled hungrily at unseen prey.
Kim heard the wolf and heard the Thunderbird.
He felt the horror in the nothingness of Sitting Crow.
He saw a dancing, singing, naked man
Inside the Thunderbird's great spirit-world.
The Thunderbirds were smiling, glad to see the man.

"What do you want?" Kim asked the Thunderbird.

The Thunderbird smiled with a rainbow's light.
"We've granted war again," he said. "We've seen
The pain our people feel; we've granted war."
He paused. The northern lights clothed spirit-light.
"But nothing's changed," he said. "Your people asked,
And then we granted what they asked of us.
They'll have the courage of a million men.

But still, there is the white man, born, then raised
On father's milk, not mother's milk, their fire
A subjugation of the Mother Earth."

"I still don't understand," Kim said, afraid.

"The ghosts all know," the Thunderbird said brightly, sad.
"They try to force their words past death's tight throat.
They care about the people that they were,
The generations birthed through nights of sexual love.
They care about the living of our Mother Earth."

Kim felt the earth become a freezing void.
He saw the felling of the forests, smoke
Above the land, the blackening of sun.

"All plants and animals derive
Their lifesap from the sun," White Rabbit sang.
Kim saw him running. "Hate destroys the world."

Kim saw the deer starve as the winter raged
Across a birdless earth that knew no spring.
He saw the earth's great cities die, a rage
So great that desperation was a spear.
The children, with their bellies huge from coming death.
Stayed huddled in their homes, afraid, insensible.

Kim's pulse was pounding in his ears, his heart.
I am the macho man, he told himself,
Then stopped the inner chant he had begun.

He saw the rising of an army made of whites
And heard the madness in the leader's voice.
He saw the war, the Indians burning homes,
White rage against the way their lives had changed,
The helicopters, tanks that moved relentlessly.

And then he saw the white men and the Indians die.
He saw them sprawled upon a battlefield,
Their faces dull with death, their tongues bright black.
The city lights went out. The people died.
The great White Bear, the shouldered world,
Gasped hard for breath, legs trembling, earth cold.

The earth was dead, was ending, void.
The White Bear kept on laboring, heart-large,
To keep alive the life that was already dead.

White Rabbit's dead, the drums said. Dead. His heritage
Is death. Our heritage is death. He's dead.

Kim wasn't macho, wasn't real, was cold.

"We've granted war," the Thunderbird said calmly.
"We shouldn't have. We feel the pain our people feel."

Kim saw he wasn't macho, wasn't man.
He was a child. He wasn't old enough
To see the ghosts or talk to Thunderbirds.

"Why me?" he asked. His question rumbled like
An echo through the centuries of man.

"There's not much time," the Thunderbird said solemnly.

The Thunderbird's bright lights surged, blinding Kim.
Infinity stretched endlessly inside his dark.

The Thunderbird, the ghosts were gone. He was afraid.
He felt the dancing madness Sitting Crow
Had wrapped around black feathers quilled into his heart.
Kim had to move. He had to stop the war.

He cried into the emptiness, "What can I do?"

The Flames

John got the call at home, the miracle
Of married love the strength of who he was.
The visions, specters, angels, demons, chants
Of hollow men and rat's feet all had disappeared.
His world was still the same. Small farmers farmed,
Small sawmills, manufacturers still sold their wares,
And even though the Warriors stayed entrenched,
The Rajah fumed with mystic chants and songs,
And Winchell raged inside his maddened world,
John still had Jane and love, normality.

"You'd better come in quick," Trish said, voice weak.

"Right now?" he asked. "More trouble? Sitting Crow?"
He waited while Trish tried to judge if he should know
The hell he had to face before he left the house.

"Right now," she said at last. "And don't delay."

A pleading filled her words. He winced to feel
The calmness he had gained begin to dissipate.

Jane watched him as he hung the phone up, turned.
"I'll wait," she said, voice soft as late spring rains.
"I'll be here when you're done and come back home."

John looked at her, his wondrous wife, and smiled.
Inside their bed she'd looked as beautiful
As she had looked inside the Lutheran church.
He heard the wings again, soft, muffled drums
Inside his head, their dark untouchable.

"I know," he said. "I've learned and won't forget."

He turned again and walked outside. Drums, wings
Were louder in the night. His sanity was gone.

2

John held wraiths back by driving angrily.
He felt eyes, bright as small suns, blazing in his head.
His wife stood dressed in white before the altar, love
A shining in her eyes, the glory of the Lord.

He parked the squad and walked into the jail.
Jill, Farley Manion sat beside his desk with Trish,
Their faces hollow with the pain they felt.
John looked into their haunted eyes and asked,
"What's wrong?" The carpenter who'd built his house,
Who'd spent each summer night upon the task,
Looked hollow, like the demons haunting John.

"The Warriors burned our house," he said. "They said
To tell you that White Rabbit's War's begun."

John looked at Farley. Jill began to sob.
John heard the drums. White Rabbit's dead, they said.
"I know that Sitting Crow's still in the Novitiate,"
He said. "The Warriors couldn't burn your house.
I've got three hundred men surrounding them."

Fierce anger burned in Farley's eyes. He held his breath.
"The whole damned tribe's at war," he said. "They've got
Their guns and torches; whites have got Cain's mark,
And now it's us or them. We'll die or else they'll die."

John looked at Trish and tried to ask for Thorn.
The chances for a peace were dwindling.
John felt as ill as he had ever felt before.
He felt the pistol barrel in his mouth,
Its odd metallic taste and rounded shape.

"They told you that they'd gone to war?" he asked.

"We live the closest to the Reservation line,"
Jill said. "We were the first, but while you sit
There's other white's besieged. Pete Wilson's leading them.
They've gone to war; you've got to stop them now."

John looked into the white man's frightened eyes.

———
231

He tried to hold on to the vision of his wife,
But drums were singing to the sweep of wings
That made the sky outside alive with birds.
He couldn't lose his sanity. He had to act.

"You're right," he said to Jill. "The time has come
To end this whole, god-awful mess for good."

What could he do? He turned and walked outside.
The demons danced for joy to see him come.
They lifted wings, scratched the air. Mule guts steamed white.
John shook his head and drove toward Hard Maple Hill.
He had to stop the madness, had to end
The hatred burning down the dream, America.

3

He saw the flames against the morning sky.
He pulled the squad onto the shoulder, parked,
And sat in silence as he watched the distant fires.
At last he reached toward the radio.
"Burt, Burt," he said. "You there?"

                                        "I'm here," Burt said.

"You've got to listen carefully," John said.
"The radicals that occupied the Legion Hall
Have gone to war. They're burning houses down.
It looks to me as if they'll cross the bridge
On County A and work toward the Novitiate."

A silence stretched between his words and Burt's response.
John saw the big white man beside the barn,
His mike in hand, his thought as careful as a child's.

"I understand," he said at last.

                        John nodded to himself.
"Then move the men around the barn," he said.
"Prepare to face a fire fight with a band
Of Warriors several hundred strong. And Burt?"

"I'm listening," Burt said.

"Be careful, please.
Hold on, but try to hesitate to fire.
We've lost one Indian; other dead won't help bring peace."

"I understand," Burt said, voice shocked. "I'm . . . signing off."

John sat inside the morning's silence in the squad.
The demons sang of horrors born before time's birth.
He closed his eyes and saw the dead at Wounded Knee,
The faces of the Cherokee upon the trail of tears,
The Long Walk nightmare of the Navajo.
He was a white man, guilty of his heritage.

What could he do? The world had lost its sense.
He gnawed the question's fire inside his mind
And watched the houses burn against the sky.
He picked the mike up once again. "Trish? Trish?"

"I'm here," Trish said.

                        "Get me the Governor,"
John said. "It's time he called the National Guard."

Trish heard the pain burned in his voice. He'd failed.
He had to act; that's where salvation was.

Creation

Inside his room the Rajah tried to find
His sense of oneness with the universe.
For days he'd raged with god-fire in his self.
First, fires had led to breakthroughs in his quest
To meld his spirit deep in universal flows
Of atoms, quarks, and other building blocks.
He now felt acids etched indelibly
Into the spiritual peace he'd always craved,
His anger dark with self-defeating hate.

He'd found Celest. He looked into himself
And saw the enemies that lurked in love.
He felt the river of the universe,
The flowing particles that were, were not —
But buried in the flow was rage, and rage
Against Jim Speltz was driving Ron, the friend
Who'd made the honorific, Rajah, real, away.

Celest was like a fading dream, he thought.
He hadn't ever really known her well.
She'd just been like his other followers,
Devout, well mannered, careful in her fasts,
And so devoted she had often made him smile.
Her body had been lean and hard and filled
With love and spirit, holy fires and verve.
And now she was his passion, symbol of the fools
Who'd wanted him destroyed. He wouldn't bend.
Truth flowed much stronger than the fools who sought,
In every land, to bend it to their whims.
But still, he couldn't seem to find his way
Past all the black despairs that plagued his days.

The words of men who plan revolt are all confused,
He told himself. The words of men who know
The doubts inside their heart are justified.
Excited men use many useless words.
The slanderers of good men hide their spite
In words that never show their substance plain.
The words of men who have no reference point
Are twisted, making all the world appear askew.

He stood up from his squat upon the floor.
He wasn't calm, he knew. He saw the minister
Inside the Methodist's brick church rise up
In rage and then collapse into his trance,
The fire of angels on the altar dazing him.
The Rajah needed peace. The Sheriff's impotence
Was caused by rebels holed up with their guns
Inside the Novitiate just seven miles away.
The man had made a prison for himself,
His fear of all the life he knew imploding like
A dying star, the Christian stake inside his heart.
The Rajah had to free Celest himself.
Then everything would be all right.
He'd start to teach again. His black despair would die.
He'd feel again the glory of his life,
The dancing of the energies of light
That moved like rivers moved, slow, fast, light, strong . . .

The children's screaming broke his reverie.
Sweat beaded on his face. His enemies!

He tried to move. A rifle barked of death.
He'd known he'd be a martyr to his cause.
He felt the calm spread outward from his inner self.
His door caved off its hinges, crashing to the floor.
A long-haired Indian stared at him with hate.

"Outside!" the Indian barked.

                    The Rajah stared.
An Indian? He had never had a convert once.
He met the Indian's stare, then went to get his coat.
The Indian didn't move. He stood as tense
As snakes about to strike their venom into blood.
The Rajah put his coat on, walked into the hall.
He stared at Indians moving through the house.
He walked outside. The moon was shining full.
The children, men, and women of his house
Were huddled close together in the cold.
Surrounding them the Indians held their guns
Against their chests, their eyes intense with rage.

The Rajah joined his people, felt their warmth

As he became a part of them, their mass.
He'd never felt so calm. He emanated peace
Into their fear; their sobbing quieted.
He turned. Toward the Reservation's borderline
Three houses were ablaze with ghost-like light.
Inside his house a fire was licking walls
As heavy smoke poured out of windows, black
And billowing toward the round, bright moon.

"Come on!" a voice demanded from the dark.

The Indians turned and ran into the night.
Car engines roared. They drove toward the Novitiate.
The fire broke through the compound's slanted roof,
It's roaring throwing heat and light at dark.

The Rajah stared in fascination at the flames.
He felt like running straight into the blazing heat.
He felt like dancing naked in the flames!

He screamed then, fought against strong hands and arms.
He broke free from his followers and ran to flames.
The universe was orange and roaring, hot as hell.
In ecstasy the Rajah fell down on his knees.
He sobbed to feel the miracle of melting snow.
He lifted arms and sang creation's life.

The universe was bitter on the tongue.
It melted flesh and bones and blended soil
Into the humanness that called itself a soul.

Inside the flames he saw the Universe . . .
As man, its dancing interweaving fate
And chance into Creation, blinding eyes
With light so bright it scorched into the soul.
It made all men one Man, a thumping heart
That beat and beat across the ages, calm,
Magnificent in war and peace, a fire
That licked away its home until it lived
Amidst the splendor of the fiery stars.

He was the prophet, Rajah, Chosen One of God.

The wall in front of him collapsed. Sparks blazed
A river made of fire into the sky.
He sobbed. Ron Zukalov was dragging him
Away from light, heat, flames, and roaring sound.

He wept to lose his dancing universe.

What Made The Sun
As Black As Sackcloth Hair[86]

Thorn sat beside his window, gun in hand,
And watched the night slip silently into the sky.
Twelve hours ago he'd been a deputy.
He'd been an Indian white man in his heart.
He'd worn a gun to keep the white man's peace
And worn the white man's badge to symbolize
The justice that the white man meted out.

But now he was a radical. He'd woken up
That morning unaware of earthquakes in his self.
He'd gone to work as usual, unaware
Of sunlight turning black as sackcloth hair.
He'd seen John Israel's vision in the church
And felt the celebration when his Aunt
Waved bread before the white man's cameras, proud
Of who she was and of the mission he'd opposed.

But when the moon and stars turned red as blood,
Their prophecy as tremulous as shrieking winds,
He'd changed inside himself, became a man
Enraged at all the long injustices
Heaped dark upon the bones of Indian lives,
And though he'd wondered at the change
And let it gnaw its queasiness into his guts,
He knew the change prevailed. He was a radical.

The white man's life was not his life. He sat
Inside the night and felt it's quivering.
The gun he'd taken from the white man touched
The dark with promises of violent change.

When he had walked away from John, he'd felt
The white man's guns in hands that flexed, unflexed.
White Rabbit's death had loosed the song of death,
And men were tense with cold and weariness
And nights of facing Indian guns and Indian hate.
He'd felt the guns in hands that longed to shoot.

And then, inside doors, safe from the white man's guns,

He'd faced suspicious Indians. He was red
Outside and white inside. He'd been a deputy.
He'd asked to talk to Sitting Crow, but Horse
Had looked into his eyes and spirit heart,
And when he'd seen, he'd said that Sitting Crow
Was in the spirit world and couldn't leave.
Thorn looked at Horse as if he'd gone insane
While Indian feelings stirred beneath his skin.

How could it be? The spirit world alive?

Thorn wove his courage strong enough to face
The dancing specter, death, and prayed to ghosts
That wanted honor in this hour of change.
He knew that Sitting Crow was in a trance.
He felt the coldness left by ghosts that once
Had passed through halls which once had known the holiness
Of Christian monks who'd dedicated lives
To celebrating glories of their God.

And as he weaved, he wondered why he'd changed,
What made the sun as black as sackcloth hair —
And as he wondered, fiery orange licked at the night.
The Reservation radicals had loosed
Ancestral memories of hate and rage.
He felt the Thunderbirds and heard their talk.
They tried to understand the white man's mind.
What would the white man do? What would he do?
Could Indians and their spirits stand the rage
Of power woven in the white man's heart?

And as Thorn saw the burning in his mind
And saw the shivering of families forced
Into the night and bitter winter cold,
He started crying.

                    Indian women sprawled
In death at Wounded Knee a hundred years ago.
The white man marched victorious upon the earth,
The sacred earth, the Mother Earth, of Indian graves.

And now the warriors with their spirits marched.

White women sprawled in death inside his mind.
Great Indian warriors died. Great white men died:
The Indian/white dilemma red as blood.

He'd been a deputy, the white man's friend.
He'd felt the Thunderbirds and saw the face
Of Sitting Crow caught, whorling, deep in trance.

And now he was a radical. A radical.

Ghosts

Celest stared out the window at the ghosts.
She'd seen them all before. Solidity against
Night darkness anchored her to earth as wings
Pulled flesh out of the hunger pangs of fasts.
And now ghosts flitted past the windowpanes,
Hair long and black, eyes dark, skin dark, mouths round.

She groaned. She felt disoriented, plagued
By arguments against the Rajah so persistent
They buzzed inside her head all day and night.
Her father was a devil dressed in human clothes.
And Trent? A man without remorse or doubt
Who turned her thought and feelings round and round.

But what was right? The fasts the Rajah preached?
A freedom trumpeted by Trent? Her father's lies?
She'd smelled her father's breath each time he'd gone
And run away to drink in Gresham at Pete's Bar.
She knew the truth. Trent never left the house.
He never let her father's drunkenness go wild.

The ghosts lit torches outside the windowpanes.
They shouted, danced, and whirled like dervishes.
They'd burn the house, she knew. The flames would lick,
And then she'd have to face her choices: Death
By flame; escape into the safety of the Rajah's truth.

What would her children say?

                          Outside the ghosts
Had started breaking glass and throwing fire.
Smoke crept across the floor to touch her flesh.

Trent Warren, looking like a ghost himself,
Cloaked black with smoke, eyes white with fear,
Came running frantically into her room.
She stared at him, detached, disoriented by
The arguments and counter arguments.
A devil-god, he'd save her life, then take her life.

She laughed out-loud. A ghost came through the windowpane.
Trent turned away from her as smoke joined flame.
"We're not the god damned white man!" cursed the ghost.
"You won't die here. Come on!"

                                    He jerked her to her feet.
She smiled. The ghost had hurt her arm. It ached.

The Indian pushed her out the window into night.
She wondered where her hidden father was.
Perhaps the ghosts had haunted him away
From her forever, loosing him from life.
The Rajah hadn't come. He hadn't come.

The ghosts had saved her. Not the Rajah. Not
Her father. Not Trent Warren. Just the ghosts.

The Song, The Dance

1

Kim felt the song possessing Sitting Crow.
It feathered, like an echo, like deep roots,
Into the shaman's heart, heart muscles clenched,
Unclenched into the ancient song of life.
Kim was the macho man, the falcon man.
He'd sung the song creation sang to make
The fullness of the universe's tiers.

But he was still a boy. He felt that truth,
Unwanted, setting like a cold, hard stone.
A god had given him a mission men
Would be afraid to undertake. But why?
Why should he be afraid? Why hesitate?

He stopped outside the dining hall's closed door.
The song was strong enough to blind him; strange enough
To make his feet move mindlessly in dance.
He heard the drums of war. White Rabbit's dead,
They said. He's dead. Kim saw the Warriors, blind
From all the rage their race had felt for whites.
Blood flowed in rivers down to distant seas:
Kim's people's blood, the white man's blood, the world.
The Thunderbirds danced in their spirit-world
And wept to see the pain and suffering.
The white man's God stared angrily upon His earth.

Kim walked into the dining hall, then stopped.
The song was power. Feather quills drove deep:
The yellow beak, the black-hole eyes, the ebony
Of feathers covering the humanness of Sitting Crow.
White Rabbit's dead, the drums said. Dead.
We'll fashion justice out of blood and death.

The warrior-shaman danced inside the storm.
He'd woken out of sleep and moved in dance,
The song a dream that rose from sleep, a ghost
Who'd taken on the flesh and bones of life.
The crow's heart throbbed inside the crow's white skeleton.

243

Kim felt the heart. He felt the heartbeat pulse.
A Thunderbird, bald head, eyes black as night,
Looked deep into Kim's eyes. The Thunderbird
Smiled calmly. "We have granted war," it said.
"We shouldn't have, but we can feel your pain."
He saw the flames danced light in winter dark.

2

Exhausted, Lena woke with Sitting Crow.
His face was drawn from pain, the hours entranced.

"It's time," he said. "The war's begun."

                                    He moved
His left foot, then his right foot. Warriors woke.
Sleep left their bodies. Drumbeats pounded flesh.
They tried to grasp the way they felt. They stared.
The power of his dance throbbed deep in hearts.
They longed to join a field of skeletons
Alive to all the power made by Sitting Crow.
They couldn't think. They couldn't feel. They moved
From sleep into the dance and couldn't stop.

"Ay yie! Ay yie! My heart is full. Is full,"
Sang Sitting Crow. "All history trails blood.
I've met with ghosts; we've met with ghosts. I dance;
We dance the dance of death, of unseen winds!"

As Lena watched her lover's faltering
She saw her mother by the fire, flames orange,
And in the flames she saw a dozen homes afire.
Her brothers, sisters danced around the fires they'd made.
They'd had enough. They wouldn't let the white man sleep.
She saw them dancing in the spirit world,
The Thunderbirds beside them as they talked
About the power of the war to come.
She saw the Thunderbirds, despairing, filled
With laughter as a naked warrior danced.
Inside her mother's death-cold eyes, death stood.
He tossed a skull into the air, and cold
Inside the flames, began to sing:

"In youth when I did love, did love,
Methought it was very sweet . . ."[87]

                                        Time whipped
Its tail and shook the gravities of time and space.
Without a thought, without care, Lena moved,
With grace, into the dance that Sitting Crow had made.

He stared at her, his crow eyes black with time.
He tried to make her stop. He tried to stop.
The death storm howled and raged as lightning struck
And flames leapt up and ate the white man's homes.
White Rabbit stood before him, mute, words torn.
The ghost said there was pain in martyrdom.
He'd tried to tell him that he shouldn't make
The dance, the song, the power that he'd made.
The world was burning. As it burned, it burned
The people that he burned to serve. He danced.

The other warriors, Superstar and Horse,
A fierce, crazed Wanda, moved their feet with grace.
Time eddied, whorled as death whorled, eddied, sang.

3

The dancing warriors didn't look at Kim.
The mesmerizing song had captured them.
Kim fought the grim seduction of the song.
He moved toward the dancing Sitting Crow.
In front of Sitting Crow, her black eyes locked
Into her dancing lover's eyes, was Lena, lost,
Her movements matching every move of Sitting Crow's.

As Kim kept struggling against the song,
He felt the end of time, of life on earth.
The heaviness upon the White Bear's back
Grew heavier than stars collapsed into themselves.
Death was a stain that started at the Legion Hall,
Then spread into Keshena, death
A string of flame that made the white man mad.

What could he do? He was the macho man.
The Thunderbird with northern lights, eyes bright

As sunlight on a sweltering August day,
Looked at him filled with sadness, hope, despair.
What could he do? He had to weave to where
Both Sitting Crow and Lena sang and danced.
He couldn't let the song entrance his melody.
He had to walk up to his hero, Sitting Crow,
And ask him if he'd stop the spell he'd made.

He didn't dance. He didn't walk. He let
The drumbeats help him weave through warriors trapped.
He stood before the shaman as he danced.

"You know you have to stop," Kim said. "The ghosts
Have told you. Thunderbirds have sent me here.
I'm just a boy. The world can't end in war!"

4

Inside the dance, the crow's mask on his face,
His feet a shuffling music on the floor,
His heart, the crow's heart fused with membrane made
Of blood and muscle, Sitting Crow looked out
At Kim and Lena and the warriors locked
Into the dance he danced, the song his being sang.
He didn't want to see the children die.
He hadn't meant to wake into the song
He'd woven deep beneath his consciousness.
He heard White Rabbit's anguished cry as he,
The living shaman, wrenched himself away
From what the shaman newly dead had tried
To tell him from the coldness of his bier.

He hated deeply in the way he danced.
But still, before his eyes danced visions of the world
Before the white man came, the struggles borne
By generations of his people as they lived
Their lives in sovereignty of who they were.
They'd celebrated, grieved, loved, hated, hoped
As season flowed from fall to winter, spring,
And summer, Mother Earth, Great Spirit, men
And women fused into a single life.

He felt the snake inside him, felt the dark

246

That writhed and twisted at the jumbled world.
He heard the words that Kim had said: "You have to stop.
The ghosts have told you." Lena stared at him.
He couldn't stand the thought of ever losing her.
He tried to see into his song, his dance.
The weave of history, emotions strong, born
Of dreams denied, of suffering and pain,
Were shuttled back and forth by women's looms,
The new-made cloth a cloth of winter night.

He was a shaman, warrior, prophet, man!
He had the force to change all history!
He danced and danced and sang and sang and sang.
Kim's friends stood, stunned, inside the dining hall.
He tried to see into the children's thoughts
Beneath the song-thought of his followers,
But all he saw was endless yards of cloth
That interwove grim darkness with the blood of flames.

What made the universe? The right of right?

He had to stop, unweave the weave, undance.
He loved too much to cause a holocaust.
The ghosts had tried to make him understand
That death was not a noble end — each man,
The chiefs and shamans, warriors, women, men,
And children, all would die. No martyrdom
Could ever solve the problems plaguing men.

He stared at Kim. Kim saw the pain in Sitting Crow,
But didn't understand the meaning in his eyes.

5

When Lena saw the change in Sitting Crow,
The way he looked at Kim, she felt her heart
Expand beyond the song and dance she danced.
She saw that Sitting Crow was locked into the song.
Hope flamed into her sense of hopelessness.
He couldn't end the song, but he had changed.
He wanted life, she saw. He wanted life!

She longed to touch the haggard face,

But in her blood the drumbeats sang their song.
Keshena's warriors danced about a burning house.
She longed to hold her lover in her arms.

She moved her feet in rhythm to a beat
Not woven by the song or dance she danced.
A frantic Sitting Crow stared at her face.
The drumbeat strengthened, faded. Dance of love.
With effort, Sitting Crow slowed down the song
And mimicked Lena's moves. The death storm howled.
The Indians killed, died; white men killed and died.
As Lena sang her love of Sitting Crow,
The song dissolved into a chant of joy.
The song and dance, alive outside the hall,
Was dying at its heart. As Sitting Crow
Slowed down he felt the joy of love — of being him:
The shaman, warrior, prophet, lover, man.

The Fire Of God On Cedar Street

1

Bill woke. He sat up in the dark, sleep lingering.
He looked into Sam Ludwig's German face.
"It's time?" he asked.

                     Sam shook his head. "Not yet,"
He said. "It's only three o'clock. There's other news.
The farmers living near Menominee
Say fires are burning near the reservation line.
The Indians claim they've started up a war."

The information percolated inside Bill's brain.
"It's started then," he said. He looked outside.
No Goddess lurked inside the night-dark trees.
His life had culminated, drawn onto this peak.
"We'll move on Tigerton at five. We'll take the town."

Sam hesitated, feeling madness burned
Into the man who sat up in his bed.
"You're sure?" he asked the madman in the bed.

Bill closed his eyes. He gathered in himself,
Each thought, each breath a wandering fire.
He saw the Goddess, nude beneath the pines
Inside his bedroom, tempting, beautiful.
"At five," he whispered. "Start to rouse the men."

Sam smiled. He'd had his chance to stop the craziness.
He couldn't turn back now. He'd wipe the smile
From Chad LeConne's inhuman, banker's face.
"At five," he said. "I'll tell the men."

                     Bill radiated force
Into the universe and felt the turning wheel
That crushed complacent lives and changed the world.

2

Outside the seven hundred men who'd come

Began the task of taking Tigerton.
Campfires were lit as breakfast coffee boiled.
They'd come all night, and now, excited, filled with zeal,
They'd got their orders: "Move. We're seizing Tigerton!"

Bill dressed, climbed down the stairs, and went outside.
Sam turned a floodlight on and covered Bill with light.

Bill felt the power coiled inside his men
And reveled in his sense of manic strength.
He waited for the crowd to grow immense,
Then took the bullhorn held by Lawrence Staub.
"We'll end this government! This awful farce
Of ruining common people's lives to benefit
The niggers, Jews, and kikes! We'll end it now!
And make God's kingdom live upon the earth!"

The roar of voices washed into Bill's blood
And made it sing with victories to come.

"We'll be God fearing, decent men,"
He said. "We won't dishonor those we love
Or battle anyone who doesn't mean us harm."
He paused, his grin surreal in artificial light.
"But if the government decides on war,
Let us, this little band of men, begin."

The roar swept through him once again. He laughed.
The crowd before him in the winter dark
Moved like a dark, huge beast upon the snow.

"From here our voices will be heard!" he screamed.
"From here! This time! This place! These men! These hearts!"

Bill reached out, touched hands that reached for him,
The power of his words an aphrodisiac.

"To war my gentle men!" he shouted. "Off to war!"

He glanced at Sam and laughed to see how dour
The German farmer looked. Bill walked toward
The jeep he'd drive to enter Tigerton.

3

Inside his truck with Lawrence Staub, Sam felt
His fear as waves that washed across his heart.
His mouth was dry and tasted sour as miles
Between the bar and Tigerton slipped past.
He tried to think about how other men
Who'd fostered revolution in America
Had felt when they had found themselves upon the brink
Of treason: Paul Revere, Sam Adams, Thomas Paine,
The names ingrained into the country's history.
He tried to feel the fire that they had felt
And tried to burn with high ideals and firm resolve.
He was his Leader's chief lieutenant,
The revolution's strong right arm, its heart.
But all he felt was fear and grim resolve.
He crossed a bridge and stopped on 45.[88]
Two hundred cars, jeeps, trucks, campers strung
Behind him in the early morning dark.

He saw Rose sitting at their kitchen table, dreams
About their life together scattered shards.
He felt her fear, the certainty of tragedy.
He loved his wife. He yearned to turn the truck,
But just behind him, eyes aflame with victory,
Fred Darrow, Franklin Timmers, young Steve Newt,
The men he'd sworn allegiance to, his friends,
Were following his lead into this dawn.

He opened up the truck door, flinched at cold.
They'd listened to the words Bill Winchell had said
And now were rooted in their consequence.
The rumble of the war planes overhead
Reverberated through Sam's consciousness.
He felt the loud percussion of the bombs,
The wreckage of the buses, cars, and trucks
Drove by Iraqis as they tried to flee.
Akimboed, stinking bodies in their trucks,
The great Oil War a desert memory
Flashed through the dark as if the huge night sky
Had turned into a television screen.[89]

He walked to Steve Newt's Plymouth. Steve grinned, laughed.

Sam didn't smile.

       "You block off 45,"
Sam said. "We're going on to town."

            Steve winked.

"Sure thing. Sam?" Steve asked softly. Sam stopped, frowned.
"Good luck," Steve said. "Take care."

           "You too," Sam said.
Bombs flared inside his chest, the morning dark.

4

Bill felt triumphant at the dawn's first light.
He sat inside the jeep he'd driven from the bar
And felt like Washington, "The World Turned Upside Down,"[90]
As British soldiers marched to their defeat.
He felt the fire of God on Cedar Street,
Because the fire of the Lord[91] burned among them.
His *citie* wouldn't be an urban place.
His people would be rural, men of land,
Who'd build white houses, bright red barns, and sheds.
Upon the street he saw the fields of oats.
Men worked the fields without their shirts;
Long scythes swept through the fields of gold.
At noon the women came with baskets filled
With fruit, sandwiches, water, homemade bread.
Machines would end their rein inside his land.
The time when labor made the man would come,
And in the holy churches, white with spires,
White congregations would praise God, their Lord.
The vision shined inside his head, a sun.

His men fanned out like wraiths into the streets
Around the downtown district, guns in hand.
Bewildered citizens awoke to find their town
Was occupied by men and women bearing arms.
Some tried to argue with the occupying force,
But most stayed in their homes and kept away
From all the hate and fear that stalked their streets.
They found their phones were dead. They were alone,

The victims of an occupying force.

Bill parked in front of First Bank, spirit burned
With joy and victory. He was the man.

He smiled and picked his axe from off the seat
And opened up the jeep door feeling good.
He walked up to the bank's glass door and swung.
The axe-head shattered glass. His men, parked down
The length of Cedar Street, cheered as glass broke.
Alarms rang out into the dawn. Bill grinned.
He was the man! He'd taken Tigerton!
The government was still asleep and didn't know,
But soon, inside the hour, the world would know.
He'd made a holy war. Now niggers, Jews,
Mad Israel would have to deal with fires he'd loosed
While Indians burned down houses in their rage.

Sam Ludwig stood beside him by the bank.
Alarms kept shrilling at the starting day.
Bill grabbed Sam's gun and shot into the air,
The sound so pure it reached the ears of God.
His men went wild. They raised their guns and fired.
They hollered, shrieked, and celebrated him.

He turned and walked into the empty bank.
His men would rise as one and stop the rot
From eating at the nation's God-true heart.

The Death Song's Continuing

1

Cold, homeless families stood outside the ring
Of heat their homes cast off, their faces dazed.
John worked the radio, his information stream
The trigger for the ambulances, squads,
And fire trucks drawn from Green Bay, Clintonville,
The towns within a two-hour drive of Shawano's roads.

At first he'd tried to find the radicals,
Intending, like a hero in a comic book,
To stop the wilding pain that burned in winter fields.
But then he'd moved toward the source of storm.
If anyone could stop the pain it was the man
Left sitting in the cold Novitiate
While other Indian leaders seared the land.
John couldn't stop the radicals until the state
Had mobilized the National Guard's full strength,
But he could end the gesture Sitting Crow
Had made to start the storm. He had the men,
And now, in spite of Thorn, he had the will.

He passed another farmhouse burning red.
He felt as fierce and angry as a wounded bear.

2

As Lena watched him, Sitting Crow unwound,
Stretched like a bird still wet from birth, untranced.

"What now?" she asked, her world compressed.
His eyes oblivious, he looked at her.

"The death dance still goes on," he said. "We've stopped,
But still it sings its way into the world."

"The song is making people die?" Kim asked.

The Warrior Shaman stretched his arms like wings
And tried to shake the blackness from his heart.

254

"It sings; it brings about the circumstance
Where death can live. It is a death song, death dance, cause . . ."

"How can we stop it then?" Kim asked. "Its birth was here.
That's what the Thunderbird came here to say."

The great black crow looked troubled as he thought.
The death storm raged, its force a part of who he was.
"I wish I knew," he whispered. "I'm alive."
He looked at Lena's eyes. "I want to stay alive."

The joy that Lena felt exploded with the words.
"We'll live," she softly said. "You want to live,
So no one here will die."

                        He looked at her,
Eyes distant from the journeys he had made.
"The white men's houses burn into the dawn.
Death isn't through with us. The song sings on."

"You wanted me to take the kids away,"
She said. "We'll leave together. Now. We'll leave the ghosts."

A bitterness welled up into his throat.
He heard the drums and felt the movement of the dance.
Fire licked its way into the sky, its flames a gut
That sucked away the comfort of a roof
And let the winter cold seep bitterly
Into the smoldering of white man ruins.
"It's not that simple locked in here," he said.
"We're outlaws occupying property.
We stay the course or face a life in jail."

A shaky Superstar sat down by Kim.
He looked as white as any white man's face.
"It's time to talk to Thorn," he said. "He knows
The white man's law. He'll get us out of here."

Hope flared in Lena's breast. The deputy!
She looked at Sitting Crow. He frowned, then sighed.
He looked as if he'd fought a war alone.
"We're still a warrior band," he said. "We're in a war."

Bewildered, Lena tried to penetrate
The black crow's mask he'd put back on his face.
She saw the death song deep within his eyes.
"But why?" she asked, her voice a fading song
Into the stirring of the warriors in the hall.

He looked at Superstar who'd suddenly
Became alert to all their nuances.

"Go bring the deputy," the crow-man said.

His chief lieutenant, like a lumbering bear,
Looked carefully at Sitting Crow, then left.

Kim saw the swirling song that Lena saw.
"The dance is starting up again?" he asked.

As Sitting Crow looked deep into the young man's eyes,
He saw the Thunderbird, the spirit-earth.
"The death song doesn't end. It changes tone,"
He said. "We haven't plumbed its depths inside this time.
The war goes on. We're still the heart of war."

"It's got to stop soon," Lena said. "We'll make it stop."

The man she loved looked through the dark crow mask.

3

Outside the stone Novitiate John sat
And tried to think his way through fierce complexities.
The key was here, where hell had started January first.
Here hate had built on hate until the ways
And place he loved had cracked and shaked apart,
Untuned from all the rhythms history
Had woven in their common daily lives.
To stop the dark unraveling John had to make
A stand and take control of things uncontrollable.

He got out of the squad and walked toward the barn.
Burt Samuelson slipped from the big barn doors.
At least a hundred men were near the barn.
The radicals could leave, and they would never know.

"Is everything okay?" John asked.

                                             Burt shrugged.
"It's quiet here," he said. "No movement there."
He pointed at the stone-white building bright with early dawn.
"The farms in sight are standing still unburned."

John pointed at the dark Novitiate.
"Has Sitting Crow tried talking yet?" he asked.

"As quiet as a tomb," he said. He looked at John.
"What's going on outside of here?" he asked.

John grimaced, pain unbidden in his voice.
"There's lots of people cold," he said. "And lots of fires.
The miracle is that there's no one dead.
With families losing homes and sheds and barns,
I figure someone's got to die real soon."

Burt frowned. "What are we gonna do?" he asked.

John looked up at the buildings once again.
"You need to get the men prepared," he said.
"We'll end this first, and then . . ." His voice trailed off.

Burt stared at him. "Thorn's trapped in there," he said.

An officer John didn't know came from the barn.
John saw disaster written in the man's grim face.
"There's news," the young man said.

                                  John held his breath.
The young man looked toward the smoky sky.

"An army led by someone named Bill Winchells' seized
The town of Tigerton," the young man said.
"The Governor is calling, wants to know
What you are gonna do about this craziness."

John smiled, his body colder than the cold
Edged sharp into the morning's winter winds.

The Aftermath

He stood and breathed the acrid smell the fire
Had burned into his lungs until he felt
Half-sick and both his eyes were watering.
The only structures left were four stone walls
Around the barn's foundation, then the fireplace built
Before he'd married Violet, ash and smoke from ruins.

He'd stood against the Indians as they'd swooped.
He'd heard their noises, woke up, grabbed his gun,
Then ran outside. They'd acted like he wasn't there.
Jim Speltz, the Gresham radical, the man
They loved to hate, who hated them, stood there,
His rifle in his hand, the Indians grim
With torches in their hands, the night so dark
It made his head pound, throbbing endlessly.

And then he'd raised his rifle to his shoulder, aimed
Into a crazed buck's chest whose face was black
With ash and felt his blood sing joyously.
No court would charge a man with murder when
He felt he had to save his life and property.

But then his finger froze. The Indian looked
At him, from dark, the black eyes bright with life,
And Jim had stared, his heartbeat hammering.
He tried to force his finger down onto the trigger's curve.
He tried to shoot the black soot man that stared at him,
Whose shadows weaved with torchlight, smoke.
But as he'd looked into the Indian's eyes,
He'd dropped his gun and ran toward the house.

By then the flames were licking at the walls.
The smoke was thick and black as oil slick sludge.
He panicked, knowing that Celest was still
Inside the living room, still dazed. He'd stopped and stared
At flames consuming wood, then turned and ran
Away into the fields and woods behind the farm.

What kind of man was he? He couldn't shoot
An Indian when the bastard looked him in the eye

258

And couldn't save his daughter from a burning house.
He hated Indians, hated all the poverty
They'd brought upon themselves, but still, he couldn't kill.

Beyond the barn his Holstein herd stood placidly,
Breath spumed into the cold. He wondered who
Had saved them from the fire. They should have died.

Out in the distance he could hear the wail
Of sirens as the Sheriff and his deputies
Fought cold and tragedy to bring back sanity.

He walked into a flowered, sun-stunned field
Of Indian paintbrushes, daisies, chicory . . .
He stank from too much booze. His head hurt, bad.
He'd spent an hour attempting to explain.
He'd tried to rape his daughter, was an animal.
He knew he'd felt a passion twisted wrong.

Why had he failed again? He hoped Celest still lived.
He'd let her go back to the Rajah's life.
His life was done, wife dead, farm burned.
He couldn't murder men when they were killing him.

He hungered, felt the darkness of his grave.
His unfired gun was lying in the snow.

The Song, the Instrument of War

They gathered at the Eau Claire Dells, eyes red,
Their weariness burned deep in faces, limbs.
They looked like people living at the end of time.
The granite cliffs, obsidian, the sun
Behind them, fell to frozen rapids, pools.

They'd burned down buildings all night long.
At first they'd roused scared families from their sleep
And forced them out into the bitter night.
But later on the news had spread. They splashed
Cold gasoline and lit the fires, home owners fled.
Twice men had stayed behind to make a stand,
But when they'd heard shots fired, they'd run away.

Pete stood above his warriors on a field stonewall
Above the river's stones and tried to feel
What strength the Thunderbirds had left them from the night.
No one had died, not yet, but in the light
They couldn't hide for long. Their trail of fire
Had been too plain. They had to move and soon.

Beth stood below Pete. They had made a war.
Inside the Legion Hall they'd lived with gods.
Beside the Eau Claire Dells they lived reality.

Pete held his gun up in the air to make
The song they'd sung with fire alive again.
"You look half dead," he said. Some smiled, some frowned.
"But we have yet to start this fight." He paused
And looked at Beth. She stood as straight and calm
As some great spirit-woman powerful with grace.
"Our greatest test's in front of us," he said.
"Tonight we'll free our warriors, Sitting Crow.
And then we'll disappear into the woods
Until the spirits gather up their strength again
And lead those brave enough to dance with war.
Lift hearts into your blood and let your blood
Pulse hot enough to make this day a song!"

The men and women warriors stirred, a beast.

They didn't shout or start a song or chant,
But light flowed back into their dulled black eyes.
They moved and made the white man quake in sleep,
The world he'd made disordered, mutinous.

Pete jumped down from his stone and grabbed Beth's waist,
And in his tiredness swung her round, her fire
The flames that made his fire alive with joy.
The others laughed. The war was still a beast alive.

"To war and Sitting Crow!" Beth shouted. "War!"
They moved toward the trucks and cars. They'd fight
Until their dreams were manifest and true,
And they were equal in the white man's world.

Hours of Waiting

When Superstar came in the room, Thorn turned
From staring at the smoke palled morning skies.
It looked as if the dawn had come from lurid fires
Of Christianity's dark vision of a smoking hell.
He didn't speak to Superstar, but tried
To see the message in the man's grim face.
All night he'd heard the sounds downstairs and felt
The fear that danced alive inside the halls.
He'd kept his fireplace fire producing heat
And watched as ruddy flames lit up the dark,
One light, and then another, flaring up.
He'd felt the deputies move from their posts
Around the grounds to new posts near the barn.
And then he'd watched dawn come, light filtered smoke
Spread from a score or more of fires, the war
That he and John had tried to end intensified.

The Warrior stared at Thorn as silently
As Thorn stared at the young man's black, grim eyes.
Spacetime was gathering upon a pin's small head.
"I've come from Sitting Crow," he said. "He wants to talk."

Thorn nodded. "What's been going on?" he asked.

The long-haired warrior looked into Thorn's eyes.
"There's spirits living here," he said, then turned.

Thorn felt a shivering upon his spine,
Then followed Superstar, dread powerful.
He'd known all night, since he had come inside
The building, held at gunpoint by a nervous Horse,
That something wrong had made the radicals
Half mad from fear . . . But he had occupied his post
And tried to understand himself, his rage.
And now, at last, he'd meet with Sitting Crow.

2

Alone, inside the room with Lena and the men
And women he had led into this place,

A brooding, weary Sitting Crow, rose up
From where he sat, the song and dance still strong
And endless in his head, and walked through halls
Invisible, not man, his spirit's ghost.
Upstairs, night washed the early morning light,
And Sitting Crow knelt down and watched the riverbank.

As one fire flickered orange into the winter sky,
And then another glow flared up, he pressed
Against the deadness of his hand flesh, tried
To weave his spirit, heart, and flesh into the stone.
He wanted hands to lose their fingers as the flesh
Of stone became the flesh of hands — and then
He wanted to transfuse the blood of stone
Into his blood, his mind, emotions, thoughts, and life —
Becoming dead like stone, alive like stone.

For weeks he'd sat within the limestone walls
A prisoner whose choice of prison freed
Him from the prison of the present and the past.

But now the drums had spoken. Warriors marched
Across ghost snow and threw their torches' fire
At memories of Indians sprawled in death.
And where was he? The warrior who had said
That there was martyred destiny in death?

At last he turned away from glowing skies
And looked into the eyes that looked at him.
He hadn't moved, though he had walked the halls.
Both Kim and Lena sat beside him in the dining hall.
A spirit that was tired, not tired, inside their eyes?
A hope that wouldn't die inside their hearts?

"We're going out," he said. "We've said that death
Was welcome if the gods were weaving strands
Of death into a warrior's robe for each of us.
Our brothers, sisters, children, fathers, mothers, wives,
And husbands light the torches of our rage.
Peace gone, White Rabbit dead, white houses burned,
We're going out into the night's great dark.
Our guards will see us come, and we may die,
But in our death we'll change our people's history

———

And gain the honor due our people's need."

He stared at them. They were his followers.
He'd seen the agony of sprawling death
Stain blood upon the whiteness of the river's ice.

He knew about Jim Jones. He'd read about
The Kool-Aid laced with poison by his followers —
The blood inside the stone was not his blood.

3

While Lena watched, as Sitting Crow's face blanched
And eyes grew vacant, as he left himself behind,
She felt the coldness of the death song once again
And railed inside herself about the loss
She felt as life swept from the dining hall.

She looked at Kim and saw the strength he had,
The macho man, the fox, the singer of life's song.
She'd fight the juggler juggling living skulls.
She'd heard the words of life from Sitting Crow.
She'd win. They'd win. Death would not be their end.
She held his hands and waited for a sign,
And when he spoke, alive again, she wept.

To life, she told herself. To life.

                              "We're going out,"
He said. "We've said that death was welcome if the gods
Were weaving strands of death into our robes . . ."

4

Thorn walked into the dining hall as Sitting Crow
Began his speech. He stopped beside the Indian kids
And watched how Superstar responded to the fiery words.
Black eyes dilated as the call for action rang.
The radical's tired face lit up and energy,
From him and others, surged into the room.
Thorn looked at Sitting Crow and felt inhuman force;
Eyes burned with worlds that Thorn had never seen.

The shaman said, ". . . and we may die, but in our death
We'll cause our people's history to shift," he said.
"And we will gain the honor due our people's need . . ."

The simple, unpresuming words moved Thorn.
He felt the glory and the courage of the man,
The angry fire that made black eyes like suns.

His speech done, Sitting Crow looked up at Thorn.
His recognition of Thorn's humanness was slow.
When eyes dulled fire he realized that Superstar
Had brought the deputy at his request.
He waved his hand at Thorn, inviting him to sit.
Thorn followed Superstar, then sat beside
The shaman, half in awe of what he felt and saw.
A silent Lena Day sat with her lover, eyes coal black.
Beside her, quiet, small, a boy sat still as stone.

"I need to know John Israel," said Sitting Crow.
"I need to see into his heart, his stomach's strength."

Thorn didn't speak. He saw John at the church,
His face lit by the vision of his wife.

"John has a dream. He wants the Indians, whites,
And people with their differences to live
Where small farms, factories, and retail stores
Provide an equal living for all families."
Thorn paused. "This episode is tearing him apart."

"What will he do when we appear outside,
Our guns held in the air without intent to fire?"

Thorn stared into the man's remarkably bright eyes.
"I didn't come in here to make a peace.
White Rabbit was my uncle. When he died . . ."

The Shaman smiled. "I've seen the pain in Neopit,"
He sang. "I bring not peace, but war." He glared.
"Still, death is not the reason that we live.
We're trapped in here. It's time I made my people free."

"We'll all face jail cells," Thorn said.

                                    "The war's not done,"
An angry Sitting Crow shot back. "I've been
Into the earth of spirits; heard their songs.
There is no giving up. We'll face the whites
And stand as warriors, test his heart
And live or die depending on the Sheriff's will."

Thorn backed away from Sitting Crow, the fire
That raged inside the leader's words so powerful
He felt his heart rage power into blood.

The fire from Sitting Crow subsided. In the hall
The warriors started getting ready, iron
Determination in the way they moved.
Their shaman, Sitting Crow, had set the time.
The hours of waiting were, at long last, done.
They'd meet their enemy and face him down.

The Wraiths Ending

1

By noon a smoke stained skiff of dirty snow.
Pete Wilson's radicals had stopped to rest.
They'd weighed the risks between a daylight raid
And night-time raid and had decided night
Would give them cover as they hit their enemies.
Three-dozen Stockbridge-Munsee joined the band
At Morgan Siding, each one fired with dreams
Of giving back the pain the whites had given them.

By noon Bill Winchell's men had moved from Tigerton
To put a barricade on Highway 29
A mile outside of Wittenberg, but men
Kept slipping north past roadblocks and the eyes
Of nervous cops who'd deputized more men
Than they had ever dreamed they'd ever need.
Bill sat in Chad LeConne's small bank and let
His men probe slowly outward through the day.
He waited patiently to face the rising storm.

All morning long John tried the barn's old phone,
But no one answered in the Novitiate.
The Governor was gathering his force.
John knew that Bill was probing, Indian radicals
Were only miles from where his deputies
Were waiting nervously for dark to come.
The radicals would strike at dusk. John thought.

The radio inside the barn kept bringing news.
The Governor declared a state emergency.
The National Guard called up six thousand men
And mobilized a helicopter group.
The nation's media descended on the state
Like locusts swarmed in Oklahoma fields
Before the Dust Bowl emptied out the land.
The Wilson radicals still hadn't moved.
Bill Winchell made a statement to the media
That his rebellion was the arm of God,
And then he'd said that Tigerton and all

267

The land his men had occupied was free,
Seceded from the U.S. government.

At last, as afternoon dimmed, newsmen's planes
Reported movement out of Morgan Siding's woods.
John sat on hay inside the barn and cussed.
The National Guard was still deployed in Madison.
John looked at Burt and said, at last, "it's time."

2

A pensive Sitting Crow stood near the door.
The stars were netting dark into the dimming sky.
In silver starlight time was not a line
That stretched across a flat geography.
It replicated, moved through seconds, minutes, hours.
It whorled and jumped about the universe.

Behind him all the people that had followed him
Into the cold Novitiate stood waiting, stress
From days of watching etched into their eyes.
He turned and looked at them, Thorn by his side
With Superstar, Kim, Lena, others linked
Behind him with the power of his shaman-force.
"We'll go," he said.

                        He didn't want to go.
Jim Jones had been a madman driven by
The awful God that breathed inside his head.
He didn't like the thought of hooded death
As Kool-Aid poisoned by a man gone mad with God.[92]
What did he want? He'd used the Novitiate
To make a symbol carved from truths inviolate.
But now? What were those truths? Why did he lead
Toward the possibility of death
When they had meant to bring new life and hope?

What did it mean to be an Indian? Why
Had Indians beat the death drums at a death
And burned their rage by burning houses built by men
That most of them had once considered friends?
Why had he spoken with the shining ghosts
And danced the crow's dance while he made

A shaman song-of-death sing to the world?

He walked through hallways littered by
An occupation locked inside a ring of guns.
He paused before the big oak door that marked
The entrance used by monks who'd locked themselves
Into the meditations that they'd hoped
Would lead to God. He felt his followers.

He took the doorknob's brass into his hands.

3

They drove from Morgan Siding down dirt roads.
They bypassed Gresham, then drove to The Rock,
A Shawano County park a mile away
From where the Sheriff's guards were sentineled.
The pines around The Rock's small falls were long
With shadows cast by sunlight's lingering rays.

They gathered round, a ring of faces grim
And haunted by the guns they'd have to face.
Beth stood by Pete upon a swell of rock
That let their followers see both of them.
They weren't the kids that they had been when they
Had faced Legune inside the Legion Hall.
They'd caused a lot of pain and felt the pain
They had dispensed as fire seared who they were.
Beth held Pete's hand and felt so confident
In love she knew they'd make it through the night
And find their happiness as fugitives.
They'd spent all day deciding where they'd run.
They'd face the Sheriff's guns, then travel north.

Pete held up his gun. The woods were murmuring
With water quietly below cascading ice.

"Remember," Pete said softly. "What we want
To do is free our people. When that's done,
We'll disappear." He paused. "Be careful now."

And then he turned and walked toward the woods,
The dark Novitiate, the deputies with deadly guns.

4

John closed his eyes and walked, his gun in hand.
His men were there, the people that he'd led
Against the dissolution of his culture's life.
And Thorn was there — a force against John's culture now,
But good beyond cohesion, representative
Of differences that boiled away false differences.

John knew his place, the black transmitter in his hand.
He pushed its button, emblematic of an age
Gone mad with speed, and talked into the night.
His eyes were locked onto the big oak door.

"I'm Sheriff Israel. We've got to keep our cool,"
He said. " There's Indians coming from the west,
And shortly Sitting Crow will leave the Novitiate.
I want the men south of the river moved
North to the barn, and everybody else
Had better keep their heads and hold their fire.

"It's not too late to save both cop and Indian lives.
But if you fire one shot, the blood will pour
So deep the Governor will have to put on boots.
I'll handle this and keep us all alive if you . . ."

He stopped. The shadows of his flitting men
Across the river ran toward the barn.
The big oak door was opening. At last.
He fumbled with his gun belt, took it off.
He held his breath, death drums inside his head.
The wraiths were gone, but flames were circling
The limestone walls and shooting sparks into the sky.

He walked across the yard toward the door.
Fear crawled inside his belly with an angry ache.

Then, Sitting Crow was out into the night,
His rifle in the air, his people crowded close.
He saw John, stopped, eyes merciless with hate.

John stood and looked at them, the Indians dragged
Into their present by their history.

———
270

"We've got to stop this madness now," he said.
"So far White Rabbit's dead. But if we shoot just once,
We'll spend a week in burying our dead.
I've pulled my men back from the river's banks.
You all can go, escape into the dark.
I won't spread death all through Menominee.
We've got to stop before momentum carries us
Into events that none of us can stop."

Then, suddenly, Pete Wilson's followers appeared.
Dark, massed, they seemed a single beast, alive with dark.
John looked at them, then looked at Sitting Crow.

He was a warrior: blue-black hair, braids strung
Down to his buttocks, eyes so strong they shined
Inside a dark that should have hid their light.
The warrior looked at how the other Indians poised
Upon the brink of death and mayhem, looked at John.

John waited, heart a drum, dread powerful.
Above earth, stars were dimmed by moonlight, night.
On earth time stretched out of its boundaries
And poised inside the mass of Indian rage,
Whites innocent and guilty; Indians innocent
And guilty, cybernetics spinning on the brink
Of unknown, unmapped brinks, fear, love, hate, man . . .

The Thunderbirds danced wildly as they tried
To find a way to end the bloodshed that was near.
A blackness raged so dark it threatened light
And made it possible that only withering
And loss would live upon the once green earth.

Then, in an instant, it was over. Sitting Crow
Threw back his head and screeched his battle cry.
Pete Wilson's mass of Indians broke away
From white Novitiate walls and disappeared,
Like ghosts, into the dark.

                    And no one fired.
The white man's guns were silent as the Indians left
The Novitiate and silence settled down
So quickly that it stunned John Israel, his men.

After Hearing the Dance of Ancient Drums

Thorn stood beside the river, sadness masking eyes.
He felt betrayed and lost, his spirit drained.
At first, when Sitting Crow had screeched to, "run!"
He'd run. But then he'd stopped on river's ice,
His rifle cold inside his shaking hands.
His warrior chief had given up without a fight,
His talk of death just that: his talk of death.
He'd tried to gain pride, honor for his tribe,
But in the end the white man's history had marched,
And Sitting Crow, his braided, blue-black hair,
Had made his warriors run away into the night,
Their spirits throbbing with the war they'd almost fought.

But Thorn? The deputy? The radical?
The man who'd turned from white men's ways to join
Rebellion just a day before rebellion died?
What now? Go back into the white man's world?
Or face the self that, in a moment's rage
Had stripped away the white man's uniform
To join his brother, Sitting Crow, his chief?

The river's skin of snow and ice became
A glow of light as moonlight spilled from clouds.
Thorn tried to warm himself by jumping up and down.
He thought he heard an osprey, wings outspread,
Against a bright blue summer sky, cry out.

John Israel walked up behind his friend.
A glowing halo circled round the moon.

"Hi John," Thorn said. John squatted on his heels in snow.

Thorn didn't turn, but kept his eyes fast on the moon.
"We change sometimes," he said. One day we're full
Of spit to do the job we've said we'd do,
And then we find we're really someone else.
A morning's sun comes up, and we don't fit our skin.
Our blood can hear the songs of ancient drums.
Our spirit's will comes out of hiding, moving us.
I've heard the drums, and now I'm caught in dance.

I don't quite understand the dance, but I'm the dance.
Here. In this moonlight spilled through clouds."

John shook his head. "It doesn't mean I'm not your friend,"
He said. "Our world is shaped by politics,
But politics can't cut the bonds we feel."

Thorn stood up from his crouch, looked at the moon.
Another cloud was threatening the light.

"You are a shaman, John," he said. "I would have sworn
The war was real. You wanted peace; you have your peace."

"Not quite," John said. "A score of homes were burned.
The Governor will howl for Indian blood.
They'll not believe this country brought this on itself."
"Your kind can't win," Thorn said. He looked at John.
"There's too much hate. You want to make the world
A better place, but poverty breeds hate,
And hate breeds hate, and fear breeds hate, and in the end
Your effort to control the hate breaks down.
The demons and the angels in your head are real,
And you can't sleep because you hear too many drums
And see too many dances that you wish would stop."
He shook his head. "My God," he finished. "Even I
Have learned how sweet it is to hate you whites."

John shrugged his shoulders. "I can only try,"
He said. "I thought of suicide. But I'm still here."

Thorn smiled. "I'm glad," he said.

                              "What now?" John asked.

"I've changed," Thorn said. "An Indian can't be white,
And white men can't be Indians. Still, the white
Man dominates. I am an Indian man."

John looked toward the ground. Cold numbed their thought.
They looked into each other's teary eyes.
At last Thorn turned and walked onto the ice.

A breeze flinched through the pines across the riverbank.

Thorn walked, his shoulders hunched against the cold.
He didn't turn around. He disappeared
Into the blackness of the night-black pine.

The Wasps

1

The helicopters, sleek, black wasps, swept low
Above the houses' rooftops: shattering sound.
Bill sat behind the banker's maple desk
And felt the sound shake through his skeleton.
Outside his men shot at the empty air,
The violence of the noise unnerving them.
He wondered where their anti-aircraft gun
Was set up, aimed toward their enemy.

Bill fought the noise and stood up from the chair
He'd used all day to issue orders, placing men
Where they would face the awful hell to come.
As noise whined down to silence, Bill's blood sang,
The God-song strong and billowing into the world.
He didn't feel the fear he should have felt,
But felt, instead, alive, his destiny alive.

He walked outside and looked into the skies,
Stars grains of salt thrown on a dome of pepper-dark.
He slowly gathered in himself, each thought
And feeling, every breath a wandering fire.
And then, a man upon a sidewalk, he sent
His God into the night against his enemies,
The eyes inside the serpent's heads malevolent.
The war of Armageddon joined at last,
The force of God against the Devil's force —
The stars, the earth, men's heart a battleground.

Bill felt as if he glowed with angel-light.
The night about him, all his men afraid
To come too near the fires that made him shine.
The helicopters swept above the rooftops, noise
The song of chaos, song of coming death,
And then he sent his fire into the air,
And God sang hearing, seeing, feeling death
Of Satan's flying minions on the earth.
The helicopters died, their human hearts a stain
Of blood upon a metal rained from skies.

Bill walked into the cold down darkened streets
And celebrated as he made his victory
Into a vision strong enough to make
His army unafraid, invincible.
Men murmured greetings to him as he walked.
They poked their heads from doorways, left the warmth
Of heated buildings, just to see him pass.

2

Sam tried to feel his death. As helicopters roared
He saw the men he'd helped to gather fire
Their useless rifles at the empty sky.
He tried to feel the moment when a bullet burned
Into his flesh, the moment when the pain
Flared like a nova deep into his brain.

Around him men he didn't know were jabbering
In tongues, excitement overlaying fear.
They'd waited all day long for enemies,
And all day long they'd fought the pall of dread
Stretched endlessly into the crawling hours.
And now the first adrenaline of battle raged
On tongues loosed from the sense they thought they said.

Sam listened to the jabbering and felt
The racing of his heart and then saw Bill
Come from the bank into the night, his eyes alive
With visions, silence like a blazoned shield.
He walked past knots of men down streets where dread
Stalked like a ravening, dark winter bear.
Bill shimmered as he walked, Sam saw, a light
So faint about him in the dark it wasn't there.
Men felt his presence, felt the victory
He sang into the empty black-wasp skies.
Sam smiled his bitterness, reality,
And walked toward his truck. He heard, far off,
The sounds of helicopters in the skies.
The army's simple strategy was clear.
They'd shatter nerves all night. They'd send the wasps
Into the skies and keep the waiting men awake
Until Bill's hold upon his men had faced the test
Of endless waiting, endless dread and fear.

Sam drove down 45 from town toward the post
A mile from 29. He tried to feel his death.
He wouldn't let the anti-aircraft gun
Kill men who flew above their ranks, he knew.

A rheumy Lawrence Staub had said, "the trick
Is if we'll stick when insides stink with fear."

Sam smiled as truck tires hummed upon the road.
They'd never stick, he thought. They couldn't stand
The fear the helicopters stung into the night.

"A man has got to stand up like a man
And let conviction rule someday," he'd said.

Three helicopters roared so low above
His head he nearly veered the truck into the ditch.
They flew toward Bill Winchell's men in Tigerton.

Sam knew he wouldn't run. His father's ghost
Sat down beside him in the truck and frowned.
His son was nothing but a fool, the spirit thought.

Sam didn't try to feel, but kept on courting death.

3

John Israel danced like a marionette.
The helicopters roared about Bill's head.
The Sheriff danced before Bill's eyes, a fool,
His grin surreal upon his painted face.
Bill fired his rifle at the dark and cursed.
The country was disintegrating in a million ways.
Morality was skewed into a rape
Of right by wrong. But in the wrong was . . . what?
The painted Sheriff dancing in the dark?

Bill found himself before the empty bank.
The copters passed again. Men tried to shoot
The shadows from the sky, but missed again.
The Sheriff danced. Bill fired into the air again.
He grinned. He laughed. The helicopters roared.

4

Sam sat beside the bonfire built on 45
And tried to understand the madness grained
In men, surrounded by an enemy,
Who'd made a fire so big its light would shine
A dozen miles away. The men were drunk
On fear and rage, and as they lurched, they seemed
Half men to Sam, eyes bright with manic energy.
Steve Newt came up and handed Sam a cup.
"You think there's reinforcements yet?" he asked.

Sam took the offered cup and sipped, his tongue
Numbed from the coffee's scalding heat. "Who knows,"
He said. "The only thing I'm sure of is, they'll come."

Steve settled back upon his heels, face blank.
"We've blown it big," he said. "We could have stopped
This at your house that night. Last night, so many men,
I thought there were enough of us to beat
The world or government or God Himself.
I didn't know how fast a helicopter was
Or how I'd feel when they fly overhead."

His words hung with a question mark in air.
Sam stared at how the darkness danced with fire.
He'd seen the banker, Chad LeConne, storm like
A madman to his bank, past men with guns,
Up to a smiling, cold Bill Winchell, death
A song Sam's leader wove into his honeyed voice.

"I want this outrage ended now!" the man had raged.
"You're not the owner of this bank. I am.
If you don't leave you'll face your punishment!"

His smile still fixed, a crazy Bill had pulled
His pistol from its holster, stuck its metal nose
Against the blanched white banker's face, and snarled.
"Get out of here or die."

                    The banker's eyes
Had grown as huge as silver dollar coins.
He'd peed his pants the minute Bill had pulled

The gun out of the holster at his side.

Sam felt the moment, felt the banker's shame,
And felt the wrong he'd let his world become.
He'd heard the question Steve had asked. What now?
They'd waited all day long anticipating war —
And now the helicopters moved much faster than a man
Could fire a gun a generation old into the air.

Then Sam had watched as Chad LeConne was shot,
His eyes surprised, Bill's glee in face and eyes.

"God's enemies will die!" A smirking Bill had said.

And Sam had stood, will paralyzed, his stomach turned
As Chad LeConne, now dead, slumped to the floor.

Sam thought about how he had lost the farm,
His need to better what his father's life
Had made undoing him, and thought about
His culpability in causing helicopter blades
To scream above the heads of men who, like
The man he was, had failed themselves, their dreams.
Bill Winchell wasn't a messenger from God.
He was a bonfire on a summer night
Attracting insects to his deadly flame.

"The time for questioning is past," he said.
"Bill's right. The country's wrong," he said. "We'll take
Our rage and bring the nation to God's throne."

Steve looked at Sam as if he'd met a man
Whose sanity was gone. Sam smiled at him,
Then got up to his feet, set down the coffee cup
Walked to his truck. They'd burn down Tigerton,
Then die or spend their lives in jail cells.

5

The phone rang. Once. Twice. John groped from his sleep
And put the black receiver to his ear.

"Lieutenant Simonson," a sharp, clipped voice.

"Is this John Israel?"

John mumbled, mind confused.
A darkened Sitting Crow before his followers:
He'd ordered them to run away into the night;
Thorn's saddened eyes beside the riverbank
As he and John searched through the night's events
To find the trust and friendship they had lived.

"We're moving in on Winchell at first light,"
The phone voice said. "The General thought you ought
To join us when we rout the radicals.
We understand those trapped in Tigerton
Will want familiar faces when we free the town."

John saw the flames of burning houses orange
Against the darkness of the winter sky.
He'd put Bill Winchell's madness from his thoughts.

He said into the phone. "I'll need a half an hour."

He hung the phone up. Jane was watching him.
"It's ending, isn't it?" she said. "It's almost done."

John looked at her. "I'm not the man I was,"
He said. "I've changed. I'm not as competent."

She didn't speak, but looked at him, her eyes
As probing as the madness that had made
Him see a living Goddess in blank windowpanes.
"I still love you," she said. "I've been alone
Since Sitting Crow kidnapped our lives. We'll be okay."

6

Each time the helicopters roared above
The roofs of Tigerton men ran outside
And fired their guns into the frozen skies.
The helicopter's roaring rattled windowpanes,
And then they came again, black swarms of wasps,
Each one so big they seemed too huge to comprehend,
A symbol of the power of the government.
At last reality stunned deep in haunted eyes.

The copters came again, and then again, the sky
Still dark before the morning's glimmering.
The men came out to see the sleek, black wasps
And didn't fire their guns, but looked bemused.
They were believers. The government was wrong.
The country was disintegrating in a million ways.

They didn't own the land. They held the land.
They'd trained for years, but now their destiny:
In morning dark the helicopters were like wasps . . .
Their sting was death, and no one had an antidote.

7

Bill stormed inside himself. He watched his men's
Resolve grow weak, then dissipate as hour
Dragged after hour through night toward the dawn.

      Indifferent bards pretend, the poet had sang.
      They pretend a monstrous beast . . .[93]
He tried to pray to God,

      O Lord my God, in You I put my trust;
      Save me from all those who persecute me;
      And deliver me
      Lest they tear me like a Lion,
      Rending me in pieces, while there is none to deliver.[94]

            But every time
He caught the fire of the prayer, life
Dissolved into the roar of helicopters black.

At last he went outside and raised his arms.
"My God, O God," he said into the dark.
"You raised the slaughtered calf's pure smoke straight up.
You gave me strength enough to raise a host.
I now beseech You as You sit upon your throne.
Raise up an angry storm of locust wings!
Let fiery death confound our enemies!
O God, my Lord, our Lord, our king of hosts!"

Three helicopters whined toward the place
Where Bill stood shouting out his prayer's rage.

Bill fell down on his knees. The government was wrong!
Bureaucracy had murdered God's great laws
And made "one nation under God" a mockery.
He heard the trees sing songs of earth's renewing Spring.
He tried to see the Goddess in the dark,
To call the trees up from a winter mist
Into a march against the army tanks
That waited for the dawn outside of Tigerton.
But when the Goddess answered with the sound
Of silence in the wake of helicopter noise,
And God, Bill's most beloved God, sat still
Upon His throne and let the helicopters fly
Untouched by pestilence or plague, Bill wept.

8

Sam found Bill knelt in prayer before the bank.
His leader's eyes had lost their focus, focusing
Instead upon a private dialogue with God.
Sam got out of the truck and stood above
The man who'd led the group of them toward
The moment when the government had moved
To end rebellion launched inside a rural bar.
The radio had bulletined the end
Of occupation at the Novitiate.
The government was focused on the man
Who'd knelt in prayer on the sidewalk, lost.

"They're coming, Bill," Sam said. "I saw their light
On 45 as I drove back here fast.
We don't have guns enough to face them down.
The men have lost their spirits since we failed
To shoot a copter down. The end's at hand."

Bill suddenly looked up at Sam. "I'll strike
Them down," he said. "I'll call forth God and make
My words ball up into a lightning bolt.
I am the instrument, the hammer of the Lord!
Their hearts will burst, make dawn a bloody, God damned red."

A group of men had come outdoors to hear Bill's words.
They felt embarrassed at their leader's crazy voice.
They tried to fend away the dawn's cold bitterness.

They were believers. They had followed God,
And now the man who'd promised God on earth
Was kneeling on the sidewalk ranting words
That couldn't stop the helicopter roar.

Bill saw the Goddess beckoning to him
From where she stood inside her copse of trees.
"My God she's beautiful, the witch," he said.

Sam looked at Bill. "You're mad," he said. He turned.
"Get out of here," he said. "Go save your necks."

The men stood still as if their blood had froze.
The sound of rifle fire was coming near their street.
God's kingdom was not yet to be an earthly place.

Sam pulled a gas can from his truck, walked to the bank.
The men stood in the winter cold and watched.
He splashed gas on the walls, LeConne's big desk.
He lit a match and threw it at the desk.
Flames roared to life, surrounding him. He laughed.
He'd lost the family farm, by God. He'd been a fool.
He wondered how his Ruth would get along.

Outside Bill saw the flames and clapped for joy.
The wrath of God had come! The wrath of God!
He gathered up himself, each wandering piece
Of fire and willed it, as a fuel, into the fire
That licked at walls and shot up, lurid, hot,
Into the winter-dusky, dawn-lit sky.
He didn't see the terror in his men.
They shied away from flames and death and loss.
He celebrated God and flames, the flames and God.

And then the men were gone. And then a jeep
Containing weary, old John Israel.
Bill turned and lifted arms and face to God,
Almighty benefactor to our humble earth.

"Praise be the Lord," he said. "Praise be the Lord."

A Second Chance

The pebbly ceiling made her feel completely lost,
The square florescent lights a faery show of light.
She tried to grasp just who she was, her arms
And body lead-like in their heaviness.

Bat wings as black as anthracite, feet webbed,
Eyes glittery kept darting through the room.
She tried to gesture them away, but teeth
Kept chittering at her inside small mouths.

Her father reached toward her naked breasts,
His face a mask of passion, eyes so bright . . .
Afraid, she tried to turn around and run,
But something held her legs in place. She screamed.

She tried to move her arms, but intravenous lines
Snaked down from bottles hung above her head.

And then remembering: the flames and smoke,
The shouting in the dark, the Indian man
Who'd picked her up and took from the house.

She was Celest. The Rajah was her father, guide.
Her father was her enemy, the man
Who'd intervened unwanted in her life.
A sheriff's deputy had found her on the road
And brought her to the hospital. She was alive.

Inside her cubicle the Rajah smiled at her.
Her stomach hurt. She hadn't eaten for a week.
The Rajah touched her face. She felt his light.
She stepped back from his outstretched arms. He smiled.
He wore a mask of bone, her helplessness.
She reached behind her back, unclasped her robe.
Her temples throbbed with her desire.

The sun's first light was filtering through dark.
She hadn't died out in the cold in snow.
The Indian man, and then the deputy,
Had saved her, given back her precious life.

In glory was the world. She'd died, but lived,
Free from her nemesis, free from the Rajah. Free.

Epilogue

I hear them still, the shaman dressed in black,
Translucent, dark, his face alive with flame.
His lady, dressed in egret white, stands still,
As cool and beautiful as early morning suns
Reflected on the waters of a placid lake.
Their wings are soft in winds of early spring,
Their voices hidden deep in winter snows
Where wilderness and wildness dominate the earth.

At night, in woods, alone, I almost see
The power Sitting Crow has gathered in his hands.
I feel the promise Lena makes as threads
Of power weave from crow wings through the skies
Into the nation's heart, a healing wind
That dances order out of chaos, peace
From frights and changes, hope from loss.

He is American. The first American. He flies
Above the earth a crow, becomes the man he is.
He sits inside the nexus where winds form
And Thunderbirds wing up-draughts as they watch
The love, hate, mourning, joy, excitement, happiness
Of women, men, and children weaving whom they are.
Beside him Lena looks into his eyes
And takes strength from the winds and feeds the songs
He sends into the world into a weft of dreams.

I hear them still. In woods, at night, alone,
I see the flames of glory in his hands,
His burning eyes, the way he shakes his head
And mutters words that no one understands.
I see the feathers growing on his back
And see the winged becoming of his lady's form
And feel the way the crow and egret knit
This earth to man and man to man, their flight
Communicating brotherhood and peace.

He sat inside his cold garage and dreamed.
He seized the stone Novitiate by force of arms,
Incited fires that blazed across the countryside,

Then slipped, wild flotsam, in a spirit-stream.
Then, in the madness of the power poured
Into his flaming dreams, he found a song
More powerful than war. He heard the Thunderbirds
Inside Kim's voice, inside his own crow-heart,

And when he faced the moment when worlds turned,
Brinked on a bloody chaos, courage called.
When peace seemed out of reach, he flashed his wings.
He sang the dance he danced. He spread black wings
And flew with Lena, egret-white, in song,
The weaving of their wings the spirit healed
Into the heart that makes Americans.

Their flight spread out across the winter fields
And brought an end to civil war and quelled
The blood-thirst, hatred cankering their worms
Inside the heart of our America.
They dance a dance of flight and crow-song/egret-song.
They dance and sing, a man and woman, birds
Of power weaving through a full moon's light.

I hear us still. In woods, at night, alone . . .

Biography

Thomas Davis is an educator who helped found the College of the Menominee Nation with Dr. Verna Fowler where he served as a Dean and Vice President of Academic Affairs. He then went on to serve as the President of Lac Courtes Oreilles Ojibwa Community College in Wisconsin and Little Priest Tribal College in Nebraska. At Fond du Lac Tribal and Community College in Minnesota he was the Chief Academic Officer and Acting President. In New Mexico on the Navajo Nation he retired as Provost of Navajo Technical University, serving as the Assistant to the President after his retirement.

Davis earned his baccalaureate degree with a double major in English and history and secondary education certification from the University of Wisconsin—Oshkosh and a master's degree in Environmental Science and Policy from the University of Wisconsin—Green Bay. His first professional job was as a teacher, and later an administrator, at the Menominee County Community School, an alternative school. It is while he was at the school that he became involved in the Coalition of Indian Controlled School Boards and the start of the Indian controlled schools movement.

He also helped found one national, Advanced Networking for Minority Serving Institutions (ANMSI), and one international, the World Indigenous Nations Higher Education Consortium (WINHEC), organization. ANMSI worked to improve technology at tribal, Hispanic, and black colleges and universities throughout the United States. WINHEC was founded to champion indigenous controlled colleges and universities from around the world. He also served on the Board and the Executive Committee of the American Indian Higher Education Consortium (AIHEC). Davis was also involved in the National Computational Science Alliance (NCSA) during its inception.

State University of New York Press (SUNY Press) published his non-fiction book, *Sustaining the Forest, the People, and the Spirit*. He has written chapters for two other publications, *Ancient Wisdom, Modern Science* (University of Nebraska Press) and *Native American Language Preservation, A Reference Guide* (Department of Health and Human Services, Administration of Children and Families, Administration for Native Americans) and published three novels: *Salt Bear* (a children's chapter book), *Inside the Blowholes*, and *The Alkali Cliffs*. Bennison Books, a publisher in the United Kingdom, published an epic poem, *The Weirding Storm, A Dragon Epic*. A new novel, *In the Unsettled Homeland of Dreams*, is being published by All Things That Matter Press. His poetry and short fiction has appeared in magazines, literary journals, and anthologies.

He has also had two plays produced and served as Editor for *The Rimrock Poets Magazine*, *The New Quiver*, and *Wisconsin Trillium* magazines and *The Zuni Mountain Poets*, an anthology of poetry written by New Mexico poets.

In addition to his work as an educator and writer, he served for a short while as the President and Chief Executive Officer of Synaptic Micro Solutions, a software firm that produced solutions for the publishing industry.

Notes

[1] Sir Isaac Newton, the great physicist and mathematician, established his laws of motion that, combined with the law of universal gravitation, led to the idea that the world and all of creation were like a great machine driven by absolute laws.

[2] Albert Einstein, in response to the quantum physics, exclaimed that God does not play dice with the universe. Einstein believed, in saying this, that the universe is governed by unified laws and principles.

[3] Planck's discovery unifies the seemingly contradictory observations that energy sometimes acts like a wave and at other times acts as if it is made up of particles.

[4] A principle in quantum mechanics holding that increasing the accuracy of measurement of one observable quantity increases the uncertainty with which another conjugate quantity may be known.

[5] A physical particle that forms one of the two basic constituents of matter, the other being the lepton.

[6] Alegieri, Dante, *The Purgatorio*, translated by John Ciardi (New York: New American Library, 1957).

[7] Nikos Kazantzakis, Greek novelist and poet who is considered one of the greatest literary figures of the 20th Century.

[8] Kazantzakis, Nikos, *The Odyssey, A Modern Sequel*, translated by Kimon Friar (New York: Simon and Schuster, Inc., 1958).

[9] Virgil, *The Aeneid*, translated by Robert Fitzgerald (New York: Vintage Classics, Random House, Inc., 1990).

[10] Chaucer, Geoffrey, "Prologue," *The Canterbury Tales* (Ruggiers, Paul G., General Editor, facsimile of the Hengwrt Manuscript (Norman, OK: University of Oklahoma Press and Wm. Dawson and Sons, Ltd., Folkestone, 1979).

[11] Homer, *The Odyssey*, translated by Robert Fitzgerald (New York: Vintage Classics, Random House, Inc., 1990).

[12] Modified from Virgil, *The Aeneid*, translated by Robert Fitzgerald (New York: Vintage Classics, Random House, Inc., 1990.

[13] A Catholic religious congregation specifically devoted to caring for the sick. The Alexian Brothers was founded in Europe during the time of the Black Death and founded a hospital in 1866 in Chicago, which was destroyed in the Great Fire.

[14] Gresham, Wisconsin

[15] The Battle of Bunker Hill was fought early in the Revolutionary War on June 17, 1775 during the siege of Boston by the British.

[16] A type of machine gun.

17 The garden at the foot of Mount Olive in Jerusalem where Jesus prayed while the disciples slept on the night before his crucifixion.

18 Angels belonging to the highest order of the nine-fold hierarchy in heaven, symbols of light, ardor, and purity.

19 *Holy Bible*, Judges 13:20.

20 *Holy Bible*, Psalms 106:37-38.

21 *Holy Bible*, Job 3:3.

22 Prophet from the book of Job in the Bible who stayed loyal to God even when God sent him grievous afflictions.

23 Friend of Job who came to comfort him after hearing about the calamities that had visited him.

24 *Holy Bible*, Job 18:10-13.

25 Third of the major prophets in the Old Testament.

26 Shawano's radio station.

27 Hero in the Book of Daniel in the old Testament who receives several apocalyptic visions.

28 Refers to the mark Cain, Adam and Eve's son, received from God after killing his brother Able.

29 Tenskwatawa was the Prophet referred to here. He was the brother of Tecumseh, the political and military leader of the Shawnee in 1768 who attempted to create a confederacy of tribes to fight against the constant incursions into Indian lands.

30 The leader of the Shawnee who worked with the Prophet, his brother, to create Prophetstown and led a confederacy of tribes against the United States in the Tecumseh War.

31 Juliet Capulet from William Shakespeare's *Romeo and Juliet.*

32 A grocery store in Shawano.

33 Eliot, T.S., "The Hollow Men," *Collected Poems 1909-1935* (New York: Harcourt, Brace and Company, Inc., 1936.

34 The Nazi leader of Germany that brought about World War II and sponsored the holocaust that murdered millions of Jews and other religious and ethnic minorities.

35 Ancient Israel's first King before David killed Goliath and ended up sparking Saul's ire.

36 The shepherd boy who became King of Israel after Saul.

37 *Holy Bible*, Psalms 43:1-2.

38 Eliot, T.S., "The Hollow Men," *Collected Poems 1909-1935* (New York: Harcourt, Brace and Company, Inc., 1936).

39 Paul was not one of Jesus' twelve apostles, but he was an apostle.

40 *Holy Bible*, Job 1:21.

[41] Wright, Frank Lloyd, *Autobiography of Frank Lloyd Wright* (New York: Longmans, Green and Co., 1932. Wright's dream of Broadacre City gave every family their own green spaces inside homes and landscapes of great beauty.

[42] Eliot, T.S., "The Hollow Men," *Collected Poems 1909-1935* (New York: Harcourt, Brace and Company, Inc., 1936).

[43] Paul was not one of Jesus' original twelve apostles, but he was the apostle who did the most to teach the gospel of Christ to the first-century world. He wrote the Book of Paul in the *New Testament.*

[44] Rough translation from *Beowulf, the Finnesburg fragment,* edited by C.C. Wren and W.F. Bolton (Exeter, England: University of Exeter Press, 1988), lines 710-711.

[45] Wright, Frank Lloyd, *Autobiography of Frank Lloyd Wright* (New York: Longmans, Green and Co., 1932).

[46] From a sermon by Winthrop, John, *Collections of the Massachusetts Historical Society* 7 (3rd series) (1838): 31–48, defining what the Puritans were attempting to accomplish by settling in the New World.

[47] Eliot, T.S., "The Hollow Men," *Collected Poems 1909-1935* (New York: Harcourt, Brace and Company, Inc., 1936).

[48] Plath, Sylvia, "Black Rook in Rainy Weather," *The Colossus and Other Poems* (New York: Alfred A. Knopf, Inc., 1962).

[49] Davis, Ethel Mortenson, "Healing Journey," *The Healer* (Sturgeon Bay, Wisconsin: Four Windows Press, 2016).

[50] Erwin Schrödinger in 1935 used a cat in a box to describe a central paradox of quantum theory. If you place a cat in a sealed box with a radioactive substance. In quantum theory even if a single atom of the substance decays, it will trigger, at least in this thought experiment, a hammer that will lead to the cat's death. An observer cannot know if the atom has decayed and thus cannot know if the cat is alive or dead inside the box. Since we cannot know, at least in quantum theory, that the cat is not both alive or dead until the box is opened, and the observer knows what really happened to the cat. But how can a cat really be both alive and dead?

[51] Zukav, Gary, *The Dancing Wu Li Masters* (New York: Bantam Books, 1979).

[52] A town in Guyana, South America, founded by the cult leader Jim Jones, where 900 followers of Jones committed suicide.

[53] The image of man being thrown into a fiery oven is from a sermon by Jonathan Edwards, an early American Puritan preacher who led the first great American revival.

[54] Graves, Robert, *The White Goddess* (New York: The Noonday Press, 1966).

55 Graves, Robert, *The White Goddess* (New York: The Noonday Press, 1966).

56 Graves, Robert, *The White Goddess* (New York: The Noonday Press, 1966).

57 *Holy Bible*, Job 30:20.

58 This poem is drawn from discussion in Hoffman, Walter James, *The Menomini Indians*, Fourteenth Annual Report of the Bureau of Ethnology (Washington DC: Government Printing Office, 1896).

59 Jehovah Witnesses.

60 Uvavnuk, an Eskimo song in *Touch the Earth*, compiled by T.C. McLuhan (New York: Promontory Press, 1971).

61 This tale has its source in work on the Trickster by Paul Radin in *The Winnebago Tribe* (Lincoln, NB: University of Nebraska Press, 1990).

62 Graves, Robert, *The White Goddess* (New York: The Noonday Press, 1966).

63 *Holy Bible*, Matthew 16:23.

64 *Holy Bible*, Revelation 14:9-10.

65 *Holy Bible*, Psalms 145:1.

66 A rifle.

67 *Holy Bible*, Psalms 28:1.

68 John Winthrop, the Puritan leader who helped found Massachusetts Bay Colony, said this when he was sailing with other Puritans reaching the shores of America in 1630, defining what the purpose of the Puritans was in coming to this new continent.

69 *Holy Bible*, Matthew 16:23.

70 *Holy Bible*, Revelation 13:1.

71 *Holy Bible*, Job 16:11.

72 *Holy Bible*, Matthew 27:46.

73 County Highway G and Highway 29.

74 Eliot, T.S., "The Love Song of J. Alfred Prufrock," *Collected Poems 1909-1935* (New York: Harcourt, Brace and Company, Inc., 1936).

75 Eliot, T.S., "The Hollow Men," *Collected Poems 1909-1935* (New York: Harcourt, Brace and Company, Inc., 1936).

76 The events described in this passage correspond roughly to events occurring during the Sand Creek Massacre when Colonel J.M. Chivington led his soldiers against defenseless Cheyenne and Arapaho.

77 Shakespeare, William, "The Tragedy of Hamlet, Prince of Denmark," *Shakespeare, The Complete Works*, G.B. Harrison, editor (New York: Harcourt, Brace and World, Inc., 1968).

78 A paraphrase from Sylvia Plath's poem, *Black Rook in Rainy Weather*.

79 This refers to one of the most iconic paintings of the 20th century by Edvard Munch, a Norweigan painter and print maker who explored intense psychological themes in his art.

[80] Crane, Hart, "The Dance," in "The Bridge," *Collected Poems of Hart Crane* (New York: Liveright Publishing Corporation, 1933).

[81] *Holy Bible,* Psalms 59:1

[82] *Holy Bible,* Psalms 59:1-2.

[83] *Holy Bible,* Revelation 22:13-14.

[84] A rock band formed in 1968 that had a psychedelic edge to its eclectic music.

[85] Tecumseh, quoted in Billington, Ray Allen, *Western Expansion, A History of the American Frontier* (New York: The Macmillan Company, 1967), p. 277.

[86] In the *Holy Bible* a cloth made of black goats' Hair: Revelation 6:12.

[87] Shakespeare, William, "The Tragedy of Hamlet, Prince of Denmark," *Shakespeare, The Complete Works,* G.B. Harrison, editor (New York: Harcourt, Brace and World, Inc., 1968).

[88] Highway 45.

[89] In 1996 Operation Desert Shield rolled over the dictator Saddam Hussein's Iraqi forces and destroyed them as they fled Kuwait after invading it.

[90] An English ballad the British army played as Lord Cornwallis surrendered to George Washington at Yorktown, Virginia.

[91] *Holy Bible,* Numbers 11:1.

[92] Jim Jones founded a church founded on what he called "apostolic socialism," although the teachings seemed to have little to do with Karl Marx and were actually related to an extreme form of Christian revivalism. When, in 1973, the church had several defections and police began paying attention to Jones and his followers, Jones moved the congregation to Guyana, South America. He intended to establish a paradise on earth. However, when investigators kept poking into the church's affairs, Jones prepared cyanide-laced grape flavored Kool-Aid and had his followers drink it, killing men, women, and children living at Jonestown.

[93] Graves, Robert, *The White Goddess* (New York: The Noonday Press, 1966).

[94] *Holy Bible,* Psalms 7:1-3.

Made in the USA
Monee, IL
30 September 2021